CHRI  XT

SERIES EDITORS

Timothy Gorringe   Serene Jones   Graham Ward

CHRISTIAN THEOLOGY IN CONTEXT

Any inspection of recent theological monographs makes plain that it is still thought possible to understand a text independently of its context. Work in the sociology of knowledge and in cultural studies has, however, increasingly made obvious that such divorce is impossible. On the one hand, as Marx put it, 'life determines consciousness'. All texts have to be understood in their life situation, related to questions of power, class, and modes of production. No texts exist in intellectual innocence. On the other hand, texts are also forms of cultural power, expressing and modifying the dominant ideologies through which we understand the world. This dialectical understanding of texts demands an interdisciplinary approach if they are to be properly understood: theology needs to be read alongside economics, politics, and social studies, as well as philosophy, with which it has traditionally been linked. The cultural situatedness of any text demands, both in its own time and in the time of its rereading, a radically interdisciplinary analysis.

The aim of this series is to provide such an analysis, culturally situating texts by Christian theologians and theological movements. Only by doing this, we believe, will people of the fourth, sixteenth, or nineteenth centuries be able to speak to those of the twenty-first. Only by doing this will we be able to understand how theologies are themselves cultural products—projects deeply resonant with their particular cultural contexts and yet nevertheless exceeding those contexts by being received into our own today. In doing this, the series should advance both our understanding of those theologies and our understanding of theology as a discipline. We also hope that it will contribute to the fast developing interdisciplinary debates of the present.

Martin Luther

Confessor of the Faith

Robert Kolb

OXFORD
UNIVERSITY PRESS

OXFORD

UNIVERSITY PRESS

Great Clarendon Street, Oxford OX2 6DP

Oxford University Press is a department of the University of Oxford.
It furthers the University's objective of excellence in research, scholarship,
and education by publishing worldwide in

Oxford New York

Auckland Cape Town Dar es Salaam Hong Kong Karachi
Kuala Lumpur Madrid Melbourne Mexico City Nairobi
New Delhi Shanghai Taipei Toronto

With offices in

Argentina Austria Brazil Chile Czech Republic France Greece
Guatemala Hungary Italy Japan Poland Portugal Singapore
South Korea Switzerland Thailand Turkey Ukraine Vietnam

Oxford is a registered trade mark of Oxford University Press
in the UK and in certain other countries

Published in the United States
by Oxford University Press Inc., New York

British Library Cataloguing in Publication Data

Data available

Library of Congress Cataloging-in-Publication Data

Kolb, Robert, 1941–
Martin Luther : confessor of the faith / Robert Kolb.
p. cm. – (Christian theology in context)
Includes bibliographical references and index.
ISBN 978-0-19-920894-4 – ISBN 978-0-19-920893-7
1. Luther, Martin, 1483–1546. I. Title.
BR333.3.K66 2009b 230'.41092–dc22
2008051379

Typeset by SPI Publisher Services, Pondicherry, India
Printed in Great Britain
on acid-free paper by
CPI Antony Rowe, Chippenham, Wiltshire

ISBN 978–0–19–920893–7 (Hbk.)
ISBN 978–0–19–920894–4 (Pbk.)

1 3 5 7 9 10 8 6 4 2

Contents

Abbreviations

ARG	*Archiv für Reformationsgeschichte/Archive for Reformation History*
BC	*The Book of Concord*, ed. Robert Kolb and Timothy J. Wengert, Minneapolis, Fortress, 2000
SA	Smalcald Articles
BSLK	*Die Bekenntnisschriften der evangelisch-lutherischen Kirche*, Göttingen, Vandenhoeck/Ruprecht, 1930, 1991
CR	*Corpus Reformatorum.* vols. 1–28: *Philippi Melanthonis Opera quae supersunt omnia*, C. G. Bretschneider and H. E. Bindseil, eds., Halle and Braunschweig, Schwetschke, 1834–60 vols. 88–94: *Huldreich Zwinglis Sämtliche Werke*, Leipzig, Heinsius, 1908–59
CSEL	*Corpus Scriptorum Ecclesiasticorum Latinorum*, Vienna, Gerold, 1866–
Deutsches Wörterbuch	J. and W. Grimm, *Deutsches Wörterbuch*, Leipzig, Herzel et al., 1854–1960
LuJ	*Lutherjahrbuch*
LQ	*Lutheran Quarterly*
LW	Martin Luther, *Luther's Works*, Saint Louis and Philadelphia, 1958–86
SCJ	*The Sixteenth Century Journal*
TRE	*Theologische Realenzyklopädie*, Gerhard Krause and Gerhard Müller, eds., Berlin, de Gruyter, 1977–2005
WA	Martin Luther, *D. Martin Luthers Werke*, Weimar, Böhlau, 1883–1993
Br	*Briefe*
DB	*Deutsche Bibel*
TR	*Tischreden*

1

'Angel of the Lord' or 'Damned Heretic': Martin Luther in the Trends of the Times

In 2000 the American magazine *LIFE* placed Martin Luther third among the one hundred most important figures of the millennium, following Thomas Edison and Christopher Columbus. *LIFE* heralded his posting of his Ninety-five Theses as the third most important event of the period, behind Gutenberg's invention of movable type and Columbus's landing in the Americas.[1] In 2003 a German television network drew more votes than national elections for a contest that found Martin Luther the second greatest German of all time, after Konrad Adenauer.[2] Such surveys flaunt their own subjectivity, but nonetheless Luther looms large in the public's imagination in parts of the Western world even yet.

One of Luther's own students ranked him higher:

Everyone who heard him knows what kind of man Luther was when he preached or lectured at the university. Shortly before his death he lectured on . . . Genesis. What sheer genius, life, and power he had! The way he could say it! . . . in my entire life I have experienced nothing more inspiring. When I heard his lectures, it was as if I were hearing an angel of the Lord. . . . Luther had a great command of Scripture and sensed its proper meaning at every point. Dear God, there was a gigantic gift of being able to interpret Scripture properly in that man.[3]

So said Cyriakus Spangenberg, preaching on 'the great prophet of God, Dr. Martin Luther, that he was a true Elijah', on 18 February 1564, Luther's eighty-first birthday, one sermon in a series Spangenberg preached twice-yearly on Luther's birthday and deathday from 1562 to 1573.

His opinion differed from that of Luther's contemporary, Johannes Cochlaeus, theologian and bureaucrat in the service of Duke George of Saxony, who concluded the first (albeit polemical) biography of Luther

[1] *LIFE* (2000), <http://www.life.com/Life/millennium/people/03.html> and <http://www.life.com/Life/millennium/events/03.html>

[2] See <http://www.german.about.com/cs/culture/a/bestger.htm>.

[3] *Theander Lutherus. Von des werthen Gottes Manne Doctor Martin Luthers Geistlicher Haushaltung vnd Ritterschafft*, Ursel, Heinrich, 1589, 70a–b.

Let the pious consider what Luther accomplished through so many labors, troubles, and efforts of his depraved intention, by whose rebellious and seditious urging so many thousands of people have perished eternally … and through whom all Germany was confused and disturbed, and let go all its ancient glory. … [4]

In his own time Martin Luther was a personality who divided the spirits. Whether Spangenberg's angel or Cochlaeus's 'enraged hornet', 'triple-jawed Cerberus', or 'disgraceful, infamous, and damned heretic',[5] this (at least initially) modest professor from a new university off the beaten path has won fame and blame ever since as an individual who changed the way many Europeans and others around the globe think. In the intervening five centuries he has been interpreted in many ways but has seldom disappeared from the stage of Western history. In the past half-century historians and theologians have tried to bring him into dialog with other contemporary or historical thinkers[6] and, through translations of his works, with readers in the two-thirds world.[7]

Following his death his own heirs[8] and other Evangelical theologians[9] attempted to interpret Luther anew; the effort continues at the beginning of the twenty-first century. As with every historical figure, these interpretations often tell more about the interpreter than the object of the interpretation. However interpreted, Luther's paradigmatic shift in defining what it means to be human and how God works in his world did create new agendas for public teaching within Christendom. He initiated reforms within the church, and his ideas impacted broader social trends that were developing in his time. This volume focuses on his theology, but his redefinition of God and the human creature cannot be separated from his impact on society and culture.

Like most historic figures, Luther worked as a member of a team. Each in the group gathered around him at the University of Wittenberg took on specific assignments in promoting their common reform program.

---

[4] *Commentaria De Actis et Scriptis Martini Luther*, Mainz, 1549 = *Luther's Lives*, tr. E. Vandiver et al., Manchester, Manchester University Press, 2002, 350.

[5] Ibid., 238, 240, 259.   [6] See the annual bibliographies in *LuJ* and *ARG*.

[7] Spanish, *Obras de Martino Luthero*, ed. Carlos Wittos et al., Buenos Aires, Editorial Paidós, 1967–85, 10 vols.; Portuguese, *Martino Luthero, obras Selecionadas*, São Leopoldo, Editoria Sinodal, Porto Alegre, Concordia, 1987–2000, 7 vols.; Korean, Won Yong Ji (ed.), Seoul, Concordia, 1981–9; Japanese, Tokyo, Seibun-Sha, 1963ff., 10 vols.; Chinese, Peter Li and Lei Yutian (eds.), Sanlian 2003ff., 2 vols. of a projected 15 have already appeared.

[8] R. Kolb, *Martin Luther as Prophet, Teacher, and Hero*, Grand Rapids, Baker, 1999; I. Dingel, 'Strukturen der Lutherrezeption am Beispiel einer Lutherzitatensammlung von Joachim Westphal', in Wolfgang Sommer (ed.), *Kommunikationsstrukturen im europäischen Luthertum der Frühen Neuzeit*, Gütersloh, Gütersloher Verlagshaus, 2005, 32–50.

[9] I. Dingel, *Concordia controversa, Die öffentlichen Diskussionen um das lutherische Konkordienwerk am Ende des 16. Jahrhunderts*, Gütersloh, Gütersloher Verlagshaus, 1996, 607–19.

Luther provided the spark and many of the ideas for this group; they in turn helped refine his thinking. His most valuable colleague, Philip Melanchthon, developed their common thought with his own creative insights on the basis of a different education and background. A study of Wittenberg theology as a whole is much needed. Nonetheless, 'Wittenberg theology' arose first of all from Luther's own thinking; therefore, this overview concentrates on his own writings.

The reception and processing of Luther's ideas began before his death, for example in disagreements with his own student Johann Agricola over the distinction of law and gospel.[10] The debates that erupted after his death over his theological legacy found some solution in the 'Formula of Concord' of 1577. A majority of his heirs found large areas of agreement in its summary of his thought (although disagreement and theological experimentation continued throughout the age of Lutheran 'Orthodoxy'). Throughout the next two centuries Roman Catholic critics continued Cochlaeus's appraisal of Luther. Calvinist opponents of Lutheran theology were gentler in their criticism but rejected certain decisive elements in his thought. His Lutheran followers gloried in his name, reproduced or echoed many elements of his thought, and defended his right to reform the church. But their dogmatic works addressed issues involved in the wider ecumenical exchange, and they cited him surprisingly sporadically. By the later seventeenth century a lay scholar and governmental advisor, Veit Ludwig von Seckendorf, defended Lutheranism with a masterful history of the Reformation but provided some historical criticism of the story's hero.[11] Lutherans of the Pietist movement treasured Luther and enlisted citations from the reformer for their own program of reform.

Enlightenment thinkers in Germany carried on the tradition of praising Luther. However, their flight from historical concretization led them in the opposite direction from that Luther had trod as he abandoned his instructors' scholastic abstractions. Thus, the praise of Lutherans like Gottfried Wilhelm Leibniz and Gotthold Ephraim Lessing lionized their champion of personal liberty and courage, but largely for reasons that betray a misunderstanding of his concerns. Their view of God and humanity took more from the thought-world of Luther's teachers than from his rejection of their dependence on Aristotle's image of humanity. That image envisaged the human being without God in the picture; Luther found too many remnants of this conception in the theology he had learned. Therefore, the halcyon years of German philosophy at the turn of the nineteenth century

---

[10] T. Wengert, *Law and Gospel, Philip Melanchthon's Debate with John Agricola of Eisleben over Poenitentia*, Grand Rapids, Baker, 1997.

[11] *Commentarius historicus et apologeticus de Lutheranismo, sive De reformatione religionis doctori D. Martini Lutheri*, Frankfurt/Main/Leipzig, Gleditsch, 1688–92.

produced new ways of thinking, in some cases, such as Immanuel Kant, with little recourse to Luther's insights, in others, such as Georg Wilhelm Friedrich Hegel, with his ideas forced into an alien framework.[12]

Eighteenth-century evaluations focused on Luther's gifts to the development of German language and literature and the human quest for freedom. Some nineteenth-century German Romantics, entranced by the Middle Ages, labeled Luther the destroyer of Western Christian unity, who also undermined public order, an interpretation in line with Roman Catholic renewal of Cochlaeus's interpretation in works published in the half-century after 1875 by Johannes Janssen, Heinrich Denifle, and, with emphasis on Luther's disturbed personality, Hartmann Grisar. But the revival of serious historical study in this period served to support a return to reading Luther from the original sources, by Protestant thinkers of various theological commitments. All profited from the fresh editing of the corpus of Luther's writings.

Luther has accompanied thinkers throughout the world during this half-millennium through republication of his works. Enterprising printers gathered his early treatises into the first printed 'collected works' of a living person (1519/20). Before his death, over his protests, Wittenberg colleagues initiated German and Latin series of his oeuvre (1539/1545–59/1557). Debates over the proper construal of his thought elicited a rival edition produced in Jena (1555–58), which dominated the market[13] until the appearance of the Altenburg (1661–4) and Leipzig (1729–40) editions. Johann Georg Walch issued a translation in eighteenth-century German (1740–53),[14] updated by Albert Friedrich Hoppe (1880–1910) for North American pastors.[15] An edition in the original German and Latin, the Erlangen (1826/1829–1857–1886), reflected new German standards for editing historical texts. In turn, the Weimar edition set even higher standards for scholarly treatment of texts and served as the basis for twentieth-century Luther scholarship.[16] More limited editions for special purposes and audiences appeared over the twentieth century, the most helpful the 'Study Edition' of the Evangelische Verlagsanstalt (Berlin).[17]

In every era and every land different accents, reflecting different concerns, have shaped the agendas of those who study Luther and attempt to

---

[12] On Kant and later Kantian interpretations, see R. Saarinen, *Gottes Wirken auf Uns. Die tranzendentale Deutung des Gegenwarts Christi, Motivs in der Lutherforschung*, Wiesbaden, Steiner, 1989. U. Asendorf, *Luther and Hegel*, Wiesbaden, Steiner, 1982, argues that Hegel's epistemology, not his metaphysics, is useful for presenting Lutheran theology today.

[13] Kolb, *Luther*, 137–50.

[14] 'Geschichte der Luther-Ausgaben vom 16. bis zum 19. Jahrhundert', *WA* 60: 427–592.

[15] Ibid., 602–6.   [16] On the Erlangen edition, ibid., 592–601.

[17] 6 vols., Berlin/Leipzig, Evangelische Verlagsanstalt, 1979–99.

bring him into dialog with their contemporaries.[18] Setting the tone and standards for this fresh look at the reformer were the theology of Luther and a biography of the reformer by a co-founder of the Weimar edition, Julius Köstlin, professor in Breslau and Halle, and the theological analysis of Theodosius Harnack, professor in Dorpat (Tartu) and Erlangen. Both reacted to the Roman Catholic criticism of Denifle and others, and they strove to make the significance of Luther's thinking for their time clear. In their wake arose a 'Luther Renaissance', developed under Karl Holl, church historian in Berlin, after World War I. Concerned about the crisis of German self-confidence following the defeat of 1918, Holl gradually moved away from the views of his mentor, Adolf von Harnack, and the 'Liberal' interpretation of Luther of Albrecht Ritschl, which focused above all on an abstract concept of God's love that paid little attention to the structure and the specific elements of Luther's thought.[19] Provoked both by Denifle's misrepresentations of Luther's positions and by the 'Liberal' dismissal of his relevance for the twentieth century of Ernst Troeltsch, Holl initiated a new wave of Luther research, based on the Weimar edition and focused on the doctrine of justification. The presuppositions he had absorbed from nineteenth-century Liberal theology led Holl, concerned about ethical performance, to reject a 'forensic' interpretation of Luther's teaching on the restoration of human righteousness in God's sight as a legal fiction. Holl and his students argued that Luther taught an 'effective' justification of the sinner instead of merely a 'verbal' pronouncement of righteousness. They failed to understand Luther's presumption that the 'verbal' pronouncement that conveys God's re-creating action of justification provides the firmest kind of reality there is.[20]

Holl's work elicited wide discussion and further research throughout Germany and beyond. Some of his students pursued Holl's agenda more faithfully than others; some fell into support for National Socialism. Others followed Karl Barth's dialectical theology, with varying utilization of Luther's ideas, and still others disciplined their historical work through a commitment to the Lutheran confessional documents. These, such as

---

[18] Cf. C.-A. Aurelius, 'Luther in Sweden', *Word & World* 18 (1998), 299–306, demonstrates much less use of Luther's image in Sweden than in Germany and elsewhere. H. Stephan, *Luther in den Wandlungen seiner Kirche*, Giessen, Töpelmann, 1907; H. Bornkamm, *Luther im Spiegel der deutschen Geistesgeschichte*, Heidelberg, Quelle/Meyer, 1955; E. Zeeden, *Martin Luther und die Reformation im Urteil des deutschen Luthertums*, 2 vols., Freiburg im Breisgau, Herder, 1952; J. Pelikan (ed.), *Interpreters of Luther*, Philadelphia, Fortress, 1968; W. Mostert, 'Luther, Martin. III. Wirkungsgeschichte', *TRE* 21: 567–94.

[19] D. Lotz, *Ritschl and Luther*, Nashville, Abingdon, 1974.

[20] J. Stayer, *Martin Luther, German Saviour: German Evangelical Theological Factions and the Interpretation of Luther, 1917–1933*, Montreal/Kingston, McGill-Queens University Press, 2000, 3–47.

Erlangen theologians Werner Elert, Paul Althaus, and Hermann Sasse, also probed new approaches to applying Luther's insights to their world. Their work continued after World War II, alongside the newer existentialist construal of Luther's thought of Gerhard Ebeling and others, who took seriously the dialectical tension that Luther made central to theological practice and his definition of God's Word as a word that accomplishes his will as it creates and upholds reality.[21]

For many in the period from Holl's initial work into the 1980s the most pressing and controversial question about Luther sought to determine when he had come to his own theological position. The revolutionary defiance of the 'young Luther' seemed more intriguing than the mature thought of the older Luther. The search for the date of the 'evangelical breakthrough' or the 'reformational discovery' reflected a Romantic concern for mastering the inner workings of this brilliant mind, a project regarded in this period as more interesting than assessing his impact. Initial attempts tended to try to find the evangelical aspects of his thought as early as possible, partially as a result of ignoring late medieval proponents of various concepts of grace. From the 1960s on, arguments for a later dating have won more support. The date claimed for the critical moment in Luther's theological development reflects more about the scholar's own definition of what element in Luther is most important than it does about Luther's actual maturing as a theologian, a process that, as with all thinkers, took place in fits and starts, in progress and regress, over a longer period.

Luther scholarship did not remain the province of ecclesiastical historians. Marxists continued Friedrich Engels' attempt to force Luther into Karl Marx's theories of history. First condemned as an enemy of proletarian revolt by the peasants (1525), he won rehabilitation as a bearer of the early bourgeois revolution through the work of Russian historian Moisei Smirin and Germans such as Max Steinmetz.[22] Heavily biased, Marxist contributions to the discussion of the social and economic setting of Luther's thought have commanded significantly less interest since 1989.

However, Western social and ecclesiastical historians have not ignored the larger social context of Luther's Reformation. Church historian Bernd Moeller provided a model of how the social setting of late medieval German cities influenced the Burghers' choices in the effort for reform,[23]

[21] e.g. G. Ebeling, *Lutherstudien*, 3 vols., Tübingen, Mohr/Siebeck, 1971–89.

[22] M. Smirin, *Die Volksreformation des Thomas Münzer und der grosse Bauernkrieg*, Berlin, Dietz, 1952; M. Steinmetz, *Deutschland von 1476 bs 1648*, Berlin, Deutscher Verlag der Wissenschaften, 1965.

[23] B. Moeller, *Imperial Cities and the Reformation*, tr. H. Midelfort and M. Edwards, Jr., Philadelphia, Fortress, 1972.

and Steven Ozment delved into the influence of municipal concerns upon Luther's own developing theology.[24] Gerald Strauss framed his own answer to the thoroughly twentieth-century question, 'how successful was Luther's Reformation?' on the basis of extensive investigation of visitation reports from Evangelical lands after the introduction of the Reformation. He found those reports as well as sermons, catechetical instruction, governmental legislation against immorality, and other kinds of evidence demonstrated a 'disappointing denouement' to Luther's call for reform because many old religious practices and a great deal of dissipation and decadence remained in the general populace.[25] Counter-evidence suggests that in some places substantial change in public behavior was reported,[26] but Strauss's method measured Luther against standards which he did not set for himself nor believed possible to attain. In 1531 he reflected on the 'success' of the Reformation in broader terms: 'Now it has come, praise God, to this: men and women, young and old, know the catechism. They know how to believe, live, pray, suffer, and die.'[27] Yet at other points the reformer shared Strauss's pessimism, sometimes expressing surprise at how little power the gospel had exercised.[28] More often he recognized that the entire history of humankind, and of God's people, recorded nothing more than the rhythm of apostasy and rebellion followed by God's call to repentance and restoration of his own to faithful living, followed by fall and sin once again.[29] The valuable contributions of social historians to the understanding of Luther's movement that have multiplied in the wake of Moeller's and Strauss's work sometimes acknowledge Luther's standard for evaluating his efforts, and sometimes do not.

Another series of vital contributions to the discussion of Luther's thought have come from Roman Catholic scholars. Josef Lortz of the Institute for European History in Mainz launched a revolution in Roman Catholic Luther studies, carried further with different nuances by a generation of careful Roman Catholic scholarship in the work of several scholars, among them Otto Hermann Pesch (Hamburg), Harry J. McSorley (Montreal), Jos Vercruysse (Rome), Daniel Olivier (Paris), and Jared

[24] S. Ozment, *The Reformation in the Cities: The Appeal of Protestantism to Sixteenth-Century Germany and Switzerland*, New Haven, Yale University Press, 1975.

[25] G. Strauss, *Luther's House of Learning: Indoctrination of the Young in the German Reformation*, Baltimore, Johns Hopkins University Press, 1978, 300.

[26] J. Kittelson, 'Successes and Failures in the German Reformation: The Report from Strasbourg', *ARG* 73 (1982), 153–75; S. Hendrix, 'Luther's Impact on the Sixteenth Century', *SCJ* 16 (1985), 3–14.

[27] 'Luther's Warning to His Dear German People', 1531, *WA* 30.3: 317.32–4, *LW* 47: 52.

[28] M. Brecht, *Martin Luther*, 3 vols., tr. J. Schaaf, Philadelphia, Fortress, 1985–93, 3: 253–8.

[29] J. Headley, *Luther's View of Church History*, New Haven, Yale University Press, 1963, 156–265.

Wicks (Chicago / Rome). Lortz argued that Luther had indeed contributed important ideas to theological discussion and that he would have remained a faithful son of the papacy if he had not been corrupted by the nominalist or Ockhamist thought dominant at his time. Had Luther only known Thomas Aquinas's doctrine of prevenient grace, that God's grace initiated and filled in the gaps in the human practice of righteous deeds that fulfill God's requirements for human beings, he would not have been driven to revolt against papal authority. The worldview Lortz had learned did not permit him to recognize that Luther introduced a new presupposition to defining salvation when he taught, against all scholastic predecessors, Thomas included, that righteousness in God's sight never had and cannot have anything to do with human performance. Human performance flows from, does not cause, God's favor toward his chosen people. Unfortunately, the rich contributions to Luther research from Roman Catholics in the late twentieth century seem not to be continuing, apart from the work of a few, including Dutch scholar Theo Bell and German scholar Hubertus Blaumeiser.[30]

Luther studies have profited also from Nordic investigation and integration of his insights into thinking on life in church and society. Gustaf Wingren, for example, highlighted Luther's appreciation for the doctrine of creation and its implications for Christian faithfulness in loving others within the context of God's callings in this world.[31] Drawn by ecumenical concerns raised in dialogs with Russian Orthodox theologians, Helsinki professor Tuomo Mannermaa advanced the thesis that Luther's understanding of justification echoes and repeats the Orthodox doctrine of salvation by divinization (theosis),[32] a theory that has been criticized for its historical method as well as inadequate metaphysical analysis.

It has been said that Luther scholarship became its own worst enemy in the course of the twentieth century: the immense mass of material discourages fresh scholarship because it demands too much preparation for carrying on the next stage of the discussion. Nonetheless, within the larger context of Reformation studies and attempts to define the transition from late medieval to early modern European thought and life, questions regarding Luther's role and way of thought remain live topics today. Debates rumble over the weight to be given to the reformer's continuity

[30] Jos E. Vercruysse, SJ, 'Luther in der römisch-katholischen Theologie und Kirche', LuJ 63 (1996), 103–28.

[31] Esp. G. Wingren, Luther on Vocation, tr. C. Rasmussen, Philadelphia, Muhlenberg, 1957.

[32] T. Mannermaa, Der im Glauben gegenwärtige Christus. Rechtfertigung und Vergottung, Hannover, Lutherisches Verlagshaus, 1989; cf. the English summary of his views, idem, Christ Present in Faith: Luther's View of Justification, Minneapolis, Fortress, 2005.

with various elements of medieval thought[33] and his own discovery of new ways to define what it means to be human, to order human society, and to practice the discipline of theology. Related to these debates is the definition of what 'Reformation' should mean, and whether it was a unitary movement or a gathering of several 'reformations'.[34] These debates have generated valuable research and helped deepen insights into particular aspects of Luther's life, context, and thought as well as helped focus the larger picture of his era and impact. However, all of them depend much on scholars' own concerns and perspectives, both in the formulation of the question that each is answering and in the specific sources chosen for study. Modern concerns, arising from social theories, ecclesiastical agendas, and personal predispositions, shape approaches to these questions.

Reshaped by the changing perceptions and concerns of nearly five centuries of thinkers, Martin Luther continues to fascinate and to inspire both negative and positive reactions, from people of widely different backgrounds and orientations because he initiated paradigm shifts in fundamental definitions of essential parts of human life. Those areas of the world with roots in the central European experience of the late medieval and early modern eras will continue to ask where Luther's voice is speaking in the heritage that runs through their minds, consciously or unconsciously. In Africa, Asia, and Latin America people have little interest in what went wrong with central European life since 1500, but Luther continues to provide texts for the life of the church, as he has since Bartholomaeus Ziegenbalg translated the catechism into Tamil in 1713. An African bishop confessed that Luther's doctrine of justification as he had learned it from missionary instructors has little to do with the lives of his people. But the bishop avowed that his people need to hear Luther's understanding of justification as the restoration of individual human worth and dignity, and his claim that all of human life is to be lived out of trust in the Word of God that conveys true worth and dignity.

This volume offers readers a personal review of key elements in recent Luther interpretation and points toward how the discussion might continue around the globe in the twenty-first century. It is not a bibliographical essay which attempts to survey or assess all Luther scholarship with its various arguments. It unfortunately cannot mention all significant aspects of the last century's analysis of Wittenberg thought. Much of the material

---

[33] H. Oberman pioneered fresh work on this in *The Harvest of Medieval Theology*, Durham, Labyrinth, 1983.

[34] e.g., S. Hendrix, *Recultivating the Vineyard: The Reformation Agendas of Christianization*, Louisville, Westminster John Knox, 2004; and B. Hamm, B. Moeller, and D. Wendebourg, *Reformations-Theorien. Ein kirchenhistorischer Disput über Einheit und Vielfalt der Reformation*, Göttingen, Vandenhoeck & Ruprecht, 1995.

in this work stems from surveys of Luther's theology taken (often without credit) from the 'theologies of Luther' by Paul Althaus, Gerhard Ebeling, Bernhard Lohse, and Oswald Bayer, to whom—among many others—I am deeply indebted and to whom I refer readers for more extensive discussions of the topics treated here.[35]

Luther's thought, as complex as his perception of human life, as nuanced as he believed the biblical message to be, defies adequate summary. This account intends to introduce his way of thinking within a single, slight volume and is therefore necessarily incomplete. Readers, it is hoped, will find reason to wend their way into those discussions through those scholars mentioned in the footnotes to fuller treatments of specific issues. When possible, we use texts available in English translation to enable readers without German and Latin to explore the texts more extensively (though the translations of *Luther's Works* are not always used). This presentation of Luther seeks to help readers begin to engage Luther's way of thinking, the Wittenberg way of practicing theology and confessing the Christian faith in teaching and living.

---

[35] P. Althaus, *The Theology of Martin Luther*, tr. R. Schultz, Philadelphia, Fortress, 1966; Ebeling, *Luther, an Introduction to his Thought*, tr. R. Wilson, Philadelphia, Fortress, 1970; B. Lohse, *Martin Luther's Theology*, tr. R. Harrisville, Minneapolis, Fortress, 1999; O. Bayer, *Martin Luther's Theology: A Contemporary Interpretation*, tr. T. Trapp, Grand Rapids, Eerdmans, 2008.

2

Set on His Way: Luther's Life to 1519

Tucked away in the crevices of the Harz mountains in the heart of Germany, the villages of the counts of Mansfeld were experiencing new growth in the last decades of the fifteenth century. Markets for copper and other metals found in the region were expanding; Mansfeld, along with areas in Hungary and the Tirol, offered a ready supply of ore. New technological developments enabled not only Mansfeld's surface beds of copper but also seams lying deeper to be tapped. Burgeoning industry attracted people from as far away as the village of Möhra, 150 kilometers south-west, whence came a young peasant, Hans Luther, with his wife, Margarete, of the merchant family Lindemann from nearby Eisenach.[1]

LUTHER'S FAMILY AND EDUCATION

As eldest brother in a relatively well-off peasant family, Hans had to yield the family farm to his younger brother. His adventurous, entrepreneurial spirit led him to Eisleben, the largest town in Mansfeld county, where his wife's brother resided, and then to nearby Mansfeld town, with two thousand inhabitants half the size of Eisleben, shortly after the birth of his and Margarete's eldest surviving child, Martin, born 10 November, probably in 1483. Hans may have begun working in the mines but soon became a leaseholder of a smelting operation, under the control of the local counts. The elector of Saxony, whose extra-territorial duties as a leading prince of the German empire included supervision of mining in the region, governed his industry. As Martin was growing up, Hans Luther was on the move up the social ladder and intimately involved in the hurly-burly of industrial and commercial expansion and its political ramifications. His business prospered sometimes, sometimes suffered losses. Hans also assumed public obligations, serving as one of four representatives of the miners before the town council. Although Martin did not experience life at court, as did his colleague Philip Melanchthon, son of the armor-maker of the elector of the Palatinate, nor life in a large city, with republican traditions, he knew what

[1] I. Siggins, *Luther & his Mother*, Philadelphia, Fortress, 1981, 20–52.

infant capitalism meant, and he recognized how princely power functioned in his world.[2]

Luther's relationships with his parents have been subject to much analysis. Some, like that of psychologist Erik Erikson,[3] attempt to impose modern theories upon a pre-modern person. Erikson's insights into the role of trust in human life provide much more helpful guidance into Luther's thought than do his attempts at analysis across the centuries; his concept of human identity gives helpful insight into Luther's view of human 'righteousness'.[4] It is fruitless to attempt to assess Luther's theological development on the basis of his relationship with his parents. They were undoubtedly strict but loving, likely disciplining their son, his three sisters, and one surviving brother with a display of genuine care and concern.[5] His mother came from the educated circle of Eisenach and must have taught her son the basics of Christian faith and living as she prepared him for school.

Certainly, these parents raised their children to be upright children of God. As a civic leader, Hans Luther probably dealt with the local clergy. He may well have shared the suspicion and exasperation often held by lay people throughout Christian history on account of their pastors. However, no records indicate he was more vocally critical of priests than others in his position. As in all eras of the church's history, anticlericalism haunted the medieval religious scene,[6] but its importance in forming popular attitudes toward the church and religious practice must be carefully nuanced. Whatever contempt for specific priests and priests in general may have been expressed in Mansfeld, Luther grew up fearing God, knowing that he was supposed to love his neighbors and that priests served as God's special instruments for mediating divine power. He heard Bible stories and worshipped the Triune God, whom he learned to approach largely through ritual.

The religious practices and beliefs of central Germany reflected the piety formed six hundred years earlier as the Frankish kingdom imposed Christianity upon adherents of traditional tribal religions. The Franks lacked sufficient teaching personnel or theological program to transform the structure and rhythms of the old worldview into a biblical understanding of reality.[7] Luther grew up believing that supernatural power touched his life

---

[2] M. Brecht, *Martin Luther*, tr. J. Schaaf, Philadelphia, Fortress, 1985–93, 1: 1–12.

[3] E. Erikson, *Young Man Luther: A Study in Psychoanalysis and History*, New York, Norton, 1958.

[4] E. Erikson, *Child and Society*, New York, Norton, 1950.   [5] Siggins, *Luther*, 9–19.

[6] P. Dykema and H. Oberman (eds.), *Anticlericalism in Late Medieval and Early Modern Europe*, Leiden, Brill, 1994.

[7] S. Hendrix, *Recultivating the Vineyard: The Reformation Agendas of Christianization*, Louisville, Westminster John Knox, 2004, 1–17.

mediated through saints, who often filled roles once assigned to Germanic deities and spirits. He believed that superhuman power was exercised not only by God but also—independently, often in defiance, of God—by demons and witches. God-pleasing rituals were vastly more important than spirits and witches, but both played a role in his perception of reality. The rituals that shaped his feeling for how life works included those performed by priests in God's name and those performed by folk practitioners, who may or may not have claimed to be on God's side. Luther's later reaction against all human attempts to manipulate divine or supernatural power through ritual strove indeed to abolish rituals that 'no longer coincided with people's cosmic understanding'.[8] Much more it reflected his desire to change that understanding by replacing human manipulation of the Creator through ritual or ethical performance with trust-filled hearkening to his Word. Attaining this conviction, however, cost young Martin much anguish and time.

No records betray when the old system of relating to God began to fail him. His education began in Mansfeld, probably in 1491; there he learned the 'trivia', Latin grammar, rhetoric, and dialectic. Like most pupils, he remembered the negative experiences, the shame of little failures. He left Mansfeld for more schooling in Magdeburg in 1496 or 1497. There he boarded with associates of the Brethren of the Common Life, a lay order from which he could learn the piety of biblical study and care of others cultivated by late medieval Dutch writers Gerhard Zerbolt and Thomas à Kempis, a piety based on the 'imitation of Christ'. In this city of 25,000 Luther gained a glimpse of how larger civil communities functioned. After a year he moved to Eisenach to complete pre-university training. He found there not only good training in the arts. His friendships with maternal relatives, with the family of a leading citizen, Heinrich Schalbe, perhaps a relative, and with a priest, Johannes Braun, provided the adolescent with support. From them he learned of the Franciscan piety fostered by Johann Hilten, a visionary prophet who died in close confinement in a monastery near Eisenach. Schalbe had known Hilten and repeated his criticism of the church.[9]

In 1501 Hans Luther's dream that his son would advance further up the social ladder by achieving a university education seemed assured. Headed by parental design for a career in law and, probably, governmental service, Martin enrolled at the University of Erfurt, Germany's fifth university, founded 1392. Erfurt, a city of 20,000, subject to the archbishop of Mainz, established its own university on the basis of an excellent school system and the presence of Franciscans, Dominicans,

---

8 S. Karant-Nunn, *The Reformation of Ritual*, London, Routledge, 1997, 4.
9 Brecht, *Luther*, 1: 12–21; Siggins, *Luther*, 51–2.

and Augustinian Hermits, who could supply instructors. During Luther's time there, Erfurt was engulfed in a battle for its own independence and inner stability against its lord, Mainz's elector-archbishop, with aid from its frequent ally and protector, the Saxon court. Culminating in 1509–10, this unrest taught Luther something of the conflicts lying at the surface of the larger political scene and the inner municipal social structure. Erfurt's artisans supported Mainz and its patricians Saxony. In the face of destruction and death among citizens and students caused by riots and their forceful suppression, Luther asked his monastic superior in 1511 how God could command respect when he inflicted such suffering. Johannes Staupitz's assurance that God intended to call people to repentance through harsh chastisement became Luther's view later, but perhaps not immediately.[10]

University students began with studies in logic and other elements of the liberal arts, under the guidance of Aristotle and his medieval interpreters. After matriculation in April or May 1501, Luther completed his first examination in the minimum period required for earning a bachelor's degree, three semesters (September 1502), ranking thirteenth in a group of fifty-seven. He immediately pursued the master's degree in the *artes*, deepening his understanding of logic, natural philosophy, mathematics, and music. With that degree in hand, in January 1505, he was prepared to enter the faculty of law. His instructors in the arts faculty, particularly Jodokus Trutfetter and Bartholmäus Arnoldi, had a reputation as leading exponents of the Ockhamist or nominalist school. Trained at the University of Tübingen, under Germany's most prominent Ockhamist of the time, Gabriel Biel, they bequeathed Luther an approach to learning labeled the *via moderna* though it is likely that, like most academicians, their teaching drew on a wide spectrum of medieval authorities, Thomas Aquinas among them.[11]

Some six weeks after beginning to study law, on 2 July 1505, Luther was returning to Erfurt from a visit in Mansfeld. It is unclear which factors in the religious atmosphere of the time contributed to his reaction to lightning striking near him a few kilometers from Erfurt, near Stotternheim. His own scrupulous, sensitive conscience fed upon the apocalyptic hopes and fears of the age, which anticipated Christ's direct intervention to either bring history to its culmination or introduce a new era of justice for all. His dissatisfaction with his own religious performance had placed a deep-seated fear of God in his heart. Terrified by the thunderstorm, he made a vow to Saint Anne, patroness of miners and smelters, protectress of those

[10] *WATR* 1: 35–6, #94, *LW* 54: 11. Brecht, *Luther*, 1: 23–9.
[11] *WATR* 4: 145, 679, #4118, 5134; 5: 653, #6419. Brecht, *Luther*, 1: 32–44.

in thunderstorms and under threat of sudden death, that he would become a monk. He and his acquaintances viewed the lightning as God's call and direction.[12]

MONK AND PROFESSOR

Among Erfurt's thirty-six churches, eleven belonged to monastic orders. Monasticism offered the shorter but steeper path to heaven that medieval theology and piety regarded as God's special gift. It enabled a select few to dedicate their lives to a particularly intense form of religious devotion, divorced from the world's ways and daily life's distractions. Luther hoped to find assurance that he stood in God's favor on the basis of the rigid, strenuous practices to which monks committed themselves. He never stated why he chose the monastery of the Observant wing of the Augustinian Hermits. Pope Alexander IV established the Hermits in 1256 to gather independent communities into a mendicant order devoted to preaching and pastoral care in cities. By 1460 separate 'conventual' and 'observant' monasteries formed within the Order as a result of the latter's reform efforts. Thus, Luther found a strict community from which he expected to receive the severest demands of the monastic ideal. Among the most important in the Order within Germany, the Erfurt monastery, established in 1273, had some fifty members at Luther's time. Its *Studium Generale* was famous for educating theologians and providing arts instruction for the university. Luther went there, however, not to continue his education but to break away from all vanity and live the arduous discipline of the monastic life. On 17 July he entered a probationary period. By year's end he took his initial monastic vows. This occasioned a serious rupture with his parents, from which his fiercely disappointed father recovered only gradually. As a novice, the hopeful candidate pledged himself to a life of simplicity, nocturnal vigils, hard work, chastisement of earthly desires, poverty, fasting, seclusion, and the discipline of seven daily prayer services. Johann Greffenstein, the monastery's novice master, directed Luther's learning of the monastic ways and counseled him against his tendencies to scrupulous self-examination and excessive self-punishment.[13]

Luther's desire to be a simple monk, as degraded and humbled as possible, was thwarted by his monastic superior, the vicar-general of the Augustinian Order in Germany, Johannes von Staupitz. They met in April 1506. Staupitz recognized Luther's potential and destined him for the priesthood and advanced theological study. The two conversed intensively over the

[12] Ibid., 1: 46–9.   [13] Ibid., 1: 51–70.

following decade, united by a bond of mutual respect and appreciation for the other's abilities and viewpoints. The suffragan bishop resident in Erfurt, Johann Bonemilch, ordained Luther as subdeacon, deacon, and then, on 3 April 1507, as priest. This office terrified Luther, for it placed him in direct contact with God and with the body and blood of God's Son when he conducted the mass. His conviction of his unworthiness of office, simply of being in God's presence, brought him near collapse in his first celebration of the mass.[14] This terror in the face of God haunted the young monk's life in the years following. He struggled with *Anfechtungen*, spiritual struggles that kept him continuously in doubt of his standing with God. He became ever more convinced that he could not win God's grace with the paltry, insufficient works he performed. Satan, Luther was certain, plagued him throughout his life with doubts about God's love for him, but in his early years these battles were intense; later Satan sent him physical suffering to continue his *Anfechtungen*.[15] At Erfurt, however, his instructors were teaching that he needed to do his best in order to win God's gifts that made his works truly worthy of salvation; he believed that he could always have done better than he had actually done. This did not reduce him to inactivity, however. His superiors conferred increasing responsibility upon him, and Staupitz impelled him into formal theological studies.

His course of study probably began in summer 1507, with study of Scripture and the primary dogmatics textbook of the medieval church, the *Sentences* of Peter Lombard, the twelfth-century compiler of the '*sententiae*' or 'opinions' of the ancient Fathers of the church. Lombard attempted to reconcile contrary opinions and formulate dogmatic orientation for his readers. Medieval systematic theology consisted of lecturing on and extending the insights of Lombard's collection to address current questions. Luther learned Lombard from an Ockhamist, Johann Nathin, who had also studied with Biel in Tübingen. Although strife within the Order soured their relationship after 1511, probably hastening Luther's permanent transfer to Wittenberg, they initially worked well together.

Staupitz summoned his young protégé to Wittenberg in 1508. Elector Frederick the Wise had established a university there in 1502, with Staupitz as first theological professor and dean. In 1506 Trutfetter came to Wittenberg for a brief stint as professor of theology. Luther followed in 1508 to lecture on Aristotle's *Nicomachean Ethics* while continuing his theological studies, leading to the Bachelor of Bible degree in March 1509. Pursuit of the degree of Bachelor of the *Sentences* followed. He returned to

[14] His letter inviting Johannes Braun to attend his first mass reveals his fears, *WABr* 1: 10, *LW* 48: 3; cf. *WATR* 4: 180, #4174, *LW* 54: 325. See *WA* 43: 381.41–382.6, *LW* 4: 340–1.

[15] H.-M. Barth, *Der Teufel und Jesus Christus in der Theologie Martin Luthers*, Göttingen, Vandenhoeck & Ruprecht, 1967, 123–83.

Erfurt to lecture on Lombard, 1509–11,[16] but turned ever more to studying Scripture.[17]

He had apparently recuperated from the earlier political conflict into which he had fallen, occasioned by Staupitz's attempt to secure the integrity of the Order's reformed wing in Germany by insulating his monasteries from indulgent administration by Roman authorities through placement of these monasteries under the reformed congregation of the Augustinian province of Lombardy, which had special papal privileges not held by the Order as a whole. This plan encountered opposition within the Order's leadership, from the papal court, and from 'refractory' members of the German province. Initially Luther sided with Nathin and his Erfurt brothers against Staupitz. With an unidentified companion, he represented this faction in Rome in November 1510. These two delivered their protest against Staupitz's plan and returned to Erfurt by early February 1511. Luther later recalled negative impressions of the impiety and open contempt for what he held sacred in the catholic faith, but the visit to the Holy City seems not to have caused any immediate revolt in his mind against elements of medieval ecclesiastical practice. Staupitz meanwhile negotiated a settlement Luther found satisfactory with Giles of Viterbo, the new Augustinian vicar-general. This apparently contributed to Luther's alienation from Nathin and transfer to Wittenberg.

As his studies progressed, Luther assumed ever more duties in the administration of the Observant Augustinians. Appointed sub-prior of the Wittenberg monastery in 1512, named director of its '*studium generale*', and delegated the responsibility of preacher for his Wittenberg brothers, he was elected district vicar for ten monasteries in Saxony in 1515. He exercised his duty as regional vicar with sensitivity to the pastoral care of his brothers, winning their respect and support, while also gaining the admiration and appreciation of students to whom he was lecturing.[18]

When Luther moved permanently to Wittenberg, in late 1511, the town of less than 2,500 inhabitants had more than three hundred years of history as a political center. The court of the Ascanian dukes of Saxony located there around 1180. The family gained a position among the seven princes who elected the emperor, a privilege confirmed by the Golden Bull of 1356. When the Ascanian family expired in 1422, the Wettin family assumed its title and territories. The Wettin elector Frederick II's sons, Ernst and Albrecht, divided his lands in 1485; Ernst's elder son, Frederick III, 'the Wise', assumed rule in 1486 and began a revival of Wittenberg, initiating the renovation of its castle (1490) and placing his university there (1502). Frederick was a learned, pious medieval Christian, concerned about church

---

[16] WA 9: 28–94.   [17] Brecht, *Luther*, 1: 90–8.   [18] Ibid., 1: 98–105, 155–61.

and about his theological faculty. In 1493 he obtained a thumb of Saint Anne and began a collection of relics that grew to over 19,000 pieces by 1520. Visiting the annual exhibition of his collection in the Castle Church in Wittenberg won remission of 1,900,000 days from purgatory. Luther never met Frederick, but the elector's circle of advisors included close associates of his young professor, Staupitz and Georg Spalatin, tutor for Frederick's nephews, later his personal secretary and counselor.[19]

Frederick had gained an imperial charter for his new University of Wittenberg at its founding in 1502; Staupitz helped win the papal charter that had been necessary for university status up to that time in 1507. The Augustinian vicar-general, along with Martin Pollich von Mellerstadt, former instructor in arts and medicine at Leipzig, organized the university. Mellerstadt served as first rector and also professor of theology. As a 'realist' and follower of Thomas Aquinas, he represented an approach to philosophical and theological inquiry shared by Petrus Lupinus and Andreas Bodenstein von Karlstadt, two colleagues whom Luther joined in 1512. Staupitz's nephew, Nikolaus von Amsdorf, taught logic according to another sytem, that of the fourteenth-century scholastic, Duns Scotus, in the arts faculty; he and Luther formed a bond as Amsdorf accepted Luther's way of thinking in the following decade. Eclectic in his use of medieval predecessors, Staupitz himself was certainly influenced by his training at the Ockhamistic University of Tübingen. Karlstadt led Luther through the examination by disputation to his doctorate in Bible, the culmination of Staupitz's plans for his protégé. The ceremonies awarding the degree took place in October 1512. A year later Luther began his thirty-three-year career as professor of exegesis with a two-year-long treatment of the Psalms.[20] Luther later recalled that his doctoral oath had obligated him to 'expound the Scriptures for all the world'.[21]

Both his monastic training and the university practice of providing students with glosses (short explanations of words and phrases) and scholia (longer comment on a text) shaped his exegetical method. The words of the psalmists, with which Luther was well familiar through daily repetition in the monastery's devotional rhythms, drove deep into Luther's consciousness the sense of God's grandeur and his compassion, his mercy for the helpless and sinners as well as his wrath against sin and every form of evil, and his concern for protecting his own against their enemies. After Luther's initial lectures as university professor, from summer 1513 into 1515, he turned to Paul's letter to the Romans, highlighting its emphases on God's anger against sin and his unconditioned favor towards his chosen, faithful

[19] Brecht, *Luther*, 1: 107–18.   [20] Ibid., 1: 120–8, *WA* 3–4, *LW* 10–11.
[21] 'Commentary on Psalm 82', *WA* 31.1: 212.12–13, *LW* 13: 66.

people. Galatians commanded his attention from October 1516 to March 1517; sometime later he embarked on lectures on the epistle to the Hebrews. Thereafter, he turned again to the Psalms. As he matured as a lecturer on the Bible in the 1510s, his method of interpreting Scripture experienced a transformation. It moved away from the formidable medieval tradition of allegory as he developed a hermeneutic centered on God's conversation with sinners, aimed at bringing their sinful identity to an end and restoring their original relationship with their Creator.

Luther, of course, did more than just lecture as a university professor. He was involved in the full range of professorial duties, including the conduct of formal examinations and exchanges of views in the form of disputations. These disputations revealed the ability of the disputant to argue and analyze logically on the basis of a series of theses proposing specific views of a topic. The practice of assessing students' skills by formal public dispute over theses composed by a professor or under his guidance by the student had begun in the eleventh century. Professors also created theses as a challenge to colleagues to debate certain views, which the author may or may not have held himself.

Luther's discontent with both the method and content of theological education began developing around 1516. His student Bartholomäus Bernhardi composed theses on grace and free will, which sharply criticized the Ockhamist view that human works could merit grace and that the human will could move itself in God's direction.[22] His disputation on 25 September 1516 aroused opposition from Luther's colleagues. During the following year, by moving them to read Augustine's works and by extensive exchange of views, Luther won over Lupinus in part, Amsdorf and Karlstadt quite completely. Luther tested his ideas on scholastic method and the primacy of an Aristotelian anthropological framework for practicing theology by drafting theses for the promotion of Franz Günther to the Baccalaureate of Bible on 4 September 1517. These theses rejected Biel's and Scotus's criticism of Augustine's 'excessive expressions' regarding sin and grace and challenged Aristotle's definition of what it means to be human. Aristotle characterized humanity in terms of human performance and independent exercise of the will rather than in terms of the creature's relationship to the Creator. Luther held that failed to take seriously the depth of sin's corrupting power.[23] Luther was advancing an upheaval in the practice of theology and the fundamental paradigm for describing reality. He had written his friend Johann Lang in Erfurt less than four months earlier,

---

[22] *WA* 1: 142–51.

[23] *WA* 1: 221–8; L. Grane, *Contra Gabrielem. Luthers Auseinandersetzung mit Gabriel Biel in der Disptutatio Contra Scholasticam Theologiam 1517*, s.l., Gyldendal, 1962, 310–47, 369–82.

'Our theology and Saint Augustine are progressing well and with God's help predominate at our university. Aristotle is gradually falling from his throne, and his final doom is only a matter of time.'[24] 'Gradually' is key to this description: Luther's positions aroused fierce criticism (though that was natural in scholastic disputations). Luther was feeling his way toward a new appraisal of God's Word, and his contemporaries found his ideas worth debating.

The stage changed profoundly with another set of theses designed to do no more than stimulate thoroughgoing theological analysis of a problem of pastoral care which increasingly unsettled Luther in autumn 1517. The well-established but ill-defined practice and doctrine of indulgences had intruded on the ecclesiastical scene as Pope Leo X attempted to fund the construction of Saint Peter's basilica in Rome through sales of indulgences. They purported to guarantee release from purgatory for purchasers or their departed beneficiaries. Leo found an agent for the sales to Germans in the person of the young scion of the Hohenzollern family, rulers of Brandenburg and other territories, Albrecht. Seeking dispensation from the pope because of his age and because he already had been appointed archbishop of Magdeburg and administrator of the diocese of Halberstadt, Albrecht needed to fund the hefty fees necessary to become the archbishop of Mainz, primate of Germany. The third new archbishop since 1504, Albrecht found his diocese strapped for funds. Therefore he agreed to sponsor sale of the special papal indulgence in German territories. Frederick the Wise, whose younger brother had preceded Albrecht in Magdeburg, wanted to thwart the advance of the rival Hohenzollerns' power, so he forbade Albrecht's preacher and salesman, the Dominican Johann Tetzel, from trespassing on electoral Saxon terrain. But Wittenberg citizens traveled to nearby Jüterbog, in Magdeburg's jurisdiction, to purchase release from the temporal punishment for their sins. Such a release was all that an indulgence could theoretically do. The theory of indulgences rested upon the presupposition that, while priestly absolution forgives eternal guilt and prepares the way to heaven, temporal punishment for those forgiven sins remains, to be worked off by human 'satisfactions', either on this earth or, after death, in purgatory. In the popular mind, according to most sixteenth-century reformers, however, indulgences were a ticket to heaven: not inexpensive but worth the price.

The underlying issue, from the reformers' point of view, revolved around the understanding of forgiveness of sins and the nature of the repentance required by medieval definition for effective appropriation of absolution. Luther had raised questions for his students three years earlier, while lecturing on Psalm 69, regarding cheap repentance and forgiveness through indulgences.[25] With his Ninety-five Theses of October 1517 he wanted to challenge what he viewed as abuses of pastoral care perpetrated by this sale of indulgences. This set of theses posed hard questions for his Wittenberg colleagues and others regarding the nature of the practice and the doctrine behind it. Since such theses did not necessarily represent the convictions of their authors, to say nothing of a full exposition of their positions, it is difficult to assess Luther's theological development in late 1517 on the basis of these Theses. Furthermore, their content was less important than their impact.

According to current custom, Luther had copies printed so that he could send them to colleagues outside Wittenberg and to Archbishop Albrecht himself.[26] Enterprising printers, sensing commercial opportunity, placed his propositions in the public arena. By December printers in Nuremberg, Leipzig, and Basel, anticipating that a wider reading public might be interested, were executing a cultural revolution, the first media event that brought a single author's ideas to a vast audience within days and weeks. Johann Gutenberg's invention of printing with movable type a half-century earlier met Luther's inquiry into the spiritual care of Christians, and the potential of the press exhibited itself in a manner heretofore never experienced. Luther became an electrifying celebrity for much of the German populace, a notorious disrupter of public order for ecclesiastical and secular officials alike.[27]

FROM DISPUTATION TO DISPUTE

The repercussions of the spread of his theses on indulgences across German-speaking lands and beyond (they were published in the original Latin and also translated into German) changed Luther's life forever. His celebrity made him a voice of hope for those whose apocalyptic dreams seemed on the verge of fulfillment, an opponent with dangerous ideas to be eliminated for those who viewed his ideas—sometimes rightly, sometimes wrongly—as a threat to the church's teaching and public order. Archbishop Albrecht, a patron of the arts not inclined to ecclesiastical politics,

---

[25] *WA* 3: 416.20–3, *LW* 10: 351.

[26] Recent debate has not resolved whether Luther actually posted these Theses on the church door in Wittenberg; see K. Aland's critique of E. Iserloh's argument against this tradition, *Die Thesen Martin Luthers*, Gütersloh, Mohn, 1983, M. Treu, 'Der Thesenanschlag fand wirklich statt', *Luther* 78 (2007), 140–4, and V. Leppin, 'Geburtswehen und Geburt einer Legende. Zu Rörers Notiz vom Thesenanschlag', *Luther* 78 (2007), 145–50.

[27] Brecht, *Luther*, 1: 175–202.

requested the judgment of his theologians at his university in Mainz and forwarded the Theses to Rome. There Leo X remanded the case to the Augustinian Order. Johann Tetzel defended a series of theses on indulgences written by his professor Conrad (Koch) Wimpina at the University of Frankfurt an der Oder, like Wittenberg a recently founded institution (1506) to serve the margravate of Brandenburg. Other German and Italian opponents emerged, most prominently Johann Eck of the also recently founded University of Ingolstadt (1472) in Bavaria, another rival principality of Saxony. They condemned Luther's for a variety of reasons: undermining of the sacramental system, challenging papal jurisdiction and authority, casting doubt on scholastic method in theology, giving assurance of salvation on the basis of God's promise in the sacraments. They misunderstood how his 'theology of the cross'[28] was informing his method and how he understood 'contrition'. They also feared that he would arouse popular disorder.[29] Wittenberg students burned a shipment of these pamphlets that came into their hands.

Luther recognized the explosiveness of the situation and published a simple exposition of his views, *Sermon on Indulgences and Grace*, in late March 1518.[30] Tetzel replied. Theologians for and against Luther began to experiment with the published tract as a means of carrying the art of disputation to a wider audience and a new level of seriousness and bitterness. Eck, who had previously expressed admiration for Luther's ideas, argued against Luther from scholastic authorities; Luther replied with biblical and patristic citations. New voices from Rome entered the fray by June: the Dominican Thomist Sylvester Mazzolini Prierias, master of the sacred palace, was commissioned to compose the case against Luther. His *Dialogue against the Presumptuous Conclusions of Martin Luther* affirmed papal authority and infallibility and condemned Luther for opposing this viewpoint. By the end of August Luther had rejected Prierias's position with arguments from Scripture, Augustine, and canon law. Prierias replied in print in November.[31] His invective caused E. Gordon Rupp to say, 'Luther never has received sufficient credit for the books he did not write,'[32] that is, Luther's polemical language, as strong as it seems to twenty-first-century readers, did not match the maliciousness and scurrility of some opponents.

---

[28] See (ch. 4) below, pp. 55–59.

[29] D. Bagchi, *Luther's Earliest Opponents, Catholic Controversialists, 1518–1525*, Minneapolis, Fortress, 1991, 20–43.

[30] *WA* 1: 243–6.

[31] Brecht, *Luther*, 1: 202–13, 242–6; cf. L. Grane, *Modus loquendi theologicus. Luthers Kampf um die Erneuerung der Theologie (1515–1518)*, Leiden, Brill, 1975, 161–91.

[32] While lecturing at Concordia Seminary, Saint Louis, 30 March 1973.

While the public disputation in print continued, forces on both sides sought to end the conflict. The German Augustinian reform chapter had a regular chapter meeting scheduled for late April 1518. Staupitz appointed Luther to conduct the public disputation at the meeting, a form of continuing education for the monks. Luther composed his 'Heidelberg Theses', defended by his fellow Wittenberg brother, Leonhard Beier, there. These made a lasting impression on listeners who came to hear his views, including future reformers Martin Bucer, Johannes Brenz, and Erhard Schnepf. No immediate ramifications of the Heidelberg encounter became apparent, but the organization of his thoughts on what Luther labeled 'the theology of the cross' proved to be a significant step in developing his hermeneutic. He called this *theologia crucis* 'our theology'.[33]

These theses focused on the relationship between God and human creatures, on the power of the human will, and on trusting God when he seems to be opposing the good, topics of great concern to Luther in his own personal struggles. But the turbulence of the attacks on him, based on differing views of authority and governance in the church, forced him to address the doctrine of the church as well. The papal court sent one of its foremost theologians, also a Dominican Thomist, Thomas de Vio, Cardinal Cajetan, to the imperial diet in Augsburg to conduct Luther's trial in September 1518. After the sessions of the diet, in which many princes had united to lodge serious grievances against Rome's alleged abuse of the German church, Luther appeared before Cajetan. Filled with trepidation because he realized the seriousness of Rome's intent to execute him as a heretic, he was also confident that God was in ultimate charge of his church. The two met 12–14 October. Cajetan disappointed Luther by refusing to discuss any theological matter. He simply demanded that the German monk return to complete obedience to the pope, retract his errors, and refrain from public disruption of the church's life. When pressed, Cajetan identified only two of Luther's errors: his rejection of indulgences, which church law supported, and his proposal that receiving the Lord's Supper gives assurance of salvation, which Scripture and tradition deny. Luther's reply repudiated Cajetan's contention on both points. Six days of waiting on Cajetan's reaction, in which he received no answer to two letters and a public appeal to the cardinal, caused Luther to fear for his life since memories of the burning of the Bohemian reformer Jan Hus in Constance at an imperial diet a century earlier were being publicly expressed. Luther fled Augsburg by night on 20 October. His case was already unfolding at the level of princely diplomacy; Karl von Miltitz, a Saxon in the pope's

---

[33] See Chapter 3. Cf. *WA* 1: 353–74; Brecht, *Luther*, 1: 213–21, 231–5.

employ, was negotiating with Frederick the Wise to attain Luther's delivery to Rome. The elector refused.[34]

Against this background Eck decided to pursue his own assault on the Wittenberg faculty, challenging its senior theologian, Karlstadt, to a public disputation over several issues, including the authority of Scripture, the continuing presence of sin in Christians, freedom of the will, and the power of the pope. Eck obtained support from Duke George of Saxony, Elector Frederick's cousin and rival, who mandated that his university in Leipzig host the disputation. Held 17 June–16 July 1519, it focused on papal power. Karlstadt did not fare well sparring with Eck; Luther did better, wielding biblical, patristic, and scholastic citations against Eck's argument. Eck brought Luther to admit that popes and councils could err. Eck was satisfied that Luther had confessed his heresy; Luther was satisfied that he was coming to clarity on how God actually governs his church. Eck appealed to the theological faculties in Louvain and Cologne to judge the outcome of the disputation. It took them more than a year, but, provoked by the Basel edition of Luther's collected works, printed in late 1518, they condemned Luther's positions at Leipzig. Throughout 1518 and 1519 individual opponents also attacked him, giving him the opportunity to sharpen his view of ecclesiastical authority and related topics.[35]

Before and after Leipzig Luther went about his duties in Wittenberg. His student, Bartholomäus Bernhardi, was serving as rector of the university in the winter semester 1518–19, leading a curricular reform that strengthened humanistic elements which had been present in the faculty for more than a decade.[36] Aristotle was giving way to broader studies in the arts and to the Bible in theology. In addition, this reform found tremendous strength, in a Wittenberg coup. Frederick was able to attract Philip Melanchthon, a young protégé of Johannes Reuchlin, the most famous Hebraic humanist north of the Alps, to a chair in Greek. After his arrival 25 August 1518, Melanchthon quickly linked with Luther, the two of them forming a team of erudition and piety working for the reform of university, church, and society. Humanist scholarship (seldom so sharply opposed to scholastic colleagues as is often intimated) had arrived in Wittenberg before 1510. Luther turned to works by Reuchlin and the French humanist Jacques Lefèvre d'Etaples for help in his exegesis of the Psalms and utilized the scholarship of Desiderius Erasmus as quickly as he could obtain newly published works. In addition, humanists began to acclaim Luther as one

[34] Brecht, *Luther*, 1: 246–73; L. Grane, *Martinus Noster, Luther in the German Reform Movement 1518–1521*, Mainz, Zabern, 1994, 23–9; Lohse, *Theology*, 110–17.

[35] Brecht, *Luther*, 1: 288–343; Grane, *Martinus Noster*, 81–136; B. Lohse, *Martin Luther's Theology*, tr. R. Harrisville, Minneapolis, Fortress, 1999, 118–26.

[36] Grane, *Modus*, 138–46.

of their own in the cause of reform even before they fully understood his message, indeed, while he was still constructing the framework for his new way of thinking about God and human creatures.[37] Humanist publishers eagerly sought to publish or republish his treatises. By 1520 some thirty tracts or books, in an estimated 600,000 copies, had carried aspects of his message to priests and populace.[38]

Like all theologians, Luther worked at clarifying his understanding of the biblical message and formulating his way of proclaiming it throughout this period. In the eight years following the reception of his doctorate, his thought matured from his own reception of late medieval thinking to a proposal for a new paradigm for understanding God and what it means to be human. His thought continued to mature throughout his life, but by 1520 its essential elements had fallen into place. He applied and extended them in specific situations the rest of his life, following the trajectory set by his education and personality. He continued to uphold his oath to 'expound the Scriptures for all the world and teach everyone', writing in 1530, 'I must indeed confess to my life's end.'[39]

[37] Brecht, *Luther*, 1: 275–97.

[38] Bernd Moeller; 'Das Berühmtwerden Luthers', *Zeitschrift für historische Forschung* 15 (1988), 65–92; 'Die Rezeption Luthers in der frühen Reformation', *LuJ* 57 (1990), 57–71; and 'Luther in Europe: His Works in Translation 1517–1546', in E. I. Kouri and Tom Scott (eds.), *Politics and Society in Reformation Europe*, New York, St. Martin's, 1987, 235–51; M. Edwards, *Printing, Propaganda and Martin Luther*, Berkeley, University of California Press, 1994, 14–40.

[39] 'Commentary on Psalm 82', *WA* 31.1: 212.12–18, *LW* 13: 66.

3

The Formation of the Theologian: The Medieval Roots of Luther's Thought

Learning theology begins at home. In Mansfeld Luther's views of God and the world took shape. The original indigenization of Christianity had little altered certain pre-Christian, pagan religious rhythms and perceptions of reality. The religion of Luther's youth focused on trust in ritual performance of sacred activities and also on moral, upright behavior that was aimed at ingratiating Christians into God's favor—not an easy task when children grew up with pictures of God as an angry judge among the only graphic depictions they encountered. To overcome God's wrath against sinners, Christians spent life striving to perform the necessary acts that could win back God's favor and aid in attaining the righteousness of obedience to his law. That was the focus of medieval Christian education.

THE PIETY OF LUTHER'S CHILDHOOD

Luther recorded no recollections of his own instruction in the faith. In addition to what he learned from praying with his parents and attending mass, he undoubtedly heard some catechetical homilies from traveling preachers before he left Mansfeld for Magdeburg. He received formal teaching in the faith in school in both places. The associates of the Brethren of the Common Life in Magdeburg implanted in him a desire to serve God by serving the neighbor and by ardent devotion to the Lord. Once he began studies in Erfurt, the city's religious atmosphere, with three dozen churches, a dozen monasteries, and some 800 clergy, framed his learning of the liberal arts, steeping him in the religious undergirding of medieval thinking. What brought Luther to the monastery lay in his perception of human fragility and perversity and God's grandeur. The depictions of God the Father or Christ as judge in the altars of his day—one of the few pictorial media making a continuing impression on medieval minds—reinforced his experience of life at the edge of sickness and dying that formed the medieval consciousness. Such depictions joined with another important medium, the liturgy of the mass, to emphasize God's total domination of his world.

That domination often seemed arbitrary and unfair, fostering in sensitive souls like young Martin a sense of awe and even terror in the presence of this Creator. His own worth and only hope, he believed, depended on his mastering his desires to stray from God's ways and his compensation for his sins. Apparently, the shortcuts to pleasing God that gave many lay people a sense of religious security did not set aside young Martin's belief that he must render perfect performance of God's demands for ritual service and ethical compliance, harsh, severe, rigorous as he imagined them to be.

MONASTIC AND MYSTICAL FORMATION

Luther entered the monastery to find a more direct, though more difficult, way to God. His foundational theological education took place within the Augustinian cloister. He threw himself with zeal and passion into monastic exercises of self-discipline and self-deprivation because he believed that his own striving to please God provided the key to finding God's approval and favor. Vital for his theological formation were the seven hours of prayer and other aspects of monastic devotional life. Daily repetition of its liturgies drilled psalms and other portions of Scripture into his head. The failure of these spiritual exercises to ease his unsettled, distressed conscience did not alter the fact that the psalmists' cries of repentance and pleas for mercy sprang automatically out of the thesaurus of his memory for the rest of his life.

Even in the midst of his scholastic studies with their intellectual mastery of things divine, Luther still felt dependence upon God and sought a suitable way to come to terms with God's awesome divinity. Searching for God devotionally led some monks into extensive reading. Luther absorbed insights from Scripture, the ancient fathers, and more recent writers, many of whose works contained elements labeled 'mystical'. Luther may not have recognized them as a special group, for his scholastic mentors, such as Gabriel Biel[1] and the Parisian Ockhamist scholastics Pierre d'Ailly and Jean Gerson,[2] had also embraced mystical elements in their discourse.

Early in his monastic education and then in teaching he gained appreciation for the *theologia mystica* through the renaissance of the thought of

---

[1] K.-H. zur Mühlen, *Nos Extra Nos. Luthers Theologie zwischen Mystik und Scholastik*, Tübingen, Mohr/Siebeck, 1972, 19; H. Oberman, *The Harvest of Medieval Theology*, Durham, Labyrinth, 1983, 340–60.

[2] S. Ozment, *Homo Spiritualis: A Comparative Study of the Anthropology of Johannes Tauler, Jean Gerson and Martin Luther (1509–16)*, Leiden, Brill, 1969, 49–83; H. Oberman, 'Simul gemitus et raptus: Luther und die Mystik', in I. Asheim (ed.), *Kirche, Mystik, Heiligung und das Natürliche bei Luther*, Göttingen, Vandenhoeck & Ruprecht, 20–5; B. Hamm and V. Leppin (eds.), *Gottes Nähe unmittelbar erfahren. Mystik im Mittelalter und bei Martin Luther*, Tübingen, Mohr/Siebeck, 2007.

Bernard of Clairvaux, the twelfth-century Cistercian preacher, whose sermons he knew by 1509. They enriched his lectures on the Psalms and especially Paul's epistles in the 1510s.[3] Likewise, devotional works by Heinrich Suso and Johann Tauler, fourteenth-century monastic devotional writers, familiarized Luther with several 'mystical' approaches to the Christian life. Steven Ozment observes 'positive points of contact between Luther's theology and late medieval mysticism where this literature emphasizes the centrality of Augustinian motifs; the concern for self-resignation, humility, and spiritual temptation; the significance of mystical vocabulary and imagery; the importance of inward, personal experience; and the role which theological methods of thought play'.[4] He did no more than flirt with the kind of mystical thought represented by the thirteenth-century Dominican Meister Eckhart but also implicit in many of Tauler's works. Eckhart strained to unite the soul with the essence of God that it might lose itself like a drop of water in the ocean of his being. Tauler held that human beings were 'one essential being' with and in God, that 'the ground of their souls' will come to rest in its uncreated source, God. Such ideas sprang from the writings of Neoplatonist Pseudo-Dionysius the Areopagite, a sixth-century body of work attributed to Saint Paul's Athenian convert (Acts 17: 34). Luther knew and occasionally cited the Pseudo-Dionysian corpus. But the 'mysticism' that helped him give voice to his own spiritual longings did not seek total separation from creaturely life and loss of identity in the depths of God's quintessence. From early on his consciousness of the total distinctiveness of Creator and creature prevented him from abiding with Dionysius in a Neoplatonic world that acknowledged no sharp divide between the Ultimate Spirit of God and sparks of spirit in the human soul.[5]

Instead, Luther was taken by fifteenth-century Parisian professor Jean Gerson's practical devotional mysticism, which emphasized the distinction between the Creator and his creatures and viewed salvation as a return to the state of Adam and Eve before the Fall.[6] The 'bride mysticism' of Bernard and others that spoke of unity with God in terms of the union of bride and bridegroom captivated his theological imagination as well. This kind of uniting with God preserves the distinct persons of Creator and creature. Indeed, the delight of the union of bride and bridegroom arises from the retention of each individual's own character as woman and man. So Luther insisted that God brings believers to himself but remains Creator

[3] T. Bell, *Divus Bernhardus. Bernhard von Clairvaux in Martin Luthers Schriften*, Mainz, Zabern, 1993.

[4] Ozment, *Homo Spiritualis*, 8.

[5] G. Ebeling, 'The Beginnings of Luther's Hermeneutics', *LQ* 17 (1993), 142–3.

[6] Ozment, *Homo Spiritualis*, 13–26, 35–46, 55–8, 90–117.

while they remain thoroughly human; this being 'in Christ' and having Christ 'in the believer' permits the believer to be fully human again. With Bernard Luther also came to recognize what he did not find in Gerson: that Christians dare not rely on their own conduct of life but rather must depend alone on God's grace, bestowed through Christ's suffering on their behalf.

His reading of the psalms in lectures, 1513–15, provided the setting for his deepening conviction of human unworthiness before God, the permeating nature of sin, and the need for God's mercy. His reading of Tauler's sermons in early 1516 made an immediate impact, giving voice to his own experience in the midst of scholastic speculation, directing him to suffering rather than action as the proper preparation for receiving God's favor. Already in the psalms lecture his 'theology of humility', nursed by Bernard and Tauler,[7] led him to find a form of self-deprivation different from that of the monastic system. Even though he still believed his own free will could generate this humbling, he acknowledged his complete perversion in his sinful 'turning in on himself'. This emphasis on the need to abase oneself before God was, however, not simply a new form of works through suffering. The cry that God would be just if he damned him served as Luther's confession that there was nothing worthy or meritorious in him before his Creator.[8] Tauler taught him to throw himself completely and exclusively on the mercy of God. This focal point began moving Luther's religious awareness from inside himself to outside himself.

Yet, for all that he absorbed from Bernard and Tauler, Luther transformed certain elements of their teaching. Bernard linked sinners with God through 'love', which embraced human action, while Luther, fearful of turning to self-evaluation that always leads to the recognition of sin, taught that Christ and sinner meet through human trust in the Savior. He alone works in human creatures effectively through this faith that centers life totally on loving God.[9] In the recent concentration on mystical elements in Luther's theology Volker Leppin's judgment cuts through prejudice and preference to observe that while his later thought cannot be understood apart from its mystical roots, Luther absorbed insights from Bernard, Tauler, and others, including their intensive preoccupation with the person of the Creator and especially the Savior, by integrating them into the framework of his law–gospel distinction of God's working through his external Word.[10]

---

[7] Ibid., 27–34; Bell, *Bernhardus*, 119–21. [8] *WA* 56: 388.4–18, cf. 246.11–247.17.

[9] Zur Mühlen, *Nos Extra Nos*, 101–16.

[10] V. Leppin, 'Transformationen spätmittelalterlicher Mystik bei Luther', in Hamm and Leppin, *Gottes Nähe*, 165–85.

Though scholasticism and monasticism failed Luther as effective avenues to peace of conscience, he found some solace in mystical writers. But finally they failed him, too, for delving deeper into himself proved to be no answer at all, humbling himself an uncertain path. He needed God to come to him and to do so through an external Word that anchored his new sense of righteousness, identity, dignity, or worth in something over which he had neither intellectual, volitional, nor emotional control. Therefore, when in the midst of prayerful contemplation of Christ's wounds a vision of Christ appeared to him, he commanded it to vanish as a Satanic creation and illusion.[11]

SCHOLASTIC FORMATION

Since Peter Lombard and Abelard, twelfth-century instructors at Paris, whose works shaped academic study of Christian teaching, university theology had existed alongside monastic instruction. It adopted Aristotelian principles in the thirteenth century as a means of clarifying biblical thinking and engaging thinkers from outside the Christian framework, such as the Arabic Muslim and Jewish scholars who had transmitted the Aristotelian corpus, for the most part lost in the Christian Mediterranean world since the fourth century. By 1300 university and monastic theologians alike blended Scripture with the earlier Neoplatonic philosophical framework, part of Augustine's legacy, and Aristotle.

Scholastic method posed questions, compared answers from ancient and recent authorities, and through logical assessment of Scripture and these authorities came to solutions to questions raised about the church's teaching. By Luther's time a number of 'schools' or 'ways' existed within the theological forum: chiefly 'Realists' who believed reality lies in divine ideas that form patterns for the shadows of that heavenly reality on this earth (*via antiqua*), and 'Nominalists', who sought to know reality on the basis of the experience of individual creations of God on this earth (*via moderna*). Within each existed various factions. Polemical exchanges served them as a pathway to truth. University professors of both the arts and theology practiced the formal academic disputation—debate—as the way to attain knowledge.

The image of such faculties as sharply divided among warring camps—realists against nominalists, followers of Thomas Aquinas (*c.*1224–74) against followers of Duns Scotus (*c.*1265–1308) and adherents of William

---

[11] *WATR* 1: 287.8–27. Cf. G. Forde, 'When Old Gods Fail: Martin Luther's Critique of Mysticism', in *idem*, *The Preached God*, ed. M. C. Mattes and S. D. Paulson, Grand Rapids, Eerdmans, 2007, 56–68.

of Ockham (*c.*1300–52) against them both, disciples of the strict moner-gist Gregory of Rimini (d. 1358) against their 'semi-pelagian' Ockhamist cousins—reflects one side of the real situation. The concrete examples of Erfurt theologians, for instance, present a more complex picture. In spite of the large quantity of good research that has explored late medieval scholastic theologies in the last half-century, Rupp's judgment that we still lack sufficient information to trace out all their influences on Luther remains valid.[12] For all theologians are 'eclectic'. None simply repristinates the thought of a single predecessor. The reputation of Luther's instructors on Erfurt's faculty as Ockhamists rests on the fact that several of them had studied with Gabriel Biel, the most prominent German Ockhamist of the period, at the University of Tübingen. Indeed, Jodukus Trutfetter and Bartholomäus Arnoldi reflected his influence in their instruction. But careful reading of their writings shows that they knew and cited favorably the Ockhamists' rival, Thomas Aquinas. They had learned that from Biel himself, who accurately and frequently cited the Angelic Doctor, in agree-ment and disagreement.

Luther's understanding of Thomas came not from reading his works extensively but rather from citations in the works of others. He also viewed Thomas through the eyes of his recent disciples, many of whom were influ-enced by the early fourteenth-century French Dominican John Capreolus. Luther's colleagues in Wittenberg, chief among them Karlstadt, and his foe from Rome, Cardinal Cajetan, also conveyed Thomas's teaching, but with less than perfect faithfulness to their thirteenth-century mentor. Thus, Luther criticized Thomas on the basis of some correct and some incorrect information. His reactions were largely critical, but only on selected topics: penance, monasticism, justification, and angels, for instance.[13] At the root of his critique, however, lay the role Thomas assigned to human merit in his definition of humanity. Thomas recognized only one kind of human righteousness, that of human performance of God's law; thus, Luther sensed a profound divide between him and this, as well as other, scholastic theologians.

More formidable influences came from those generally labeled 'Ockhamist', especially Biel. Luther reacted sharply against his instructors' views of salvation, but many marks of their formation remained. Lecturing on Genesis 1 in 1535, he revealed that something of their linguistic theory lingered in his mind: 'we assign names to objects which have already been

---

[12] *The Righteousness of God: Luther Studies*, London, Hodder & Stoughton, 1953, 87–101.

[13] D. Janz, *Luther on Thomas Aquinas*, Stuttgart, Steiner, 1989; *idem, Luther and Late Medieval Thomism*, Waterloo, Wilfrid Laurier University Press, 1983; cf. L. Grane, *Modus loquendi theologicus. Luthers Kampf um die Erneuerung der Theologie (1515–1518)*, Leiden, Brill, 1975, 161–91.

created'.[14] But for the rest of his life the chief impact of his instruction in Erfurt lay in Biel's understanding of Luther's most pressing question: his identity in God's sight. Biel had tried to balance biblical doctrine regarding God's grace and human performance by insisting that 'out of purely natural powers' (*ex puris naturalibus*) sinners could 'do what is in them' (*facere quod in se est*). By doing their best they could win 'congruent merit', a worthiness or righteousness before God that is not truly worthy but nonetheless accepted by God as the basis for receiving his grace. Among his many definitions of God's grace Biel followed the Aristotelian tradition and placed at the center of his description of salvation the gift of a 'habit' (*habitus*), a disposition. It supplied power to perform acts that are truly worthy or righteous in God's sight. These acts have condignent merit, worthiness that makes the sinner righteous before God. God's sacramental absolution covers the eternal guilt of those sins that continue to emerge from the sinner. Doing one's best is possible, Biel taught, because the *synteresis*, the highest power within the human creature that directs thought and action, retained a spark of goodness that directed the mind and will toward the good.[15]

If Biel's doctrines of the human creature and of salvation offended Luther—caused him to stumble into the depths of self-deprecation and self-doubt—Biel's image of God as almighty Creator and of human dependence on his self-revelation laid foundations that never disappeared from the reformer's way of thinking, even if the construction he built on these foundations differed significantly from Biel's. Biel followed Ockham in teaching that God's foremost characteristic is his unlimited, unconditioned power and that God could do anything he pleased according to his 'absolute power'. No timeless law, existing eternally alongside God, defined the good. God defined the good. To prevent fears that God might act arbitrarily, Ockham and Biel taught that God limited his own alternatives by restricting his options. In relationship to his creatures God acts according to his 'ordered' or 'ordained' power, confirmed in covenants made in nature and revelation for his human creatures.[16] Luther transformed these ideas but remained convinced of God's absolute power and lordship and of human dependence on God's revelation of himself.[17] Aristotle had needed

---

[14] WA 42: 17.21, LW 1: 22; cf. 'Disputation on John 1: 14' (1539), WA 39.2: 11–12, WATR 4: 679, #5134, WATR 5: 653, #6419. On Luther's continuing use of Ockhamist logic, see G. White, *Luther as Nominalist: A Study of the Logical Methods used in Martin Luther's Disputations in the Light of their Medieval Background*, Helsinki, Luther-Agricola-Society, 1994.

[15] B. Gerrish, *Grace and Reason: A Study in the Theology of Luther*, Oxford, Clarendon, 1962, 114–37; Oberman, *Harvest*, 57–89, 146–84.

[16] Oberman, *Harvest*, 30–56.

[17] e.g., Genesis lectures, 1539, WA 43: 71.19–27, LW 3: 274.

an eternal law for preserving order for the world and thus security for human beings, for he could not imagine a personal creator. Biblical writers relied instead for that order and security on the Almighty Creator. Scotus's maxim, 'nothing created must be accepted by the Creator', reflecting the comparison of God with the potter or the father, who alone is responsible for pot or child (Isa. 45: 9–13), informed this view of God.[18] Luther may have appropriated it through Ockhamistic instruction or from Scotist masters in Erfurt. So Luther commented on God's treatment of Ishmael: God 'owes nobody anything. Before him, let no one boast or glory in his righteousness and merit.'[19] In the Scotist and Ockhamist traditions this God had made a decision unconditioned by human effort, in pure grace, to reward human performance and thus deliver sinners from their sin. Here Luther slowly parted company during the 1510s. He gradually repudiated Biel's doctrine that God's covenant with sinners demands performance of their best efforts before further grace can be forthcoming as an aid to truly righteous performance.

Biel followed Ockham in positing that God must reveal what we know about him because human reason cannot reach up or out to grasp God. In his omnipotence, as Creator, his human creatures cannot grasp God fully. Therefore, human creatures depend upon what God tells them about himself, in Scripture and through the church's teaching office. The human mind comes to hear or read what God has said and grasps it by faith, defined chiefly as the intellectual comprehension of what God reveals. With this revelation the *synteresis*, the ultimate guide for human decision-making (located by Biel in the intellect, not the will), perceives God's truth and acts upon it. Faith, the basic knowledge of the content of God's revelation, is acquired by the intellect through hearing, but this *fides acquisita*, as mere knowledge, is insufficient for salvation, Biel believed. Sacramental grace had to infuse faith that is active in love (*fides infusa per dilectionem operans*) for the justification of the sinner.[20] Luther came to define faith first of all as the trust which grasps God's revelation, though its object always determines whether faith is true or not. Furthermore, Luther defined this relationship with God in faith as the central, determining factor of human life, a strikingly different understanding than Biel's, by which human performance defined human worth. Nonetheless, human dependence on God's Word remained crucial for Luther's conception of the relationship between God and human creature.

[18]   W. Dettloff, *Die Entwicklung der Akzeptations- und Verdienstlehre von Duns Scotus bis Luther*, Münster, Aschendorff, 1963.

[19]   *WA* 43: 166.26–8, *LW* 4: 43.

[20]   Oberman, *Harvest*, 38–42, 57–89; Zur Mühlen, *Nos Extra Nos*, 18–19.

The doubt which Biel's system created in Luther regarding his own identity before God sparked his revolt against scholastic theology. But the problem of his own righteousness formed only one part of a larger problem with what he had been taught. Scholastic theologians did not properly present the biblical view of the relationship between the Creator and his human creatures, Luther contended. Scholastic theology's reliance on Aristotle permeated its method and content and necessarily obscured God's power and majesty as well as what was proper for human creatures with their potential and limitations. Therefore, Luther often railed against 'reason' as a means of asserting human control over God's revelation. He did not reject reason itself, as God's gift for the proper conduct of human life. He consistently accorded reason a vital role in governing the horizontal relationships of human beings among themselves and with other creatures.[21] He appreciated Aristotle's works when used for specific purposes. But at the most fundamental level, Luther's world and Aristotle's were antithetical, for Aristotle knew no personal Creator and therefore defined humanity in terms of human performance of proper acts.[22] He could not create a system in which God stands at the center of human life.[23] Although Luther embraced and applauded both 'reason' and 'Aristotle' at times, at other times he rejected both because they obscured God's truth with false lenses for viewing reality.[24] He broke with this understanding of who God is and what it means to be human by edging away from defining original sin as lack of original righteousness to a view of it as the absence of a proper trust in God. He no longer defined grace as an internally located gift from God; it became instead his favor, his merciful disposition toward sinners. Hints of experimentation in these directions occur as early as lectures on Lombard's Sentences (1509), but these must be viewed in retrospect as only the background of later experiments with interpreting Scripture and formulating its message that then blossomed into his own theology.[25]

---

[21] *WA* 10.1.1: 527.11–528.16; *WA* 12: 548.14–549.11; *WA* 40.3: 612.35–613.10. See Gerrish, *Reason*, 12–27; H. Junghans, *Der junge Luther und die Humanisten*, Göttingen, Vandenhoeck & Ruprecht, 1985, 143–71, traces Luther's struggle against Aristotle's dominance of his thought; Ebeling, *Luther*, 76–92; B. Lohse, *Martin Luther's Theology*, tr. R. Harrisville, Minneapolis, Fortress, 1999, 196–205.

[22] W. D. J. Cargill Thompson, *The Political Thought of Martin Luther*, Sussex, Harvester, 1984, 82–4.

[23] T. Dieter, *Der junge Luther und Aristoteles*, Berlin, de Gruyter, 2001, 193–213. Luther criticized Augustine for defining human performance as the basis for righteousness before God, although Augustine did not know Aristotle.

[24] *WA* 40.3: 608.15; *WA* 42: 21.9–35, *LW* 1: 26–7; *WATR* 1: 178–9, #411; *WA* 1: 226.10–31. Dieter, *Aristoteles*, esp. 632–42 and Gerrish, *Reason*, 28–42, 69–113.

[25] Zur Mühlen, *Nos Extra Nos*, 1–25.

AUGUSTINE, AUGUSTINIANISM, AND
OTHER FATHERS

As an Augustinian monk Luther learned to treasure Augustine but not necessarily to understand him. Indeed, Augustinians took their namesake seriously, but before editions of the Fathers began to appear in the early sixteenth century, members of the Order read him somewhat haphazardly. Some Augustinians reproduced his thought on grace and sin more accurately than others; all agreed on the centrality of love and emphasized the human will more than the intellect. Their various positions coincided generally in doctrines of human depravity and divine predestination, the issues raised by Augustine's criticism of the teaching of his contemporary, the British monk Pelagius. Pelagius taught that human beings could attain righteousness before God with little or no help from God's grace. A distinct tradition of theological Augustinianism crossed over the lines of membership in specific orders; several prominent late medieval thinkers echoed Augustine's rejection of Pelagius's understanding of the free will and the contribution of human works to salvation.

Luther arrived at the Augustinian cloister in Erfurt as Johann Jeuser von Paltz was laying aside his duties as director of theological studies there. Paltz followed his own teacher, Johannes von Dorsten, in presenting theology in a framework reflecting both Aristotelian influences and pious, pastoral concern for God's people. He held that the church guaranteed salvation through the practice of its sacramental system and encouragement of personal piety, with requirements for pleasing God set at a level sufficient to accommodate most people's ability to perform, so that no sincere Christian had to fear exclusion from the merit that insured grace. Since Luther never mentioned Paltz in his writings, it is impossible to determine how much Paltz's influence shaped his younger monastic brother, but the themes of his teaching must have remained in conversation during Luther's years there.[26] It is also impossible to ascertain how many of the bevy of other late medieval Augustinians Luther had perused. By 1519 he knew the fourteenth-century fiercely anti-pelagian theologian Gregory of Rimini, reading him with profit and appreciation.[27] Before that, Staupitz had led him into Augustine; Luther annotated the works collected in his *Opuscula*, *De trinitate*, and *De civitate Dei* about 1509, perhaps for lectures in the monastery.[28]

---

[26] B. Hamm, *Frömmigkeitstheologie am Anfang des 16. Jahrhunderts. Studien zu Johannes von Paltz und seinem Umkreis*, Tübingen, Mohr/Siebeck, 1982.

[27] Janz, *Medieval Thomism*, 158–65, D. Steinmetz, *Luther and Staupitz*, Durham, Duke University Press, 1980, 13–34.

[28] *WA* 9: 2–27.

By 1515 his attention focused above all on Augustine's anti-pelagian writings, *Contra Julianum* and *De spiritu et littera*.[29] Along with his exegetical works, particularly comment on Psalms and John, these treatises clarified and reinforced Luther's understanding of sin and grace although precisely how his influence impacted Luther cannot easily be determined. In reflecting on his coming to terms with the concept of God's righteousness in Romans 1: 17, Luther recalled that only Augustine among the Fathers had helped although he did not date precisely when he found this critical assistance in the Fathers since it may not have been on first reading.[30] He knew Augustine's works well enough by 1516 to identify *De vera et falsa poenitentia* as falsely attributed to the bishop of Hippo.[31]

Luther's use of specific concepts of Augustine's changed over the years. For example, by 1517/18 he was developing his own use of the maxim, 'The Word comes to the element, and it becomes a sacrament', integrating it into his maturing theology of God's Word.[32] Indeed, even toward his favorite Father Luther exercised a critical eye. His standard was not what was old and time-honored, but what was true, scriptural, conveying Christ's gospel. Therefore, he could also criticize Augustine, particularly for not fully understanding how God justifies sinners: Augustine believed grace produces good works and thus held onto a concept of righteousness by grace-assisted human performance, which Luther rejected.[33]

Although his works throughout his career reveal his respect for the Fathers, Luther frequently exercised critical judgment, particularly against those whose writings taught that human merit contributes to salvation or who held what he regarded as false interpretations of other points in Scripture. His biblical lectures continued the conversation with Jerome, begun by 1509,[34] throughout his career. As late as 1539 he expressed appreciation for Lombard's collections of patristic citations while

---

[29] Grane, *Modus*, 46–62.

[30] *WA* 43: 537.18–25, *LW* 5: 158; cf. *WA* 54: 186. Cf. W. Bienert, ' "Im Zweifel näher bei Augustin?" Zum patristischen Hintergrund der Theologie Luthers', in Damaskinos Papandreou et al. (eds.), *Oecumenica et Patristica*, Stuttgart, Kohlhammer, 1989, 281–94, Junghans, *Junge Luther*, 123–43, and Grane, *Modus*, 23–63.

[31] *WABr* 1: 65.

[32] K.-H. zur Mühlen, 'Die Rezeption von Augustins "Tractatus in Joannem 80,3" im Werk Martin Luthers', in Leif Grane et al. (eds.), *Auctoritas Patrum: Contributions on the Reception of the Church Fathers in the 15th and 16th Century*, vol. 1, Mainz, Zabern, 1993, 271–81.

[33] *WABr* 6: 100, #1818, *WATR* 2: #1572, *WATR* 1: #347.

[34] M. Brecht and C. Peters (eds.), *Martin Luther. Annotierungen zu den Werken des Hieronymus*, Archiv zur Weimarer Ausgabe, Cologne, Böhlau, 2000; cf. R. Mau, 'Die Kirchenväter in Luthers früher Exegese des Galaterbriefes', in Grane et al., *Auctoritas Patrum*, 1: 117–27.

noting Lombard's weakness on the topics of faith and the justification of sinners.[35]

Controversy over Luther's 'fairness' in citing the Fathers has shown that, like other Protestant reformers, the Wittenberg theologians neither canonized their work nor rejected it entirely. They viewed the Fathers as witnesses to the faith, as fallible as they saw themselves, and sought to glean from them what testified to the truth and leave aside, sometimes with sharp criticism, what might be used to undermine the church's proper teaching, as they understood it. They 'deparentified' the Fathers[36] because they acknowledged only God as the authoritative Father, whose teaching remains unalterable. Luther's authority remained Scripture; he cited Augustine to affirm that it alone is the authority and utterly reliable source of God's truth.[37]

BIBLICAL HUMANISM

Luther's doctoral oath pledged him to deliver the biblical message to the church faithfully. He pursued study of Scripture not only with the resources at hand in the scholastic and monastic traditions of exegesis. He turned to the newer methods and aids developed by the 'biblical humanists', who emphasized textual study on the basis of the original languages and whole texts rather than Latin citations assembled by earlier scholars. This broader interest in ancient sources and good style began to focus specifically on Scripture and the Fathers with the work of Lorenzo Valla's *Adnotationes in Novem Testamentum* (1444). This movement 'back to the original' elicited the first printed editions of ancient church fathers and Erasmus's edition of the Greek New Testament.

Humanists generally sought not only to argue logically with the tools of dialectic but specifically to argue persuasively with the tools of rhetoric. They began influencing thought in universities and monasteries in the fourteenth century; Luther absorbed those influences from monastic writers, from scholastic authors, from his Eisenach mentor, Johannes Braun, and from a circle of scholars, including prominent advocates of humanist reform of learning around his own monastery and university in Erfurt, Nikolaus Marschalk and Johannes Crotus Rubeanus. With them he learned

[35] *WA* 50: 443.21–3.

[36] S. Hendrix, 'Deparentifying the Fathers: The Reformers and Patristic Authority', in Grane et al., *Auctoritas Patrum*, 1: 55–68.

[37] *WA* 50: 524.13–18; citing Augustine's letter to Jerome, *CSEL* 34.2I: 354.4–15. Cf. K.-H. zur Mühlen, 'Die Auctoritas patrum in Martin Luthers Schrift "Von den Konziliis und Kirchen" (1539)', in Grane et al., *Auctoritas patrum*, 2: 141–52.

Ovid, Virgil, Terence, Quintilian, Cicero, and other classical authors. Representatives of this movement had come and gone in Wittenberg's faculty before and during Luther's first years there.[38]

Signs of Luther's use of humanistic helps for his teaching occur early. His glosses on Peter Lombard from 1509 demonstrate a familiarity and capacity for critical judgment with the works of Augustine and other Fathers that came from reading newly printed editions.[39] Humanist tools also proved useful as he increasingly turned to the study of Scripture. By 1509 he had read Johannes Reuchlin's introduction to the Hebrew language, *De rudimentis hebraicis* (published 1506): he used Jacques Lefèvre d'Etaples' *Quincuplex Psalterium* (1509) for his first Psalms lectures.[40] He must have begun to learn some Greek in the same period and purchased the first edition of Erasmus's Greek New Testament, the *Novum Instrumentum* (1516). He read and used Erasmus's *Paraphrases* of the New Testament. He finally began to correspond with the older scholar although by 1516 he sensed a different spirit, another definition of reform, in his more famous colleague. Erasmus soon realized the gap as well.[41] Other recent and contemporary humanist authors, including Johannes Baptista Mantuanus, commanded Luther's attention. His own Latin style betrayed humanistic influences. As his views drew him into public controversy, he slowly changed the ground rules for theological discussion by going back behind scholastic collections of citations for arguing dogma (Lombard's) and canon law (Gratian's) by appealing to older, purer sources.[42]

Not only did Luther embrace many of the humanists' concerns and methods; many of those engaged in humanistic pursuits embraced his cause as his calls for reform began to spread. Not without ambiguity and imprecise understanding of what he was really proposing, many his age or younger greeted Luther enthusiastically and supported him, lavishing praise upon him, at least until the crisis of his condemnations by pope and emperor.[43] South German and Swiss humanists regarded him as a contemporary Elijah, reported Ulrich Zwingli in 1520; his older contemporary in Freiburg, Ulrich Zasius, shared this view.[44] The next generation of the movement provided the shock troops for the spread of his message.[45]

---

[38] Junghans, *Junge Luther*, 17–108.   [39] Ibid., 108–23.   [40] Ibid., 171–273.

[41] Grane, *Modus*, 115–19.

[42] T. Dost, *Renaissance Humanism in Support of the Gospel in Luther's Early Correspondence* Aldershot, Ashgate, 2001; Grane, *Martinus Noster*, 59–80, 86–113.

[43] Junghans, *Junge Luther*, 288–304; Grane, *Martinus Noster*, 29–37, 137–87.

[44] See Zwingli's letter to Oswald Myconius, 4 January 1520, in *CR* 94: 250; cf. a reference to a no longer extant similar reference in Zwingli's correspondence with Ulrich Zasius's, in Zasius's letter to Zwingli, 13 November 1519, ibid., 222.

[45] L. Spitz, 'The Third Generation of German Humanists', in A. R. Lewis (ed.), *Aspects of the Renaissance: A Symposium*, Austin, University of Texas Press, 1967, 105–21.

Not all his humanistic supporters remained in Luther's camp. Most notably, as papal opposition grew more strident and Luther's responses grew sharper, Erasmus made the distance between himself and the Wittenberg theologian clearer. His vanity and the upstart's rising popularity may have contributed to this, but Erasmus recognized that his plan for reform concerned fundamentally moral and institutional issues, whereas Luther's struck at the heart of papal doctrine. For Erasmus doctrine was not an issue if abuses could just be abolished and misrepresentations caused by scholastic methods clarified. The formal break waited until 1524/5, when common enemies and shared interests in moral and institutional matters no longer could hold Luther and Erasmus together. But it is too much to speak of the 'disintegration of the reform party' at that point. Some humanists remained loyal to Erasmus, some straddled the fence, but most favored 'our Martin'.[46]

JOHANN VON STAUPITZ

Alongside his reading, his contemporaries influenced Luther, especially Johann von Staupitz. He had initiated the Wittenberg doctrine and given him everything he had, Luther claimed.[47] The Augustinian Observants' German Vicar General and his fledgling protégé had developed a mutual respect in the 1510s as Staupitz nursed Luther's troubled conscience and compelled him to become Staupitz's successor on the Wittenberg faculty. Like countless contemporaries, the Saxon nobleman cannot easily be pigeonholed into one late medieval school of thought. His writings betray familiarity with Ockhamists and Thomists, the range of Augustinian theologians of his time, mystical and monastic thinkers, and humanistically inclined colleagues and friends. Exchanges with Staupitz certainly bolstered and buttressed—perhaps initiated—Luther's acquaintance with these currents.

Perhaps the most outstanding characteristic of Staupitz's practice of theology, however, lay in his concern for good pastoral care, for comforting scrupulous, distressed, distraught believers like Brother Martin. Staupitz's conception of the gospel arose out of his conviction that God had unconditionally chosen the elect and arranged for their salvation through the death of Christ without any reference to their merit or performance. The doctrine of God's predestination, he counseled, assured Christians that God had committed himself irrevocably to their salvation; his treatment

---

[46] Grane, *Martinus Noster*, 189–229, 243–9, 269–97.
[47] *WATR* 1: 245, #526; 1: 86.6–7, #173; *WABr* 3: 156.36–8, #659; 11: 67.5–8.

of justification flowed from this foundation. When Luther came to him fretting about his inability to do his best in order to earn grace, Staupitz pointed him to God's merciful decree of salvation, which he was conveying to this troubled conscience through the wounds of Christ. Luther should look to them. Slowly Luther's understanding of unconditioned grace, the impossibility of human contribution to salvation, and the total perversion of the sinner's relationship to God through sin came close to Staupitz's. Both insisted that embracing God involves both cognitive and emotional engagement with him.

But there were profound differences between the two as well. Luther departed earlier from the exegetical method Staupitz employed. He never regarded election as the foundation of God's justification of sinners but only a 'wall of defense for its clarity'. He emphasized that justification comes through faith alone, whereas Staupitz defined human love for God as that which grasps God's gracious gift in Christ.[48] Without Staupitz Luther might have lacked some impetus or idea that proved vital to the definition of his theology. More likely, the most profound impact he made on Luther's practice of theology stemmed from his consolation of Brother Martin on the bad days, both from its content—the wounds of Christ, the unconditional nature of God's grace—and its method—the assurance of God's love through Jesus his Savior, given without requirement or restriction, simply because God is like that. Staupitz gave him practice in thinking in fresh ways about God's disposition toward him and Christ's work.

THE MEDIEVAL ROOTS

In his mixing and matching ideas from several antecedents,[49] Luther conformed to the pattern of every significant thinker in human history. From various perspectives, in answer to different questions, his thought may be assigned to one medieval school or movement or another. In fact, like all intellectuals he composed his own brew of the traditions he inherited, but, indeed, with insights and assertions sufficiently dissimilar to the body of any predecessor that one may attribute to him a new paradigm or pattern for viewing the relationship of God and his human creatures as presented in Scripture.

That does not mean that he freed himself completely from the questions posed or the answers given by those from whom he learned. It does mean that the combination of his personality (with its intense consciousness of

---

[48] Steinmetz, *Luther und Staupitz*, 35–140; M. Wriedt, *Gnade und Erwählung, eine Untersuchung zu Johann von Staupitz und Martin Luther*, Mainz, Zabern, 1991, 32–250.

[49] Lohse, *Theology*, 18–29, summarizes these factors.

God's presence and power, and the scrupulosity fostered and strengthened by his upbringing), his scholastic education, his efforts to please God through the monastic way of life, and his engagement with Scripture in the context of Ockhamistic and monastic ways of thinking, gave him new perspectives on God and humanity. This perspective fits neatly neither into the performance-driven religiosity of medieval thought nor into the Cartesian world which developed a century later. His call to turn from self to God reflects his context and projected itself into coming generations. It did not repristinate the old tradition nor prevent much of Western thought from returning to definitions of humanity in terms of humanly produced merit. Nonetheless, it has commanded significant elements in Christian and Western thought ever since.

4

In Via Vittembergensi: *Luther Develops His Hermeneutic*

No question so occupied Luther scholars in the first half of the twentieth century as the identification of the moment of Luther's 'conversion' to his new theology, to an evangelical understanding of God and humanity. This query sought to pinpoint not only a magic moment in Luther's intellectual and spiritual development; it also would determine the most vital, defining element in his thought. Therefore, the 'tower experience' or 'evangelical breakthrough' was found to have taken place either when the scholar's favorite aspect of the reformer's thinking first might be detected or when it seemed to have established itself firmly in his teaching.

Recent archeological finds have moved the 'tower' in which Luther was purported to have 'discovered the gospel' some hundred meters.[1] More seriously, most historians now recognize that no single 'experience', whether in a tower or not, determined Luther's way of thinking. Instead, it is better to speak of an evangelical maturation rather than a dramatic breakthrough, both because seeds for many of his mature ideas lay in the influences reviewed above and because the process of his construction of a new blueprint for public teaching developed over a longer period. In fact, Luther's pulpit and lecture podium became laboratories: he spent his entire career doing experiments in how best to formulate the building blocks of his teaching.[2] The shape of his own way of practicing theology appeared in fairly clear form by 1520. He sometimes piled up terms that he thought might best express his concepts, using terminology inherited from the past and trying new language harvested from Scripture or his experience. During that period in which he was constructing his hermeneutic some elements in it appeared and then faded back into his old way of conceiving of God and humanity. Some insights occurred to him in one context and failed to appear in others because his scholastic ways of thinking remained

---

[1] M. Treu, 'Waschhaus—Küche—Prioret. Die neuen archäologischen Funde am Wittenberger Lutherhaus', *Luther* 76 (2005), 132–40.

[2] G. Ebeling, *Luther, an Introduction to his Thought*, tr. R. Wilson, Philadelphia, Fortress, 1970, 13–58. See the helpful analysis of vital texts in V. Leppin, *Martin Luther*, Darmstadt, Wissenschaftliche Gesellschaft, 2006, 107–17.

instinctive. Only gradually did new formulations permeate his thought structures.[3]

In the 1510s he was mixing together ingredients from monastic, mystical, scholastic, patristic, and humanistic sources in the mortar of his assignments as professor and monastic administrator with the pestle of his own personality and experience. What emerged from his new constellation of the biblical definitions of God and human creature constituted a new paradigm for interpreting Scripture and proclaiming its message to the people of God. With his colleagues in Wittenberg he constructed a new 'way' of practicing theology, in which he strove to 'speak like an apostle' rather than like a metaphysicist or moralist. That kind of speaking embraced both hermeneutical method and content.[4]

HOW TO READ THE BIBLE IN WITTENBERG FASHION

All medieval theologians were biblical theologians. None tried to formulate his thought apart from Scripture. None admitted that he permitted any other sources, even Aristotle, to dominate what Scripture and the church's tradition say. Theological instructors in university and monastery strove to press God's truth from the Bible's pages no matter how dependent they were on philosophers, pagan and Christian, to aid them in conveying what they found there. Luther began his career by following the models for biblical exegesis practiced by both monastic and scholastic predecessors, not only for scholarship's sake, but also to extract from Scripture the solution to his own spiritual struggles. His attempt to use methods at hand brought him so deeply into its message that he found the Bible turning on him. The Bible seized Luther and asserted its mastery over him despite his desire to tame it to serve his own efforts to please God.[5] Obviously, this is an oversimplification of his own insight into the mysterious interaction between God's control of life and responsible human engagement with all God's gifts, Scripture included. Its mastery is exercised through the interpreter's exercise of the tools of interpretation. But Luther did experience a change in his understanding of his relationship to the text he was charged with interpreting, perhaps as early as the mid-1510s.

---

[3] Cf. E. Herrmann, ' "Why then the Law?" Salvation History and the Law in Martin Luther's Interpretation of Galatians 1513–1522', Ph.D. dissertation, Concordia Seminary, Saint Louis, 2005.

[4] L. Grane, *Modus loquendi theologicus. Luthers Kampf um die Erneuerung der Theologie (1515–1518)*, Leiden, Brill, 1975, 198–9.

[5] G. Ebeling, 'The Beginning of Luther's Hermaneutics', *LQ* 17 (1993), 130.

Many scholars have defined Luther's revolutionary move in biblical interpretation as his setting aside the allegorical method of seeking meaning in
its text. 'Allegorical method' encompasses several approaches to the text.
Fundamentally, it rests on the presupposition that the meaning intended
by God, as author of Scripture, is often hidden behind words that describe
historical happenings no longer of significance for later readers.[6] Meaning
itself has more than one level; words point to an immediate, concrete referent, but that referent can also point to an abstract truth behind it, according
to allegorical theory. Before Christ's time Jewish exegetes, such as Philo,
approached the biblical text in this way in order to make it meaningful
for contemporaries living far from the culture of Abraham or David. They,
like early Christians, lived in a Neoplatonic thought-world, which viewed
human history as but a fundamentally inconsequential accident of eternal
spirit and meaning.

The third-century Alexandrian theologian Origen faced the same challenge, particularly in regard to Old Testament texts. The two testaments
constituted the fundamental division in Scripture, the Old foreshadowing things to come, the New the source of truth in its highest revealed
form. Most medieval exegetes followed Origen, seeking the text's true
meaning on the basis of its literal sense in three higher levels of significance. Augustine sought to explain texts on the basis of faith, love, and
hope, on the levels of four senses: historical, allegorical (figurative interpretation), analogical (the correlation of Old and New Testaments), and
aetiological (causal explanation). His contemporary John Cassian (360–
430/435) defined the levels of meaning of biblical texts as tropology (moral
application to individual lives), allegory (foreshadowing Christ, the sacraments, and the church), and anagogy (pointing to the mysteries of heaven).
Cassian's definitions largely determined medieval usage of the terms.[7] This
method diminished the concrete and historical in favor of ideas on an
abstract level. Despite their concentration on the concrete things of the
created order, Ockhamist views of reality did not by and large counteract
this ascension to the abstract. Luther learned allegorical method in both
monastery and university. He began his exegetical lectures at least partially
bound to seeking the ideas behind the concrete detail of the text.

Luther's Psalm lectures (1513–15) echoed many predecessors in illus-
trating the method with the example of Jerusalem. Allegorically Jerusalem
represents good people, Babylon the bad; tropologically, Jerusalem denotes
virtues, Babylon vices; anagogically, Jerusalem signifies heavenly rewards,
Babylon hellish punishments. Luther also contrasted the deeper meanings

---

[6] Herrmann, 'Why', 14–66.
[7] S. Preus, *From Shadow to Promise, Old Testament Interpretation from Augustine to the Young
Luther*, Cambridge, Belknap, 1969, 21–3.

of Mount Zion in the forms of the killing letter and the life-giving spirit. Historically, the letter refers to Canaan, allegorically to the synagogue, tropologically, to the righteousness of the Pharisees or the law, anagogically to future bodily glory. The spirit represents the faithful of Zion, the church, the righteousness of faith, and spiritual glory.[8] But even as he used this method, he was also searching the author's original intent, which he believed often prophesied of Christ.[9]

Allegorical exegesis did not dominate medieval biblical study completely. The twelfth-century Victorine school, influential particularly in some monastic circles, accentuated the literal meaning of Old Testament texts. The early fourteenth-century Augustinian monk Hermann von Schildesche, who taught briefly at Erfurt, proposed a careful program for assessing the historical and non-historical dimensions of Scripture's literal sense and the use of figurative interpretation in each.[10] Whether copies of his 'Compendium of the Meanings of Sacred Scripture' were still available in the monastery library at Luther's time is unknown. Luther did know the commentary of Hermann's contemporary, the Parisian Franciscan Nicholas of Lyra (c.1270–1341), and attacked Lyra's approach, which legitimized the synagogue alongside the church, asserting that the psalms are filled with literal prophesies of Christ.[11] Luther was following Paul of Burgos (c.1351–1435), who criticized Lyra's position, arguing that Christ alone establishes the Bible's literal meaning.[12] Allegories continued to embellish Luther's sermons throughout his career, but instead of abstracting higher truths from the historical sense, he continued that strand of medieval interpretive tradition that regarded Old Testament figures prophetically, as pointing to what Christ was to do and what his church would be like.

In the midst of this use of allegorical and figural interpretation in his psalms lectures in 1513–15, Ebeling insists, Luther was struggling for linguistic and conceptual clarity but still confusing the historical definition of law as Old Testament with its theological function as evaluation of human performance. He continued to define 'gospel' as bound to the historical event of Christ's incarnation although he began to add to his definition the power to forgive sins and restore life in Christ. In these lectures he was practicing a 'hermeneutical syncretism',[13] viewing Scripture in terms of three concrete, historical 'advents' of Christ: in the flesh, in the believer's soul, and at the Last Day. This permitted him to take seriously simul—at the same time—the prophetic words of the Old Testament both for the

---

[8] WA 3: 11.3–12.10, LW 10: 3–4.   [9] Ebeling, 'Beginnings', 454–60.
[10] C. Ocker, *Biblical Poetics before Humanism and Reformation*, Cambridge, Cambridge University Press, 2002, 94–106.
[11] Herrmann, 'Why', 78–80; cf. F. Beißer, *Claritas scripturae bei Martin Luther*, Göttingen, Vandenhoeck & Ruprecht, 1966, 70–3.
[12] Preus, *Shadow*, 79–101.   [13] Ebeling, 'Beginnings', 457.

expectant people of God before Christ's coming and for New Testament believers. The former held the faith which would be fully revealed, while the latter were able to grasp the completion of God's revelation in Christ.[14] Yet in context, affirming the 'spirituality of the letter' or literal sense was not revolutionary. Monastic interpreters had done that for two centuries. Sixteenth-century humanists were already changing biblical exegesis by finding 'a literary method for handling the narrative construction of the Bible as a whole . . . where discrete biblical meanings congealed in a coherent body of knowledge'.[15] Luther contributed to that search by providing a metanarrative that recognized the dilemma of the sinner and delivered God's salvation, categorizing the biblical message as law that condemns sinners and gospel that resurrects children of God.

Over the following decades Luther's presupposition that God's Word is a living, creative instrument became intimately connected with defining this metanarrative of God's interaction with his human creatures. As he abandoned the allegorical method as his orienting hermeneutic, he slowly became convinced that Scripture's meaning lay not in 'the system of signification of the text's exoteric or esoteric meanings but rather in what the text actually *did* to him and for him'.[16] He proposed that the story of God's creation, redemption, and sanctification of fallen humankind proceeds out of Scripture and into the life of the congregation through the use of its message. This message functions in oral, written, and sacramental forms as the law kills and the gospel makes alive. 'Alive' for him meant living by faith in Christ, in the vertical dimension of life, and loving the neighbor in its horizontal dimension. His thought attracted attention because it struck his contemporaries, friends and foes, as a radical challenge to old tenets for interpreting Scripture and conducting the Christian life.

This complicated process was beginning when Luther turned from psalms to Pauline texts in 1515. There he naturally had less material for allegory. He subjected this method to discriminating but sharp critique in commenting on Galatians 4: 24 in 1517. He dismissed the Quadriga, as the fourfold method of interpretation was called, because the apostles and the earliest Fathers had not employed it. However, he used it to elaborate and apply texts.[17] He began to recognize intermittently that God

[14] S. Hendrix, *Ecclesia in Via*, Leiden, Brill, 1974, 268–71; J. Vercruysse, *Fidelis Populus*, Wiesbaden, Steiner, 1968.

[15] Ocker, *Poetics*, 211.

[16] G. Forde, 'When Old Gods Fail: Martin Luther's Critique of Mysticism', in *idem*, *The Preached God*, M. C. Mattes and S. D. Paulson (eds.), Grand Rapids, Eerdmans, 2007, 63.

[17] *WA* 2: 550.8–552.32. Cf. G. Ebeling, *Evangelische Evangelienauslegung, eine Untersuchung zu Luthers Hermeneutik*, 3rd edn, Tübingen, Mohr/Siebeck, 1991, 283–7. Cf. T. Maschke's critique of Ebeling's position, 'The Understanding and Use of Allegory in the Lectures on the Epistle of Saint Paul to the Galatians by Doctor Martin Luther', Ph.D. dissertation, Marquette University, 1993. It is correct that Luther changed his use of allegory from application to

was confronting him in the text with his powerful and active Word that killed sinners through the law and brought them to new life through the gospel that conveyed God's promise in the work of Christ. In 1515 or 1516 he became convinced that the law was not simply Old Testament revelation, the gospel a New Testament improvement upon it. Leaving behind this 'salvation-history' understanding of God's working through 'law' and 'gospel', he began to view the gospel as the delivery of the promise, especially through Christ's spiritual advent in faith to both Old and New Testament believers.[18] His fundamental distinction in Scripture no longer separated Old and New Testaments as historical expressions of one message from God. Instead, Scripture's critical distinction lies in God's two actions of condemning and promising, his requirements for human performance, the law, and his action in Christ to deliver from sin, the promise which creates faith in Christ.[19]

Moreover, Luther was no longer seeking the substance (*res*) behind the sign (*signum*) in God's use of human language.[20] He took the material, created order ever more seriously as God's good gift for humankind, believing that God revealed himself and performed his will through selected elements of that created order. Therefore, human language functions as God's re-creating Word because his promise not only teaches but also actually performs or executes his saving will.[21] The promise delivers Christ, that is, the benefits of his death and resurrection, when it is preached or bestowed in sacramental form. This new perspective brought him to view his own exegetical activity differently: no longer as scholarly mastery of the text but rather as the occasion for delivering God's action. By 1519, when he brought his Galatians lectures of 1516/17 to print, he could warn readers that this was not the kind of traditional commentary they might expect but instead his 'testimony', his confession of faith.[22]

Luther was very familiar with the concept of God's promise from his scholastic training. Biel had taught that the stability of God's world rested upon his 'pact' or 'covenant', which expressed his utterly reliable assurance that he would manage the world and human life in specific ways. But his promise of salvation was conditional upon human performance.[23] Luther found peace only when he came to understand that God's promise of life

---

illustration, but he also replaced it as a primary tool with a concrete, historically oriented focus on God's promise in Christ.

[18] Herrmann, 'Why', 113–29, 147–93; cf. Preus, *Shadow*, 184–99.

[19] Herrmann, 'Why', 194–235.

[20] O. Bayer, *Promissio. Geschichte der reformatorischen Wende in Luthers Theologie*, Göttingen, Vandenhoeck & Ruprecht, 1971, 240–1, identifies this as the 'reformational turn in Luther's hermeneutic'.

[21] WA 4: 321.35–6; 284.32–3.   [22] WA 2: 449.16–31, LW 27: 159.

[23] Oberman, *Harvest*, 160–84.

and salvation falls upon his chosen children without condition based on their actions. God's covenant is a gift from the sovereign, not a contract between roughly equal partners. (Thus, he anticipated recent research on ancient near-eastern 'suzereignty' covenants.)

In the late 1510s Luther's understanding of God as a God who creates reality through his Word slowly fused with his view of that Word as a message and instrument which condemns sin and promises and creates life. This teaching on God's Word found its center in the 'Word made flesh' (John 1: 14), Jesus Christ, and in the Holy Spirit's delivery of the benefits won for sinners by Christ's death and resurrection through human words, in oral, written, and sacramental forms. Luther's preface to the Old Testament (1523) reminded readers that Christ directed people to the Scriptures and their testimony of him (John 5: 39) as did Paul (1 Tim. 4: 13; Rom. 1: 2; 1 Cor. 15: 3–4).[24] He looked upon Scripture less as a source of information than a tool to accomplish the Holy Spirit's work. Luther repeatedly identified passages in Scripture as the Holy Spirit speaking,[25] and the Spirit spoke with specific purposes in mind. Therefore, 'John's gospel and his first epistle, Saint Paul's epistles, especially Romans, Galatians, and Ephesians, and Saint Peter's first epistle are the books that show you Christ and teach you all that is necessary and salutary for you to know.' It was on this basis and 'in comparison to these books' that Luther labeled James's epistle 'an epistle of straw'.[26] Describing this epistle itself, he found it 'a good book because it sets up no human teaching but vigorously promulgates the law of God' even though the ancients rejected it as canonical and it fails to teach justification, Christ's passion and resurrection, and the Holy Spirit.[27]

Luther believed that Scripture serves as God's conversation with those who hear it, read it, and receive its promise. Living in a semi-literate society, he emphasized the oral delivery of God's Word from the biblical pages to the ears of his hearers, but he did not ignore the Holy Spirit's coming to readers of the biblical text.[28] Luther equated Scripture with the Word of God,[29] despite his broader definition of that 'Word' that encompassed

---

[24] *WADB* 8: 10.1/11.1–12.22/13.22, *LW* 35: 235–7. See R. Kolb and C. Arand, *The Genius of Luther's Theology*, Grand Rapids, Baker, 2008, 161–6.

[25] *Avoiding the Doctrines of Men*, 1522, *WA* 10.2: 91.12–92.7, *LW* 35: 152–3; *On the Councils and the Church*, 1539, *WA* 50: 545.35–547.11, *LW* 41: 51–2, P. Althaus, *The Theology of Martin Luther*, tr. R. Shulz, Philadelphia, Fortress, 1966, 35–42, 72–102, 338–41.

[26] Preface to the New Testament (1522), *WADB* 6: 20.33–35, *LW* 35: 362.

[27] Preface to James (1522), *WADB* 7: 384.1/385.1–386.30/387.30, *LW* 35: 395–7.

[28] *WA* 33: 147.26–148.1, *LW* 23: 97. Cf. M. Thompson, *A Sure Ground on Which to Stand: The Relation of Authority and Interpretive Method in Luther's Approach to Scripture*, Carlisle, Paternoster, 2004, 76–8.

[29] Sermons on the Sermon on the Mount, 1532, *WA* 32: 305.22–30, *LW* 21: 10; Sermon on 1 Corinthians 15, 1532, *WA* 36: 500.25–501.10, *LW* 28: 76–7; Commentary on the Johannine

all forms of the delivery of the Bible's message. In Scripture alone could Christians find the genuine source and final judge for what to believe and proclaim.[30] He held that Scripture has but one consistent message since God neither contradicts himself nor confuses his people.[31] While granting that some passages of Scripture are obscure upon first reading, and certainly to those outside the faith, he affirmed the clarity of the biblical message regarding Christ in the eyes of those whom the Holy Spirit guides. Its writers did not write obscurely, but they did treat mysteries beyond human comprehension. In addition to its 'external clarity', its message is internally clear to the faithful.[32] Luther's reliance on Scripture alone as the only authoritative source for all teaching did not mean that he believed that the Holy Spirit communicates only through reading the biblical text. What the Holy Spirit delivered to the church in Scripture informs and does its work through the tradition of the church and through contemporary use in the oral, other written, and sacramental forms of the biblical message.[33]

The preface to his German works offered readers special instructions for reading Scripture themselves. Adapting the monastic pattern of *lectio, meditatio, oratio*, he combined the reading and pondering of the first two, prefaced and permeated by prayer, and added *tentatio*, the *Anfechtung*, or spiritual struggle that formed his own piety. Bible reading must take place within the framework of praying for the Holy Spirit's enlightenment. It involves repeated consideration of the text. Prayer and meditation emerge out of the struggles of everyday life with Satan and the doubts he nurtures.[34]

The preface to Paul's letter to the Romans that Luther composed in 1522 offered readers a hermeneutic for their meditation on the biblical text. It consisted in definitions of eight terms. If readers did not understand these terms, 'reading the book has no value'.[35] 'Law' refers to all God's expectations or demands for human creatures, including what is in the depths of their hearts. 'Doing' the law produces upright works; 'fulfilling' the law meets all God's expectations perfectly—and is impossible for sinners (Rom.

Epistles, 1537, WA 46: 542.6, 548.32–3, LW 22: 6, 14; A. Buchholz, *Schrift Gottes im Lehrstreit. Luthers Schriftverständnis und Schriftauslegung in seinen drei großen Lehrstreitigkeiten der Jahre 1521–28*, Frankfurt am Main, Lang, 1993, 15–38, 61–74. Althaus, *Theology*, 1–8; O. Bayer, *Martin Luther's Theology: A Contemporary Interpretation*, tr. T. Trapp, Grand Rapids, Eerdmans, 2008, 66–90; B. Lohse, *Martin Luther's Theology* tr. R. Harrisville, Minneapolis, Fortress, 1999, 187–95.

[30] WA 10.2: 139.14–18. *Three Symbols*, 1538, WA 50: 282.11–17, LW 34: 227–8.
[31] Thompson, *Sure Ground*, 147–90.
[32] WA 18: 606.1–609.14, LW 33: 24–8; Beißer, *Claritas, passim*; Buchholz, *Schriftverständnis*, 74–138; Thompson, *Sure Ground*, 191–247.
[33] Thompson, *Sure Ground*, 249–87.
[34] WA 50: 658.29–661.8, LW 34: 285–8; Bayer, *Theology*, 13–41.
[35] WADB 7: 2.17–19, 3.16–18, LW 35: 366.

3: 20). Faith in Christ is the key to this righteousness in God's sight, and only he can bestow it. Sin is, above all, unbelief, 'the root, sap, and chief power of all sin' (John 16: 8–9). 'Grace' is God's favor, his loving disposition through which 'he gives us Christ and pours into us the Holy Spirit with his gifts'. Grace, God's attitude of mercy toward his people, bestows gifts, which remain imperfect as believers combat evil desires and sins in the struggle for repentance (Rom. 7: 7–25). 'Faith' is 'a living, daring confidence in God's grace, so sure and certain that believers stake their lives on it a thousand times'; it is 'a living, busy, active, mighty thing', always engaged in carrying out God's commands in order to praise and thank him. 'Righteousness' is God's gift through faith, the relationship of trust in him. 'Flesh' refers in Scripture to all desires turned against God, where as 'spirit' refers to living and working inwardly and outwardly in the service of the Holy Spirit.[36]

Luther found his distinction between 'law', which kills sins by judging sinners guilty, and 'gospel', which restores human life to those trapped in sin, vital for the practice of theology, that is, for preaching and pastoral care. He detailed how God's Word works as a seemingly weak and foolish word from the cross and how it creates and interacts with human trust (1 Cor. 1–2). He placed God's actions in the anthropological context of two dimensions of human life, the relationships with God in his 'right-handed' realm and those with other creatures in his 'left-handed realm', in which people live in two distinct ways, 'passively' as a child of God and 'actively' as a sibling of other human beings and as one called to care for God's creation. Gradually developing this new configuration of ideas, Luther matured as a biblical interpreter; his hermeneutical 'breakthrough' occurred as the maturation of this view of God and human creature progressed. It combined axioms regarding God and his means of dealing with sinful human creatures through law and gospel, in the context of his theology of the Word of the cross, and regarding what it means to be human in his distinction of two kinds or dimensions of human righteousness and its correlative, the two realms or spheres of human life.

LAW AND GOSPEL

Luther did not invent the comparison of law and gospel as a significant element of Christian thinking, but his innovative pairing of them as a fundamental hermeneutical presupposition transformed their definitions and use. Medieval tradition had understood the two terms as a description of two phases of salvation history, with the gospel of Christ replacing the law

---

[36] *WADB* 7: 2.18, 3.20–12.26/13.26, *LW* 35: 366–72.

that had foreshadowed it.[37] The third rule of Tyconius, a fourth-century North African interpreter, summarized by Isidore of Seville (c.560–636), taught that the law or letter sets forth precepts to be performed; the spirit, or grace, gives aid to do them.[38] Augustine spoke of the killing letter of the law and differentiated 'Spirit' and 'letter' not as merely the literal and spiritual senses of a passage; instead, the letter was the law without grace, the spirit the gift of grace and the fulfillment of the law within it.[39] At the beginning of Luther's psalms lectures stands a definition of 'gospel' as God's rod of iron which directs, convicts, reproves and upholds, which crushes, subdues, and disciplines the undisciplined (Ps. 2: 9). Interpreting Psalm 72: 1, Luther recognized the necessity to die spiritually with Christ on the basis of Romans 6: 4–5 and 8: 10–11, although this dying was not connected specifically to 'law'. He defined the gospel as the judgment and righteousness which reveals what is to be condemned and what God has chosen as it teaches believers how they must live. Gospel replaces law as all that Christ does in ruling his church, but not yet as his saving promise of salvation.[40] On Psalm 82: 5 Luther contrasted law as a word of figures and visible shadows to the gospel, a word of 'internal, spiritual, true things'.[41] These and other passages reveal that Luther had not yet begun to distinguish law and gospel as precisely delimited terms for two active words of God that accomplish very different goals.

Luther's Romans lectures reveal a new contrast of law and gospel: the law 'shows nothing but our sins, makes us guilty, and thus produces an anguished conscience'; the gospel provides the remedy with its gift of peace that comes from the Lamb of God through faith.[42] Similar passages appear in his Galatians lectures in 1516/17.[43] Instead of equating law with the Old Testament, the first stage of the history of God's revelation of himself and his salvation of sinners, Luther was identifying the law as that word of God which sets forth the Creator's demands for human performance. These demands condemn human sinfulness. 'Gospel' no longer was chiefly the fulfillment of Old Testament figural prophecy (though it remained that, too). No longer the replacement of Moses's law with the perfect law of Christ, 'gospel' came to designate the promise of God which re-creates sinners as God's children and restores the loving, trusting relationship between them and their Lord.[44] No longer a matter of salvation-history,

---

[37] Herrmann, 'Why', esp. 14–66.   [38] Preus, *Shadow*, 24–5.

[39] *De spiritu et littera*, esp. ch. 4.6–5.8, *CSEL* 60: 157–60. Cf. Herrmann, 'Why', 74–81.

[40] *WA* 3: 463/4, *LW* 10: 405.

[41] *WA* 4: 9.28–35, *LW* 11: 160; cf. *WA* 4: 133.32–136.32, *LW* 11: 285–8; cf. Ebeling, 'Beginnings', 138–40.

[42] *WA* 56: 424.1–26, *LW* 25: 416; cf. *WA* 56: 338.13–339.3, 424.8–17, 426.5–9.

[43] *WA* 57.2: 59.18–20, 72.5–19, 73.21–4, 80.24–30.   [44] Herrmann, 'Why', esp. 236–47.

the proper distinction of law and gospel became God's way of addressing the existential situation of fallen human beings: One word ends sinful identity. Another word raises up the new identity of children of God for those whom God has chosen to give the gift of trusting him. Thus, each Testament contains both law and gospel. The death and resurrection of Christ, the promise he delivers, made that possible. Years later, in 1542/3, Luther related at table that he misunderstood what it meant that the righteous live by faith until he learned to differentiate the righteousness of the law from that of the gospel, that of Christ from that of Moses. He had confused the 'abstract' and the 'concrete' until he began making this distinction.[45]

With this operating principle in place by 1518, as Luther continued preaching and teaching in Wittenberg's churches and his monastery, this distinction of God's two actions through his two words informed his application of every biblical text to his hearers' lives. Introducing his 'Short Form' of the Decalog, Creed, and Lord's Prayer in 1520, Luther noted that 'three things are necessary to know to be saved: first, what he should do and not do; second, when he sees that he cannot do or not do these things by his own strength, that he know where to seek and find it, so that he may do and not do these things; third, that he know how to see and gain it'. Sick people must diagnose their illness, then seek the remedy, and consequently desire and strive for healing.[46] The law reveals sin; the gospel reveals God's help and deliverance; those who trust the gospel proceed to practice the life of faith. This distinction is less a definition of terms than a lively guideline to their use.[47]

The following year the introduction to his postil (book of sermons on the appointed lessons for the church year) sketched guidelines for parish preachers' delivery of God's action in law and gospel to their parishioners. He informed his preacher-readers that all Scripture and the understanding of all theology depends on the proper understanding of law and gospel. 'Every law, especially God's, is a word of wrath, the power of sin, the law of death' (Gen. 6: 3); given as God's good gift to guide life, the law sets loose God's anger at the human failure to be the human creature he fashioned.[48] Law's promises rest on human performance; therefore, it threatens sinners with punishment. This elicits in sinners an inner hatred of the law as it reveals the sinner's identity as an impious enemy of God. It turns all sinners into liars who cannot recognize the truth about themselves

---

[45] WATR 5: 210, #5518.

[46] WA 7: 204.13–27. Cf. Luther's Prayerbook (1522), WA 10.2: 376.12–377.14. Althaus, Theology, 251–73.

[47] Bayer, Theology, 56–62; Ebeling, Luther, 110–24; Lohse, Theology, 267–76; Kolb and Arand, Genius, 148–59.

[48] Althaus, Theology, 169–78.

or God. In contrast, Luther defined the gospel as 'a word of grace, life and salvation, righteousness and peace'. It offers only blessings, remission of sins; it makes it possible to fulfill the law through Christ the Savior. It has a power which heals and restores sinners.[49] Particularly the German translation of this 'instruction on how to seek and wait upon the gospel' instructed preachers regarding the centrality of Christ in God's dealing with sinners. Christ serves as both 'sacrament' or gift of God bringing life and salvation to his chosen people, God's promise in person, and as 'example', personifying the Creator's expectations for all human beings. Preaching the gospel delivers the presence of Christ to hearers as both gift and example.[50] By 1516 Luther could mention Augustine's position that the gospel that conveys Christ as 'sacrament' not only signifies or points to Christ but also actually delivers the benefits of his death and resurrection.[51] Luther was beginning to understand God's proclaimed Word as his active instrument to effect new life by actualizing the presence of Christ and the benefits of his death and resurrection in their lives.

Luther often noted that this use of law and gospel leads to obedience to God's commands, to good works. His *Meditation on Christ's Passion* (1519) marshaled the medieval tradition on contemplating Christ's suffering and death but transformed its content. Such meditation begins with 'a terror-stricken heart and despairing conscience', continues by 'transferring your sins to Christ' through trusting that he has suffered for you, and concludes with faith's practice of the love that Christ kindles.[52] Six years later, his critique of his colleague Andreas Karlstadt outlined the five chief parts of Christian teaching for parish pastors: (1) preaching the law to reveal sin and terrify the conscience (2) preaching the gospel to bestow the forgiveness of sins (3) putting to death sinful desires (4) works of love toward the neighbor, and 5) continuing to emphasize the law for those without faith.[53] The significance of law and gospel standing together in distinction or contrast lay in their use as a description of God's two actions toward sinners, the destruction of the old identity as sinner and the creation of a new identity as child of God.

This mature distinction of law and gospel showed different faces in different contexts, as it guided Luther's preaching throughout his career. Twice in the 1530s he published sermons delivered in Wittenberg that formally

---

[49] *WA* 7: 502.34–505.35. Cf. Luther's sermon of 3 February 1521, *WA* 9: 507.27–508.15, 575.30–576.12, 577.14–578.17, 608.21–610.20.

[50] *WA* 10.1: 8.12–18.3. N. Nagel, '*Sacramentum et Exemplum* in Luther's Understanding of Christ', in C. Meyer (ed.), *Luther for an Ecumenical Age*, Saint Louis, Concordia, 1967, 172–99, demonstrates how Luther gradually transformed and then largely abandoned this medieval distinction, 1509–22.

[51] Bayer, *Promissio*, 91–3.   [52] *WA* 2: 136–42, *LW* 42: 7–14.

[53] *WA* 18: 65.9–66.11.

treated the topic of the distinction and how it is to work. The reformer composed the first in 1532, while his adherents were engaging Roman Catholic treatments of salvation and the role of human performance in countering sin. Wittenbergers heard the second in 1537, during a public controversy between Luther and his former student Johann Agricola over Agricola's denial that the law had any place in the life of the Christian.[54] He had caught Luther's rejection of salvation by works of the law and so thought it best to ban any mention of the law from preaching to believers, assigning to the gospel the task of bringing Christians to repentance while at the same time comforting them through that gospel.

Certainly, both sermons have common elements. The first reminded hearers that God's law expresses his will for how they were to act in daily life and that Christ freed his people from the law's curse but not from obedience to it.[55] It also defined the law quite broadly, as anything that reveals the disruption of the human relationship with God and his good gifts: thus, the law not only accuses but also terrifies and crushes consciences through 'war, pestilence, poverty, and shame' as well as guilt.[56] The second noted the gospel's redeeming power,[57] but it highlighted both the law's accusing and condemning power and the necessity of informing Christians that forgiveness leads to fulfilling the law through obedience to God's commands.[58] The first sermon focused on the gospel which Luther perceived his Roman Catholic opponents to be denying; he insisted that the law's demands on troubled hearts no longer torture and smother believers. Christ, the gospel pronounces, is 'your treasure, your gift, your help, comfort, and savior' and rescues believers from despair over their sins.[59] The second sermon reflected Luther's anxiety that Agricola's position undercut the distinction of law and gospel, imposing upon the term 'gospel' the task of instructing human performance which is properly the work of the law, and emptying the law of its power to call believers to repent of their sins.

These two sermons illustrate the situational nature of Luther's distinction of law and gospel. Both reflect the preacher's conviction that distinguishing law and gospel is 'the noblest skill in the Christian church', without which both messages can be lost.[60] Both reveal that the situation of the hearer determines how the distinction functions concretely at any time. Sinners resisting God's call—trusting and gaining orientation from

---

[54] T. Wengert, *Law and Gospel: Philip Melanchthon's Debate with John Agricola of Eisteben over poenitentia*, Grand Rapids, Baker, 1997, *passim*; M. Edwards, *Luther and the False Brethren*, Stanford, Stanford University Press, 1975, 156–79; Lohse, *Theology*, 178–84.

[55] WA 36: 12.6–13.27, 15.16–25, 30.24, 37.25–7.

[56] WA 36: 17.23–4, 16.19–25.   [57] WA 45: 148.4–149.32.

[58] WA 45: 147.37–148.19, 151.5–28, 148.33–150.29.   [59] WA 36: 22.18–21, 15.30–16.25.

[60] WA 36: 8.14–10.18, 25.1–34; cf. 36: 28.12–16, 33–8.

something other than their Creator—need to hear the law that condemns them, so that they may be turned to God. When sinners already despair of their substitutes for God—when their trust in their own works and powers fail—they need the life-giving promise of an end to their identity as sinner and the gift of a new identity in Christ. Whatever abstractions may reproduce passages of Scripture accurately, Luther found them of very limited use. The application of God's message directly to the concrete situations of sinners, both secure and despairing, was his concern.

He made that clear by emphasizing the oral and sacramental forms of God's Word, which bring God's action directly to the receivers, and by proclaiming that the benefits of Christ are truly present in proclamation and sacrament 'for you', 'for me', 'for us'. This personal engagement with the hearers of his Word, Luther believed, is God's natural communication with his people. He set this understanding of God's verbal approach to sinners into what he and modern scholars have labeled the 'theology of the cross'. Based on 1 Corinthians 1 and 2, it treats not only Christ's death on the cross but above all the proclamation or delivery of that death to sinners through God's Word.

THEOLOGY OF THE CROSS

Luther accentuated the power of the gospel to re-create sinners in God's image. But on the basis of 1 Corinthians 1 and 2 he told hearers that God's Word from the cross appears to sinners to be foolish and impotent. He developed this insight into his first major public statement of theological method in the 'Heidelberg Theses', presented to his Augustinian brothers in 1518. He chose this first formal opportunity for the public presentation of his concerns for reform not as an occasion for further criticizing abuses, such as indulgences, though that issue occasioned his defense at Heidelberg. He did more there than oppose his opponents' teachings: he offered a substitute for the scholastic framework for practicing theology.[61] Luther's own 'crosses' and the problem of human suffering and service to others became his occasion for raising questions addressed within the framework of his 'theology of the cross', but the Heidelberg Theses focused on the dissonance between God's wisdom and way of doing things and human wisdom and definitions of power. 'True theology and recognition of God are in the crucified Christ.'[62] For on the cross, Luther believed, God justified both sinners and his own modus operandi among his human

---

[61] Grane, *Modus*, 151; G. Forde, *On Being a Theologian of the Cross, Reflections on Luther's Heidelberg Disputation, 1518*, Grand Rapids, Eerdmans, 1997.

[62] *WA* 1: 362.15–19, *LW* 31: 53.

creatures. These theses developed thoughts that had appeared in his Psalms lectures[63] and wove them into a statement of method for conducting the theological enterprise. Luther did not believe that God's mercy and goodness reveal themselves only in the cross, but the cross illuminates the more ambiguous encounters with the Creator's providential goodness in the course of his supplying the needs of daily life. For 'no one has seen God; only the only-begotten God has made him known' (John 1: 18);[64] when God's providence seems inconsistent or unreliable, his exhibition of his fatherly concern for sinners in the crucified Christ clarifies what his disposition really is. This *theologia crucis* came to function as Luther's alternative to what Gottfried Wilhelm Leibniz later labeled 'theodicy', the human defense of God in view of the mystery of how evil can exist when God is both good and almighty.

Luther's 'theology of the cross' describes 'theologians of the cross' who listen humbly to what God says to humankind and do not try to master or complete his revelation of himself. The Heidelberg Theses reject 'theologies of glory'; such theologies assert human mastery over a person's own worth and dignity by trying to attain them through human efforts or attempting to exercise mastery over God's disclosure of himself in Christ and Scripture through 'rational' explanations of that which God does not explain. God functions as Creator also in salvation, for 'the love of God does not find but creates that which is pleasing to it' (thesis 28). Lives that appear most religious may be defying God if those good works command the person's trust, diverting trust from God as Creator and Savior (theses 1–9).[65] The human will on its own cannot contribute to obtaining grace; it actively does evil but can only passively, that is, with God's assistance, do good (theses 13–15). The law, inadequate to produce life, can only evaluate human living, resulting in death and condemnation for all that is not in Christ (thesis 23). Luther left the law's goodness and wisdom unchallenged but soberly assessed its ability to produce God-pleasing trust in him.

Most importantly, the Heidelberg Theses sought to foster a clear-sighted analysis of human life, especially of the problem of evil, a topic Luther later treated more extensively in his *On Bound Choice* (1525). He struggled with theodicy, confronting but not solving the problem of the existence of evil. Recognizing that God the Creator exceeds the human creature's capacity for understanding, he proposed a distinction between the 'hidden God' and the 'revealed God': one and the same God, two aspects of God which never

---

[63] WA 4: 450.39–451.26; 3: 279.30–2.

[64] Luther used this concept of God's revelation in preaching on John 1: 18 in 1537, WA 46: 665.34–673.30, LW 22: 148–58.

[65] WA 1: 353.15–32, LW 31: 39–40.

opposed each other—the one the majestic Creator beyond human grasp, the other the giver of all good, even the gift of knowledge of himself.

Luther used the term 'hidden God' in three different senses. The term can describe God as he really is in his totality, inaccessible to human imagination (though Luther could also designate sinful reshapings of that God, images of the Creator that conform to human desires and fantasies, as the 'hidden' god). On the other hand, Luther described God's revelation of himself in Jesus of Nazareth and in the seemingly weak and impotent Word in its several forms as God 'hiding' himself, for instance, in crib and cross, as baby and criminal. For God, Luther insisted, reveals himself by hiding and acting 'under the appearance of opposites'. In his effort to take into honest account the mysteries that confronted him as God's Word and his own experience claimed his attention, Luther turned already during his Psalms lectures (1513–15) to the assertion of opposites that are simultaneously true.[66] After Heidelberg Luther emphasized ever more strongly that the God whose own power and wisdom appear weak and foolish to sinners (1 Cor. 1: 18–25) makes his strength perfect in the weakness of his people (2 Cor. 12: 9), another instance of God accomplishing his good will under the appearance of opposites.

This led Luther to reject the explanations and excuses lodged for God by theologians who wanted to master reality with their own wisdom (thesis 19); those who deserved the title 'theologian' focus not on the invisible things of God but on the visible, seen through suffering and the cross. So theologians of glory label evil good and good evil; theologians of the cross align their thinking with God's view of reality and call things what they are.[67] Luther explained in defending these theses that God's power, godliness, wisdom, justice, and other such attributes are invisible, but knowledge of them does not as such make one wise regarding the personal relationship God has established with his people. That comes through looking to the weakness and foolishness of the cross.[68] Suffering marks the Christian life, and the fact that it often seems to be undeserved and contrary to God's promise raises doubts in Christian minds. Luther's 'theology of the cross' called believers to patience in suffering and to peace with their sufferings in view of the fact that God accomplishes his purposes through both his own suffering on the cross and his people's in the midst of battling evil. Often Christians suffer in the context of bearing one another's burdens—or crosses—and this provided Luther with a means of consolation for sufferers.

---

[66] S. Ozment, *Homo Spiritualis: A Comparative Study of the Anthropology of Johannes Tauler, Jean Gerson and Martin Luther (1509–16) in the Context of their Theological Thought*, Leiden, Brill, 1969, 130–8, 178–81.

[67] *WA* 1: 354.21–2, *LW* 31: 39–40.   [68] *WA* 1: 362.1–33, *LW* 31: 52–3.

Indeed, Luther believed that God's revelation presents paradoxes (statements that assert ideas contradictory according to reason but revealed to be true by Scripture) and praised this form of the Creator's communicating with human creatures. The tension between law and gospel is not strictly speaking a 'paradox' but rather an address of God's gift of identity and his expectations for human performance on two levels of reality, divine and human. That God can be responsible for everything while demanding total responsibility of his creatures is, however, a paradox. This is not classical dualism, which ranges good and evil against each other at more or less equal levels. God is always in charge and control. Luther concluded early in his career that the mystery of what it means to be human, in relationship to the Creator, cannot be grasped by human logic.[69]

Similarly, the mystery of evil reflects the paradox of almighty God's absolute goodness coexisting with evil. Luther believed that the final answers to questions regarding evil in human life cannot be resolved if both God's goodness and his power are maintained, in accord with Scripture's presentation of who God is. Therefore, his theology of the cross asserted that human beings can do no more than cling to God in trust when evil comes from inside or outside, when they are victims of evil and when they perpetrate evil. Trust clings to God when reason's attempts at mastery over such questions, and thus over life's most serious problems, fail. Luther did not try to make excuses for the omnipotent Creator when evil struck. He simply trusted that God, who sacrificed himself on the cross for sinners, will demonstrate his love in the end.[70] Thus, faith, specifically faith in Jesus Christ, defies the human reason that demands proofs through experimental, experiential signs or logic. Apart from faith reason can do many good things. It can grasp the historical meaning of biblical texts. The Holy Spirit is required, however, to help human beings experience true understanding in the heart.[71]

That led Luther to write a year after Heidelberg that 'the cross of Christ is the only instruction in the Word of God there is, the purest theology'.[72] For at the heart of God's revelation of himself stands Christ's cross. It manifests God's essence, which Luther redefined as his mercy and steadfast loving-kindness. 'The cross puts everything to the test.' 'The cross itself alone is the judge and witness of the truth.'[73] For God's truth revolves

---

[69] Ebeling, 'Beginnings', 140–2.   [70] See Chapter 7, below.
[71] WA 24: 17.29–18.25.

[72] *D. Martin Luther: Operationes in Psalmos 1519, 1521*, II, ed. G. Hammer and M. Bersack, Cologne, Böhlau, 1981, 389.15–16.

[73] Ibid., 325.1, 341.15. Luther continued to use the concepts of this *theologia crucis*, R. Kolb, 'Luther's Theology of the Cross Fifteen Years after Heidelberg: Lectures on the Psalms of Ascent', *Journal of Ecclesiastical History* (forthcoming).

around his disposition toward his human creatures, even after they have fallen into sin. That disposition is gracious, seeking ardently to return them to himself. Distinguishing God's Word in the categories of law and gospel under the parameters of the theology of the cross presumes the existence of two conversation partners, God and his human creatures. Therefore, Luther's view of God's Word leads inevitably to his definition of who God is and what it means to be human.

LUTHER'S CREDAL FAITH IN GOD, FATHER, SON, AND HOLY SPIRIT

In the course of his evangelical maturation two axioms emerged that mark Luther's comprehension of God. Attempting to abandon speculation beyond or behind the biblical text, he found that he could not formulate his understanding of God apart from an understanding of God's relationship with his human creatures. The God human beings can know is the God who reveals himself by conversing with his human creatures. God and his human creatures are so linked that each belongs to the practical definition of the other. God and his creatures are totally distinct, but the definitions of their essences are bound together. Corollary to that definition, Luther's understanding of what it means to be human centered on the relationship human creatures have with their Creator. Being human is first of all 'to fear, love, and trust in God above all else'.[74] This explanation of the first commandment in the *Small Catechism* served as Luther's fundamental definition of what God had wrought in making human beings in his own image. God is ever present in human history 'for' his people (*pro me, pro te*).[75]

Second, Luther held an intensely personal view of God. God's *persona* or personality, his character traits, became ever more important for the reformer. His lectures on the Psalms equated what God does with his essence and his self-communication[76] and defined this essence as goodness and giving, above all in relation to his human creatures, even when they bring his wrath upon themselves.[77] Lecturing on Romans (1515/16), Luther cast off a perception of God's righteousness as strict judgment of right and wrong, as he struggled to formulate a new definition of God's righteousness and human righteousness, what made each what they are

---

[74] *Small Catechism*, Explanation to the first commandment, BSLK, 507, BC, 351; Bayer, *Theology*, 150–72, 339–41; Ebeling, *Luther*, 9–11, 226–67; Lohse, *Theology*, 35–41, 207–18, 240–7.

[75] G. Kalme, ' "Words Written in Golden Letters"—a Lutheran Reading of the Ecumenical Creeds', Ph.D. dissertation, Concordia Seminary, Saint Louis, 2005.

[76] WA 4: 262.32–3, LW 10: 398; WA 3: 406.38–408.18, LW 10: 346–8; WA 3: 152.7–153.18.

[77] WA 55.2.1: 45.6–46.14, 3: 35.7–32 [LW 10: 40–1]; 4: 269.25—30, LW 11: 403.

by nature or definition. God's own righteousness is that which bestows righteousness on sinners who recognize their own sinfulness and cry out to God for deliverance.[78] Furthermore, Luther conceived of God's disposition on a most personal level. After becoming a father himself in 1526, he increasingly described God's love for humankind in terms of parental affection and concern.[79]

Although he never ceased to proclaim God's wrath against the sin that ruins his human creation as an earnest expression of his righteousness and his love for human creatures,[80] Luther held that God's essential disposition toward his creatures is love, mercy, his personal favor, based on nothing but his own desire to show kindness and compassion. 'The Giver of all things', he has 'given himself to us all wholly and completely, with all that he is and has.'[81] 'What a kind, fine God he is, nothing but sweetness and goodness that he feeds us, preserves us, nourishes us.'[82] God is always in action in relationship to his human creatures, and his actions aim at showing them his kindness.

Despite his occasionally expressed discomfort with the word 'Trinity', a symptom of his desire to return to Scripture alone and forsake terminology invented by theologians,[83] Luther fully embraced and reaffirmed the catholic tradition's understanding of God.[84] However, he sharply rejected attempts to relate the three-fold nature of God to some imaginative human plumbing of the divine essence, as some scholastics had ventured.[85] He rejected all speculation into the inner workings of the 'immanent' Trinity and concentrated on the 'economic' Trinity, recounting how God acts in behalf of his human creatures throughout history rather than exploring the mechanics of the relationship among the three persons of the Godhead. 'We confess the deity of Christ and of the Holy Spirit, thus believing in the Holy Spirit just as we do in the Father. Just as there is one faith in three Persons, so the three Persons are one God,' he wrote in 1522, introducing the Apostles Creed in his *Prayer Book*. His confession of God reiterated the ancient confession of the church. His trust renounced all alternatives to

[78] *WA* 56: 215.16–17, 231.9–10, 290.15–291.14, 233.5–34, *LW* 25: 201, 215, 218, 277–8; cf. Grane, *Modus*, 63–103.

[79] B. Stolt, 'Martin Luther on God as Father', *LQ* 8 (1994), 385–95.

[80] U. Rieske-Braun, *Duellum mirabile. Studien zum Kampfmotiv in Martin Luthers Theologie*, Göttingen, Vandenhoeck & Ruprecht, 1999, 74–7.

[81] C. Arand, 'Luther on the Creed', *LQ* 20 (2006), 1; cf. *WA* 23: 505.37–9, *LW* 37: 366.

[82] Genesis sermons (1524), *WA* 24: 39.23–5; cf. 24: 57.28.

[83] *WA* 46: 436; 39.2: 287, 305; and in the Disputation for Georg Major and Johann Faber, 1544, *WA* 39.2: 305.15–26; cf. his sermon, 16 June 1538, *WA* 46: 436.5–17, 28–36.

[84] See D. Bielfeldt, M. Mattox, and P. Hinlicky, *The Substance of the Faith: Luther's Doctrinal Theology for Today*, Minneapolis, Fortress, 2008.

[85] *WA* 10.1.1: 181, 185; 37: 41.

God, the Father almighty, maker of heaven and earth, and placed confidence 'only in the one, invisible, inscrutable, and only God, who created heaven and earth and who alone is superior to all creation'. Jesus Christ, he professed, is 'the one true Son of God, begotten of him in eternity with one eternal divine essence ... Lord over me and all things which he created together with the Father in his divinity'. 'The Holy Spirit is truly God together with the Father and the Son.'[86]

He repeated that confession in 1537 and 1538, in his Smalcald Articles,[87] and his exposition of *The Three Creeds of the Christian Faith*. There he wrote, 'Jesus Christ is real, eternal God by nature, not made, uncreated, having been from eternity onward, arisen, begotten (or however one may call it), a different Person from the Father, but not a different God from the Father, rather equal to him in one single, eternal substance.'[88] On the basis of this presumption about the nature of God, this definition dwells on God's actions in providing creatures with their daily needs, rescue from sin and new life, the gift of trust and the assurance of everlasting life.

He reaffirmed this emphasis on God's actions, while confessing 'the sublime article of the majesty of God, that the Father, Son, and Holy Spirit, three distinct persons, are by nature one true and genuine God, the Maker of the heaven and earth', in his 'doctrinal last will and testament', his *Confession concerning Christ's Supper* (1528).[89] In 1528/9, in sermons preparing for the composition of his catechisms, Luther continued to emphasize God as One who does all things 'for us'. His concept of faith had changed from focusing on acceptance of dogmatic premises to trust in God's person, as he exercised responsibility for sustaining his creation, restoring sinners to fellowship with him through Christ's death and resurrection, creating trust and obedience in his chosen people.[90] Earlier he had underscored God's fatherly love, coupled with his omnipotence, that comes to the aid of his people. In the *Small Catechism*, he capitalized 'CREATOR' to summarize not only God's almighty power and parental love but also his initial responsibility for the existence of everything and his continuing responsibility for upholding and sustaining creatures by his creative Word.[91] The independent, self-sufficient, unconditioned Creator has the whole world in his hand.

Nonetheless, in the *Small Catechism* Luther defined him as the One who has created 'me' and then added immediately 'together with all creatures', continuing with his providing, sustaining actions in everyday life,

---

[86] WA 10.2: 388.20–395.8, LW 42: 24–9.   [87] BSLK, 414–15; BC, 300.

[88] WA 50: 278.16–20, LW 34: 222.   [89] WA 26: 500.10–15, LW 37: 361.

[90] R. Schwarz, *Fides, spes, et caritas beim jungen Luther, unter besonderer Berücksichtigung der mittelalterlichen Tradition*, Berlin, de Gruyter, 1962, 291–413.

[91] Bayer, *Theology*, 91–115.

giving, preserving, providing, protecting, shielding, and defending 'me' and others.[92] The Catechism's exposition of the Trinity continued with the confession that Jesus Christ is 'Lord', the one who overcomes sin and death 'that I may be his own and live under him and his rule',[93] and that the Holy Spirit 'calls me by the gospel, enlightens me with his gifts, makes me holy, and keeps me in the one true faith', along with all God's chosen people, the church.[94]

Indeed, throughout his career Luther's Trinitarian faith expressed itself clearly even though his special concern for the comfort of sinners brought him to regard God's saving work in Christ as the heart of that faith, 'the best of God's assets, the foundation, ground, and totality, around and under which everything is gathered and found'. 'In Jesus Christ the whole fullness of the Godhead dwells bodily or personally, so that whoever does not find or receive God in Christ shall nevermore and nowhere have or find God outside of Christ.'[95] As the one who delivers the benefits of Christ, the Holy Spirit likewise played a prominent role in his preaching and teaching. Charles Arand points out that Luther's presentation of the Trinity presumes that believers first encounter the Holy Spirit as he reveals Christ to them, and that their understanding of God's love in Christ illumines their understanding of the Father and his creative gifts.[96]

The Catechism's failure to treat the Trinity as a whole and the inner relationships among the three persons does not, however, result in a 'naive tritheism' for two reasons. God's actions and the disposition or character behind them reveal the oneness which unites the three persons in one Godhead. Luther insisted that it is one God who in the three articles of the Creed 'has revealed and opened to us the most profound depths of his fatherly heart, his sheer, unutterable love. He created us for this very purpose, to redeem and sanctify us.' Furthermore, the Father 'has given us his Son and his Holy Spirit, through whom he brings us to himself', working in and through his Word.[97] Luther followed the ancient Greek Fathers in teaching that the Son, begotten of and sent by the Father, sends the Spirit. He brings sinners back to the Father through the work of the Son. By emphasizing God's actions and thus the 'economic' Trinity, Luther preserved God's relationship to creation and 'assures us that God is not simply a detached, ambivalent divine being who stands aloof from the

---

[92] Arand, 'Creed', 2–6; A. Peters, *Kommentar zu Luthers Katechismen*, vol. 2: *Der Glaube*, ed. G. Seebaß, Göttingen, Vandenhoeck & Ruprecht, 1991, 56–91; Althaus, *Theology*, 105–18; cf. *BSLK*, 510–11, *BC*, 354.

[93] Arand, 'Creed', 6–8; Peters, *Kommentar*, 2: 92, 174; *BSLK*, 511; *BC*, 355.

[94] Arand, 'Creed', 8–10; Peters, *Kommentar*, 2: 175–250; Althaus, *Theology*, 43–63; Lohse, *Theology*, 232–9; *BSLK*, 511–12; *BC*, 355–6.

[95] *WA* 50: 267.5–13, *LW* 34: 207.   [96] Arand, 'Creed', 12.

[97] *Large Catechism*, Creed, 64–5; *BSLK*, 660–1; *BC*, 439–40; Bayer, *Theology*, 235–50.

world'. Upon this presupposition Luther affirmed the 'immanent' Trinity and thus the unity of the three persons and their equality.[98]

The concept of the Creator as actor in human history, who had fashioned all reality and used it according to his good pleasure, permeated Luther's thought. This perception of the goodness of the created order and God's comfort at working within and through it counteracted the Neoplatonic elements he inherited from Augustine's legacy. Not emanation of divinity from the Godhead but active, personal demonstration of creative power and love informed Luther's view of God and all reality.[99]

God's Word formed reality, as the Creator's agent and instrument for creating—and re-creating sinners into his children. 'God created [the essence of each individual created person or thing] through the Word so that it grows without ceasing and we do not have any idea how. . . . It is an eternal Word, spoken from eternity, and it will be spoken always. As little as God's essence ceases, so little does his speaking cease.'[100] Luther asserted that God has the whole world on his lips: 'the earth has its power only from God's Word', for 'you see soil on which nothing grows; it is still soil and dry earth, empty, for God is not giving his word or command that it bear and that something can grow. Therefore, the reason that not all land bears fruit in the same way is due not to the ability of the land but to God's Word, for where it is, there is the power to be fruitful. The entire world is full of the Word that drives all things and bestows and preserves power.'[101]

Luther's intellectual grandfather, Gabriel Biel, had also struggled with the question of how to adjust God's omnipotence with human freedom or responsibility. Biel had resolved it with a doctrine of contingency, which permitted Almighty God to establish the system in which human beings were free to make decisions although he also conceded that everything in creation happens within the framework of divine cooperation. Biel's effort at harmonizing and homogenizing divine omnipotence and human freedom recognized that if God should withdraw his power, human free will collapses. But for all practical purposes, Biel believed, human beings can exercise control over their lives because God has released them to a world in which they are responsible.[102] Instead of harmonizing and homogenizing God's responsibility as Creator for his universe with the human responsibility the Creator bestows upon his creatures, Luther held them

[98] Arand, 'Creed', 14, 10–21.

[99] Ebeling, 'Beginnings', 142. Cf. R. Flogaus, *Theosis bei Palamas und Luther*, Göttingen, Vandenhoeck & Ruprecht, 1997, 285–380.

[100] On Gen. 1: 9–13, WA 24: 37.12–14, 23–5; cf. O. Bayer, *Schöpfung als Anrede*, Tübingen, Mohr/Siebeck, 1990.

[101] Gen. 1: 9–13, WA 24: 38.11–18, 44.20–45.13.

[102] Grane, *Contra Gabrielem*, 69–76, 119–23.

in tension, applying his affirmation of God's exercise of responsibility for the welfare of his people in what he labeled 'gospel', and directing human responsibility according to the 'law'.

TWO KINDS OF RIGHTEOUSNESS

Luther had learned from his instructors what they had learned from Biel: that God is omnipotent, responsible for everything in his creation, and that human beings are held responsible for 'doing what is in them', for doing their best. In his struggle to deal with Biel's homogenization and harmonization of human performance with divine grace, Luther became ever more convinced that nothing good remains in fallen human creatures in terms of being able to please God with their own efforts. Therefore, Biel's concept of a *synteresis* that preserved a spark of goodness—a foothold for human powers to move toward God—caused him to stumble over the demand to do his best. Luther's language in his early Psalms lectures both embraced and rejected Biel's view as the young professor strained to formulate ideas that did not fit Biel's paradigm within the boundaries set by his language. Ozment observes that these lectures contain Biel's terminology regarding human merit and preparation for grace alongside elements that find salvation in trust in Christ alone.[103] At the same time Luther viewed human sinfulness in such a way that he could see human beings as God's creatures and thus develop a positive appreciation of human creatureliness when it is liberated from sin.[104] But these ideas required further maturation in the years after 1515.

When Luther was trying to explore how to relate to God within Biel's framework of humanity as defined by Aristotle—memory, intellect, will, and the governing *synteresis*[105]—he was driven to focus on human powers. He never denied that these organs for exercising humanity exist and are significant, real components of being human, but he found that these components have life and breath in relationships, first with God and then with other creatures, above all, the human. The concept of a *synteresis*, as a controlling spark of goodness that can command and generate good acts in mind and will, gave way to trusting God as the fundamental constituting element of humanity. His new orientation to what it means to be human laid aside his concept of faith as one virtue among several, coming to believe that trusting God establishes fundamental human identity, as he asserted in explaining the first commandment in the *Large Catechism*.[106]

---

[103] Ozment, *Homo Spiritualis*, 182, 139–83.   [104] Ibid., 190.

[105] L. Grane, *Contra Gabrielem. Luthers Auseinandersetzung mit Gabriel Biel in der Disputatio Contra Scholasticiam Theologiam 1517*, s.l., Gyldendal, 1962, 283–309, 320–37.

[106] *BSLK*, 560–7; *BC*, 386–90.

Luther described the critical point in his evangelical maturation in different fashion several times at the distance of more than a decade. In 1532 he
recalled his struggle with the scholastic definition of humanity as defined
by the righteousness of human performance. In that belief-system God's
righteousness consisted of his condemnation and judgment of those who
had merited evil by their works. Luther's discovery that God is righteous
because he is fundamentally a forgiving Father (although he judges justly)
permitted him to distinguish two dimensions of humanity, one, at the core
of that humanity, the relationship with God, the second, a direct result from
that core relationship, the relation with God's creations, above all, other
human creatures.[107] His preface to his Latin writings (1545) recounted his
uncovering in Romans 1: 17 new definitions of the righteousness of God
and the human creature. The creature is righteous 'passively', that is, as a
result of the gift of God. Created apart from the merit of any human performance, human beings are what they ought to be—righteous—because
God created them as his own. Sinners are restored to righteousness
through God's acting according to his essence and nature—righteously—
by justifying sinners for Christ's sake. This, Luther said, opened for
him 'the gate of paradise'.[108] In 1531 he dubbed the distinction of this
passive righteousness in relationship to God from the active righteousness of human performance in relationship to other human creatures
'our theology'.[109] This radical departure from Aristotelian psychology,
which defined what it means to be human apart from any relationship with a Creator, proceeded from Luther's intensely personal view
of the Creator and his creative Word. It intertwines with his concepts
of God and human creature, of law and gospel, of justification and
sanctification.

Earlier hints of his experiment with the language of this distinction occur, for instance, in the Romans lectures. There he distinguished
between the passive justification of God that takes place when faith recognizes the truth of his Word (Ps. 51: 6, cited in Rom. 3: 4) from God's active
bestowal of righteousness on human beings.[110] In 1516 he had commented
on Galatians 2: 21 that Paul had a new definition of righteousness, not as
'virtue that renders to everyone his due', but as 'faith in Jesus Christ'.[111]
The topic became public in a tract, *On Three Kinds of Righteousness*, issued

---

[107] Psalm 51: 14, WA 40.2: 444.36–445.29, LW 12: 392.

[108] WA 54: 186.3–16, LW 34: 337.

[109] Galatians lectures, WA 40.1: 45.24–7, LW 26: 7. See F. Cranz, *An Essay on the Development of Luther's Thought on Justice, Law, and Society*, Cambridge, Mass., Harvard University Press, 1959, 41–111.

[110] WA 56: 224.13–228.22, LW 25: 208–15.

[111] WA 2: 503.34–6, LW 27: 240–1; cf. T. Bell, *Divus Bernhardus. Bernhard von Clairvaux in Martin Luthers Schriften*, Mainz, Zabern, 1993, 266–9, on Bernard's influence on this development.

in autumn 1518. It approached the definition of being human by exam-
ining what has gone wrong with humanity: human evil takes shape as
criminal sin, essential sin, and actual sin. Corresponding to criminal sin
is an external righteousness, which consists in the practice of deeds that
roughly correspond to God's demands, but motivated by something other
than trust in God. Luther later called this 'civil' or 'civic righteousness',
praising its service to society, noting its failure to live the full human life
which focuses on God. Essential, inborn, original righteousness, a gift from
God, determines the individual's identity, the core of being human, the
disposition of trust in God. This is passive righteousness, granted freely and
unconditionally by God. From this passive righteousness, from its trust in
the Creator, flows the active righteousness of human obedience, aroused
by faith, meeting God's expectations for human performance as expressed
in his commands.[112]

Although this treatise applied the topic only to life after the fall, Luther
elsewhere pointed out that Adam and Eve in Eden were righteous in God's
sight by grace alone, for God's gracious disposition, not any performance
of their own, caused their creation. They did not earn God's favor by
keeping his commands. They were receiving God's love and favor from the
moment God created them. 'God gave him this command (Gen. 2: 15–17)
as a sign . . . for he had to know and remember that he had a lord over him.
He could not become upright through obeying the command, but he could
become a sinner. This is an important proof that no law can make a person
upright, but rather it is given to him so that he can keep it and prove that
he is already upright and lives hearkening to God. The law does not bestow
uprightness; rather, those who are already upright practice the law.'[113]
God's law had nothing to do with the human being's becoming human,
acceptable to the Creator. Only the Creator's gracious favor did that. He
gave his law as an instrument for evaluation of the human performance that
resulted from the gift of humanity that he restores through his Word.[114]

Luther saw this pattern of God's creative claiming his own people in
Abraham's life. God simply chose Abraham, without merit on the patri-
arch's part. He clung to God's Word alone,[115] demonstrating that 'if some-
one is converted and becomes upright, a Christian, we do not initiate that.
No prayer, no fasting helps. It has to come from heaven, from grace alone,
when God hits the heart through the promise of the gospel so that it feels
this Word and has to say that it never before occurred to him or came to his

---

[112] WA 2: 41–2/43–7. Kolb and Arand, Genius, 21–128; Ebeling, Luther, 141–74, discusses
this concept under the titles 'person and work' and 'faith and love'.
[113] Gen. 2: 15–17, WA 24: 72.15–23.   [114] Gen. 2: 15–17, WA 24: 73.19–32.
[115] Gen. 12: 3, WA 24: 249.21–2.

mind that such grace should fall upon him. . . . Those who want to become righteous should not say, "I want to begin this matter and do good works, so that I can attain grace," but rather, "I will wait until God wants to give me his grace and his Spirit through his Word." '[116]

In Luther's world very few people had not received God's promise of new identity through baptism, so it apparently did not make sense to discuss the civil righteousness of non-Christians. Therefore, he sharpened his thinking about the distinction of the ways in which Christians are truly human under the title *On Two Kinds of Righteousness*. Righteousness in God's sight consists of trusting and thus possessing Christ and his righteousness, as promised to Abraham, won in his death and resurrection, instilled by grace alone as the Father draws us in faith to Christ. Although he would later maintain that God's initial gift of faith assures believers that God regards them as totally righteous in his sight, in 1519 Luther still believed that this 'alien (in Latin, 'belong to another', that is, Christ) righteousness' begins and then grows throughout human life and is perfected only at death. Later, Luther viewed the gift of righteousness in God's sight as complete when God claims the believer through his forgiving, justifying Word. In contrast, he always believed that 'proper' (in Latin, 'one's own') righteousness, which proceeds from alien righteousness in the performance of good works, does grow—and sometimes regress. In spite of the battle with Satan that brings reversals, believers improve in the practice of God's design for human life in its horizontal dimension. This proper or active righteousness does not merit God's favor but responds to his love by living as his children. Fruit and consequence of alien righteousness, it is the fruit of the spirit that the Holy Spirit has created anew. Active righteousness works at killing off sinful desires and practicing good toward others. That the larger portion of this tract treats active righteousness demonstrates that, despite his protests against the 'works-righteousness' which claimed to be meritorious in the relationship with God, Luther did teach that believers demonstrate their righteousness in relationship to other creatures in the new obedience to God that loves the neighbor by doing good works.[117] He consistently and continually emphasized that passive righteousness naturally produces active righteousness. Because of the mystery of continuing sin in believers' lives, he continually called them to repentance through the demands for human performance in God's law. Repentance enabled them to enjoy the gift of righteousness in God's sight bestowed by the gospel of Christ.

As 'sacrament' Christ gives believers their passive righteousness; as 'example' he reveals the shape of active righteousness. In 1524 Luther

---

[116] Gen. 12: 1–2, WA 24: 244.21–6, 29–30.   [117] WA 2: 145–52, LW 31: 299–306.

proclaimed, 'he was a human being full of love, mercy, and grace, humility, patience, wisdom, light, and everything good. His whole essence was dedicated to serving everyone and harming no one. We must bear this image and conform to it. In this image belongs also his death and suffering and everything attached to it, his resurrection, life, grace, and power. . . .'[118] Luther largely avoided the language of 'imitation' of Christ, particularly because monastic celibates based their avoidance of marriage on Christ's not marrying. Nonetheless, in the respective callings in human life that God gives, Luther demanded that hearers follow Christ in obedience to God's commands for human living.[119]

On the other hand, he used this distinction to reinforce the dependence of believers on God alone. Lecturing on Galatians (1531), he said, 'I do not seek active righteousness. I ought to have and perform it; but I declare that even if I did have and perform it, I cannot trust in it or stand up before the judgment of God on the basis of it. Thus I put myself beyond all active righteousness, all righteousness of my own or of the divine law, and I embrace only the passive righteousness which is the righteousness of grace, mercy, and the forgiveness of sins.'[120] If trust in God did not serve as the central orientation of life, deeds would be off target, he believed. 'They should be done only as fruits of righteousness, not in order to cause righteousness. Made righteous. we must do them, not the other way around.'[121]

THE WHOLE LIFE OF A CHRISTIAN IS A LIFE OF REPENTANCE

Luther's profound conviction of his own sinfulness, his inability to turn himself to God and please God, arose within the context of a monastic piety. It focused both on the purity of the monk's inner disposition toward God in contrition for sins and on the outward practice of the sacrament of penance. All late medieval Christians encountered God's Word directed at themselves personally most often in the sacrament of penance (even though many seldom availed themselves of it). Monks encountered this sacrament, above all, as a demand for sufficient contrition in order to

---

[118] On Gen. 1: 24–7; *WA* 24: 49.23–51.8. Luther continued by asserting that the human creature is either in God's image or in the image of the devil; see also *WA* 24: 153.15. Such statements anticipate his later comments on Genesis in his lectures (1535–45) and the view of Matthias Flacius Illyricus, see Lauri Haikola, *Gesetz und Evangelium bei Matthias Flacius Illyricus. Eine Untersuchung zur lutherischen Theologie vor der Konkordienformel*, Lund, Gleerup, 1952, 97–192.

[119] G. Wingren, *Luther on Vocation*, tr. C. Rasmussen, Philadelphia, Muhlenberg, 1957, 171–84.

[120] *WA* 40.1: 42.26–43.15, *LW* 26: 6.   [121] *WA* 40.1: 287.17–23, *LW* 26: 169.

qualify for forgiveness and as a prescription for works of satisfaction to complete its task of reconciliation between sinner and God. Biel's insistence that the pious could produce perfect contrition for sins out of their purely natural powers and that they had to confess each mortal sin to the priest in the sacrament drove Luther to despair. His solution to this problem arose out of his rethinking of *poenitentia*. *Poenitentia* designated both the sacrament of penance and the repentance that turned sinners from false gods and false obedience to serving God, through the change of disposition that focused obedience on him.

Several authors helped Luther abandon his understanding of *poenitentia* as a ritual action in which his performance held the key to unloosing God's grace. He redefined it as his disposition of submission to God grounded in trust in the gift of Christ's forgiveness and life rather than in his own efforts. From Bernard of Clairvaux[122] and Johann Tauler[123] Luther had learned that to be a monk meant to practice repentance through continual remorse—self-accusation—for sin and turning to Christ. Particularly Bernard redirected his thinking to the conviction that trust in God formed the center of human life.[124] Jacques Lefèvre familiarized Luther with the definition of Christian experience as the killing of the flesh and vivification of the spirit.[125] When he launched his critique of indulgence practices in 1517, he had become convinced that 'the whole life of Christians is a life of repentance'.[126] His understanding of repentance matured over the next decade; his *Small Catechism* described it as the drowning and dying of the 'old creature' in us with all sins and evil desires and the emergence and resurrection of a new person who lives before God in righteousness and purity forever.[127] This struggle over life and death, between God and Satan, permeated the Christian's daily existence, Luther's own experience taught him, because the mystery of sin and evil continues in the lives of the baptized.

Luther slowly came to the conviction that repentance centered in the promise God had first given the believer in baptism, this promise of

---

[122] Bell, *Bernhardus*, 62–71, 124–33.

[123] V. Leppin, 'Transformationen spätmittelalterlicher Mysik bei Luther', in B. Hamm and V. Leppin (eds.), *Gottes Nähe unmittelbar erfahren. Mystikim Mittelatter and bei Martin Luther*, Tübingen, Mohr Siebeck, 2007, 165–85; Bayer, *Promissio*, 45–6, 64.

[124] Bell, *Bernhardus*, 91–106.

[125] *WA* 3: 29.9–30.8; 4: 403.27–407.17, 468.1–5; cf. Bayer, *Promissio*, 39.

[126] *WA* 1: 233.10–11, *LW* 31: 25. V. Leppin, ' "Omnem vitam fidelium penitentiam esse voluit", Zur Aufnahme mystischer Tradition in Luthers erster Ablaßthese', *ARG* 93 (2003), 7–25, demonstrates that in 1517 Luther was echoing Tauler's conviction regarding the continuing necessity of humbling oneself before God; cf. M. Brecht's response, 'Luthers neues Verständnis der Buße und die reformatorische Entdeckung', *Zeitschrift für Theologie und Kirche* 101 (2004), 281–91.

[127] *Small Catechism*, *BSLK*, 516–17; *BC*, 360.

resurrection through forgiveness of sins to new life that in the face of the unexplainable continued sinfulness of believers must be repeated daily. This concept was beginning to emerge in 1520 in his *Babylonian Captivity*.[128]

Critical to the development of Luther's view of repentance was God's role as the one who with human language, in direct address to sinners, speaks law, which kills, and gospel, which makes alive, in its unfolding. Preaching in 1514, he reflected his teachers' focus on an inner word from God, with little appreciation for the external, spoken word which conveys the gospel. By the 1520s he had come to understand that God speaks his re-creative Word though human language and human agents.[129]

As he tinkered with the ideas forming in his head after issuing the Ninety-five Theses, Luther synthesized thoughts that had been percolating through his writings for months. During 1518 and 1519 the indulgence controversy aided him in coming to view the word of absolution as a word of power that actually conveys what it promises—forgiveness of sins, life, and salvation—in the wake of the experience of God's wrath against sin that produces contrition.[130] This word that God speaks through the voice of the priest functions as the Holy Spirit's tool to create trust.[131] This faith grasps the promise which God's own person guarantees. Two significant contrasts with his previous formulations appear. First, earlier the orality of the Word had seemed its weakness, as Augustine taught, but Luther now recognized that as God's gift for human creatures its very externality made it a powerful instrument.[132] Second, the disposition of the sinner in humility no longer plays a causative role in what God does. His re-creative word is unconditioned and creates, as Luther later said, 'out of nothing'.[133] The word is not just any utterance of God. Luther bound absolution to the promise coming from Christ, who has given his life for sin and been raised to restore human righteousness (Rom. 4: 25) and has offered the promise of bearing all sinners' burdens (Matt. 11: 28).[134] This promise grasps the Christian heart, which clings in consolation and peace of conscience to this word and defies the gates of hell on the basis of the promise.[135]

With these elements in place as the nervous system or circulatory system of his body of doctrine, Luther proceeded to his tasks of preaching, exposition, and public dissemination of his message. Trained in the art of the university disputation, he viewed sharp conflict of opposing views as

[128]   WA 6: 534.3–535.16, LW 36: 67–9. Cf. Bayer, *Promissio*, 32–6.

[129]   WA 1: 22.37–23.20; see Bayer, *Promissio*, 17–23; Bayer, *Theology*, 66–90.

[130]   WA 1: 543.14–19. Cf. Bayer, *Promissio*, 168–9; Bayer, *Theology*, 40–56. *Resolution of the Disputation on ... Indulgences*, 1518, WA 1: 541.12–543.30, 593.40–596.39.

[131]   Bayer, *Promissio*, 197.   [132]   Ibid., 178–9.

[133]   WA 42: 439.9–13, LW 1: 149; Bayer, *Promissio*, 198–9.

[134]   Bayer, *Promissio*, 208–12.   [135]   WA 2: 715.15, 26–9.

a natural way of seeking the truth. This method, when placed into the situation in which his opponents not only challenged his views but threatened both his life and the welfare of the church as he saw it, resulted in what is often seen as 'coarse' and 'abusive' polemic. Mark Edwards demonstrates that his polemic functioned as a carefully honed instrument to accomplish his purposes.[136] Even more fundamental to his preaching and teaching was the concern for proper consolation of consciences and admonition to proper living—good pastoral care—that shaped his entire approach to Scripture.[137] With this way of practicing theology, his *via Vittembergensi*, in place but always adapting to new situations, Luther proceeded to fulfill his doctoral oath, confessing his faith and proclaiming God's Word, for the last quarter-century of his life.

---

[136] *Luther's Last Battles: Politics and Polemics, 1531–1546*, Ithaca, Cornell University Press, 1983, 163–208, cf. Edwards, *Brethren*, 197–205.

[137] G. Ebeling, *Luthers Seelsorge an seinen Briefen dargestellt*, Tübingen, Mohr/Siebeck, 1997, *passim*.

5

The Emergence of the Reformer: Luther's Decisive Turn to Reform

As Luther forged the orientation for his thinking discussed in Chapter 4, on the basis of the factors discussed in Chapter 3, his routine at the university continued apace, but not without serious interruptions and distractions. The indulgence controversy had made him a cause célèbre throughout western Europe. The legal processes of church and empire sought an end to the threat he posed to good order in the years following the posting of the Ninety-five Theses.

After returning to Wittenberg from Leipzig, Luther experienced mounting challenges from opponents loyal to the papacy. They included Jerome Dungersheim and Jerome Emser from Leipzig, advisors to Duke Georg, cousin and rival of Frederick the Wise; Johann Cochlaeus from the young university at Frankfurt an der Oder, which belonged to Frederick's rival, Elector Joachim of Brandenburg; and Johann Eck, professor at another rival, young university, that of the dukes of Bavaria, Ingolstadt. Their criticisms centered on Luther's undercutting papal authority and thus order in church and society. They addressed only tangentially, if at all, the issues of pastoral care and concern for the consolation of sin-ridden consciences that stood at the heart of Luther's calling. From the beginning the two sides talked past each other because their concept of the Christian faith differed fundamentally.[1]

PROPAGATING THE WITTENBERG MESSAGE

In the midst of teaching, university reform, duels with foes, and political negotiations being conducted by Elector Frederick and other secular governments, in 1518–20, Luther set to exploiting his new-found celebrity and the technology that had fostered it. Gutenberg's invention enabled him to pursue his calling as a public teacher of the church in new, imaginative,

[1] M. Brecht, *Martin Luther*, 3 vols., tr. James L. Schaaf, Philadelphia, Fortress, 1985–1993, 1: 330–48; D. Bagchi, *Luther's Earliest Opponents, Catholic Controversialists, 1518–1525*, Minneapolis, Fortress, 1991, 45–91.

ways as well as in old forms. Even in print he adapted several medieval genres of edification as he responded to special requests from colleagues or in executing his monastic duties. Devotional treatises illustrate the intensity of his pastoral concerns already at this stage of his career; catechetical sermons reveal his desire to educate the people in both biblical teaching and proper behavior. These writings combined his strong instinct to care for believers' spiritual welfare, cultivating the peace of the gospel in their lives, with his insistence that Christ's peace produce a life of obedience to God's plan for life. His distinction of law and gospel, as well as elements of the theology of the cross, informed these treatises; his distinction of two dimensions of human righteousness asserted itself explicitly more slowly.

Two devotional works—the preface to a partial text of the *German Theology* that arose from Taulerian circles, published in 1516, and a commentary on the seven 'penitential psalms' of 1517—marked Luther's print debut. Both emphasized Christ's presence as the savior of sinners in the Christian life.[2] Lent 1519 gave him occasion to appropriate the medieval genre of meditation on Christ's passion. His treatise expressed his distinction of law and gospel, focusing through Christ's suffering on the believer's sin and God's merciful giving of himself to sinners. Luther criticized medieval forms of meditation, which practiced self-righteous condemnation of the Jews or ritualistic efforts to show sympathy for Christ. Rightly contemplating Christ's passion yields a terror-stricken heart and despairing conscience. Sinners do not stand as safely distanced observers of Jesus's suffering but recognize their personal involvement in his crucifixion. Such a stance throws sinners totally into God's hands, resulting in hearts filled with love for him. This identifies God in a new way as kind and loving; it identifies the sinner as God's own. That strengthens and encourages believers to fight against sin and to make Christ's life and name integral to their own daily living.[3]

Luther composed his adaptation of the medieval *ars moriendi*, devotional tracts to aid the terminally ill in preparing to die, in May 1519, employing this same law/gospel structure as it focused on Christ's crucifixion to prepare believers for death. 'Luther's sermon stands within an old tradition, but at one decisive point he breaks away and concentrates on one concern: only faith in Christ's cross helps in the final hour.'[4] In autumn

---

[2] *WA* 1: 153, 158–220.

[3] *WA* 2: 136–42, *LW* 42: 7–14; cf. the manuscript, 'Duo sermones de passione Christi', *WA* 1: 336–45.

[4] W. Goez, 'Luthers "Ein Sermon von der Bereitung zum Sterben" und die spätmittelalterliche ars moriendi', *LuJ* 48 (1981), 97–114, at 114; cf. *Sermon on Preparation for Death*, *WA* 2: 685–97, *LW* 42: 99–115; N. Leroux, *Martin Luther as Comforter*, Leiden, Brill, 2007, 45–80.

1519 Luther adapted another medieval devotional genre, the consolations of the fourteen 'auxiliary' saints, by outlining seven vices and seven virtues (another medieval devotional category) to aid readers in repenting of sin and turning to Christ in faith. Each chapter reminded readers of their sinfulness and vulnerability to Satan, the world, and sinful desire, but also demonstrated how Christ's death reverses those evils. The subsequent rehearsal of 'blessings' from all directions repeated the message that God had spent his wrath on the cross and set believers on the path of true living. Luther's strong doctrine of creation expressed itself in the initial comment on the blessings 'within us', the first of which are gifts for this body and life, including reason, knowledge, and eloquence. Trust in Christ crowns those blessings and impels believers to speak publicly about Christ, serve him with good works, and suffer evil.[5]

Luther's catechetical writings of this period reflected this same law / gospel / good works structure. As a monk he had undoubtedly often preached catechetical sermons, not only on the core of medieval catechesis, the Apostles Creed, the Lord's Prayer, and the Ten Commandments (he apparently abandoned the 'Ave Maria', the fourth part of the core of medieval cathechesis, early), but also on the sacraments, of which some early printed catechetical handbooks had provided a list. Published in Latin, his sermon on penance (1518) fitted into the controversy over indulgences;[6] his 'Sermon on Proper Preparation for Receiving the Sacrament of the Eucharist', also in Latin, asserted that all sins should be regarded as mortal offenses, breaking the sinner's relationship with God, and that faith in Christ, not Moses' law that demands performance, creates a proper relationship with God.[7] Subsequent catechetical writings expanded and deepened these stepping-stones as he sharpened his law / gospel distinction.

Luther's instruction on the Ten Commandments, delivered to the Wittenberg public between June 1516 and March 1517, published first in Latin, then German, revealed his understanding that the first commandment defines all sinners as idolaters because they rely on God's creatures rather than God, and that this idolatry provokes all other sins.[8] The manner in which the law / gospel distinction permeates Luther's way of thinking became clear in his published version of the subsequent public *Exposition of the Lord's Prayer*, which did not appear in print until 1519 because Luther

---

[5] *WA* 6: 104–34, esp. 119.33–122.6, *LW* 42: 121–66, esp. 144–7. Cf. Leroux, *Comforter*, 1–43.

[6] *WA* 1: 319–24.

[7] *WA* 1: 329–34. He continued to develop his teaching on proper repentance and use of confession and absolution, e.g. in *Brief Instruction on How to Confess Sin*, *WA* 2: 59–65; *Sermon on the Sacrament of Penance*, *WA* 2: 713–23, *LW* 35: 9–22; *Explanation of Confession*, *WA* 6: 157–69.

[8] *WA* 1: 398–521, esp. 399.11–22.

tried to involve other members of the embryonic team he was gathering, Johann Agricola and Nikolaus von Amsdorf, in preparing his sermons for publishing. Dissatisfied with their attempts, he composed his own version. It began with a rejection of ritualistic use of prayer; Christians pray as their faith throws itself totally upon their Father, not upon its own religious exertions. Luther's treatment of individual petitions of the Our Father contained an exposition of why the petition is necessary in view of sinners' sinfulness and vulnerability in an evil world as well as how God gives the baptized assurance of forgiveness and salvation in Christ. Luther viewed the Lord's Prayer as a weapon against Satan and sin. Praying commits believers to wage war against their own sinfulness and evil in the world around them.[9]

Sermons on penance, baptism, and the Lord's Supper followed in 1519. This trilogy delivered law and gospel to readers but also indicated that Luther's conviction regarding the re-creative power of God's Word in the sacraments had not yet taken complete command of his thinking. For instance, in his *Sermon on Baptism* Augustine's understanding of the signification of sacramental signs led him to say that baptism is an external sign or token that separates Christians from others by placing them under Christ's leadership in battling sin. It *signifies* dying to sin and resurrection in God's grace, drowning the old creature, raising up the new, but it *effects* that new life only gradually in the battle against sin. This sacramental word does not change the fundamental reality of human existence, at this stage of Luther's development.[10]

'So that no one again accuses me of forbidding good works, I state that believers should have remorse and regret over their sins, confess them, and do good works,' even though trusting in Christ remains the most important focus for Christian living.[11] Luther began early in his career to provide concrete instruction for living a God-pleasing life in love for neighbors. In addition to ethical direction in treatments of the Ten Commandments and the Lord's Prayer, he wrote a *Sermon on the Estate of Marriage*, in 1519. Although his full-fledged understanding of God as Creator does not emerge clearly, Luther began by affirming marriage's place as God's created order for human life. Sin has made it a vital hedge against lust, to be sure, but fundamentally the institution of the family follows God's original plan for human community. God preserves and governs this godly relationship. Raising children properly is holier than all religious performance of fasting

---

[9] *WA* 2: 80–130, *LW* 42: 19–93.

[10] *WA* 2: 727.20–731.257 (2: 727–37), *LW* 35: 29–34 (35: 29–43); cf. *WA* 2: 713–23, *LW* 35: 9–22; *Sermon on the Sacrament of the Holy, True Body of Christ and the Brotherhoods, WA* 2: 742–58, esp. 742.15–743.26, *LW* 35: 49–73, esp. 49–51.

[11] *WA* 2: 719.24–8, *LW* 35: 17.

and other good works. Parents should not worship their offspring nor spoil them but raise them strictly and responsibly as children of God.[12] Within the setting of his concern for proper teaching of God's Word, Luther strove to cultivate the daily Christian life.

THE WITTENBERG PROGRAM FOR REFORM

In 1520 invitations to write on specific topics kept coming to Luther; he responded to many of them. In the course of these writings he formulated five treatises that summarized his program of reform, his way of applying his interpretive framework to the whole of theology and the life of both church and society. Though not planned or organized as a comprehensive overview of his reform, they indicated how his message was taking concrete shape. The first met Spalatin's request for a refutation of the accusation that Luther discouraged good works. *On Good Works*, published in June 1520,[13] was followed in August by another writing probably generated by secular counselors at the electoral Saxon court. The *Open Letter to the German Nobility of the German Nation, concerning Reform of the Christian Estate* placed traditional complaints of the German diets against Rome into Luther's own theological framework.[14] *On the Babylonian Captivity of the Church* appeared in October, a treatment of the sacramental system and the concept of the priesthood which administered it, provoked by Roman Catholic challenges to his teaching on the church.[15] In an effort to stave off escalation of the confrontation with the papacy Luther was persuaded to write an open letter in a reconciling tone to Pope Leo X. He then appended a discussion of his concept of the central teaching of Christianity; he chose the title *The Freedom of the Christian* to express his doctrine of justification and the fruits of faith that flow from Christ's restoration of the sinner's righteousness in God's sight.[16] Fifteen months after this treatise had appeared in November 1520, Luther issued his *Judgment on Monastic Vows*, explaining his rejection of this form of religiosity.[17]

The *Open Letter* repeated the *gravimina*—grievances calling for reform—that the imperial diet had sent several times in recent years to the papal court. This treatise framed them, however, with Luther's critique of the medieval church, its piety and policies. This treatise did not treat strictly doctrinal matters but church structures and governances, and popular piety and ritual observances. Luther began by expressing his

---

[12] *WA* 2: 166–71, *LW* 44: 7–14.   [13] *WA* 6: 202–76, *LW* 44: 21–114.

[14] *WA* 6: 404–69, *LW* 44: 123–217.   [15] *WA* 6: 497–573, *LW* 36: 11–126.

[16] *WA* 7: 3–38, 42–73, *LW* 31: 333–77.

[17] *WA* 8: 573–669, *LW* 44: 251–400; B. Lohse, *Martin Luther's Theology*, tr. R. Harrisville, Minneapolis, Fortress, 1999, 137–43.

reliance on God alone for his efforts to relieve the 'misery and distress of suffering Christendom', announcing that this treatise addresses papal usurpation of God's power in governing his church. The papacy defends that power with three walls, Luther claimed. The first concerned the assertion of papal power over temporal governments; here Luther articulated an early form of his distinction of two realms, 'the heavenly' and 'the earthly', within human life. God is lord of all, and all Christians are truly of the spiritual realm, in one body, all contributing members (1 Cor. 12: 12–13). The community places the bishop in his responsibilities. Therefore, secular authorities, as baptized believers, are priests of God and serve him in a proper and useful place as they carry out the responsibilities of governing society in godly fashion. Those with responsibilities for leading the church should not interfere with the exercise of secular power. Not yet a fully developed formulation, these quite circumscribed remarks on church and society point to a reshaping of the medieval understanding of how God provides for human creatures within the structures of daily life.[18]

The second wall was the claim that only the pope can interpret Scripture properly. Popes had not done so; furthermore, the 'office of the keys' (Matt. 16: 16; 18: 15–20) relates to forgiving or binding sin, not exercising power in the church, as medieval theologians claimed. Luther did not argue that Christians may interpret Scripture in any way they individually please but that all have access to the Holy Spirit's teaching through its pages, without priestly mediation. The third wall was the assertion that the pope stands above the judgment of all other Christians, an argument reinforced in the fifteenth century to counteract the power of councils. Not even the pope stands above correction if he acts against Christ (2 Cor. 13: 8).[19]

The list of twenty-seven grievances that followed embraced twenty-three directly relating to the practice of the faith, including the luxurious lifestyle and the size of the papal court, papal usurpation of ecclesiastical powers that belonged properly to German bishops, simony, and papal intrusion into secular affairs. Luther criticized some pious practices, including pilgrimages, special vows to perform certain pious acts, clerical celibacy, monasticism, masses for the dead, abuses of excommunication and the interdict, the ecclesiastical festivals that provided occasion for drunkenness, gambling, and laziness, begging as a meritorious work, and masses for pay. In addition, he called for a solution to the Hussite schism through negotiations with the Bohemians, for university reform on a humanistic model, and for German imperial freedom from papal domination. Finally, he urged prohibition of luxurious, extravagant clothing, foreign spice imports, usury,

---

[18] See Chapter 10.   [19] WA 6: 405.12–415.18 (404–69), LW 44: 124–39 (123–217).

gluttony and drunkenness, and brothels.[20] Moral issues, including waste, economic exploitation, and abuse of God's gifts of body and sexuality, came under the preacher's purview as matters of God's design for humanity. Although this subject matter did not lend itself to extensive use of the distinction of law and gospel, it did give opportunity for some halting steps in experimenting with the distinction of the two realms of human life. The treatise does not explicitly employ the distinction of two kinds of righteousness.

That was not true of the central piece of this reform program, *The Freedom of the Christian*. Without using the term 'two kinds of righteousness', the work unfolds its argument along lines set by this distinction as it defines God's justifying action toward sinners as, first, liberation from sin—thus restoration to the dignity and activity of human creatures as God designed them—and, second, liberation for living in trust toward God and service or love toward others.[21]

Two theses summarized Luther's view of what it means to be human, behind which stood his understanding of how God deals with sinful human creatures: 'a Christian is a perfectly free lord of all, subject to none', his definition of the human relationship to God, and 'a Christian is a totally responsible servant of all, subject to all', his definition of the relationship among human beings. He designated the vertical relationship of trust in God as a 'spiritual, inner' relationship, the new creature; identifying the 'bodily' nature as flesh, carnal, outward, 'the old creature'. He did not equate this latter with the horizontal dimension of life, or earthly matters.[22] Those who live apart from trust in Christ are truly enslaved; all things force them to submit, take them captive, as they try to use these things to give life meaning.[23] God designed human creatures to live out of God's love, trusting in him, orienting all of life in this trust toward him. 'The gospel of God concerning his Son, who was made flesh, suffered, rose from the dead, and was glorified through the Spirit who sanctifies', or bestows new life. Where this word from God is missing, there is no help. Where it is present, so are all blessings—the full enjoyment of humanity. To preach Christ means to feed the soul, make it righteous, set it free, and make it whole, provided it believes what is proclaimed. Faith alone is the saving and efficacious use of God's Word (Rom. 10: 4; 1: 17). Trusting in one's own efforts destroys faith, for it diverts human reliance to personal performance

---

[20] *WA* 6: 415.19–469.17, *LW* 44: 139–217. Cf. similar admonitions to governments in *On Good Works*, *WA* 6: 242.20–245.18, *LW* 44: 95–7.

[21] Luther contrasts the two dimensions of humanity particularly clearly at *WA* 7: 61.1–62.36, Latin (31.17–34.22, German), *LW* 31: 360–1.

[22] *WA* 7: 49.20–50.31 (20.25–22.2), *LW* 31: 344–5.

[23] *WA* 7: 57.32–58.3, *LW* 31: 355–6.

rather than God's disposition of love. Therefore, to be human means to view oneself as God's new creature. Therein alone is the true realization of a person's humanity.[24]

Luther set his definition of humanity within the framework of God's address to human creatures in commands and promises, his distinction of law and gospel. Commands help sinners recognize their helplessness, leaving them in distress. The promises give assurance that God gives them mercy, righteousness, peace, and freedom through Christ. Trust in God's promises therefore constitute the heart of humanity; the performance of his commands attracts the sinner's focus to personal accomplishment. Faith functions in this way because it regards God as God, trustworthy and faithful. Faith first renders sinners totally dependent on God's mercy, so that they let God be God, who alone creates life; as a result faith causes them to recognize that their performance of his will can only flow from their recognition of their dependence on him and his nature as their loving Maker. The root of all sin is the belief that sinners may secure God's favor through their own performance rather than relying on his favorable, loving disposition toward them. Thirdly, faith unites believers with Christ in the manner in which a bride is united to her bridegroom. This is not an ontological absorption into the other, as some medieval mystics envisioned salvation, but a union as mysterious as husband and wife becoming 'one flesh' (Gen. 2: 24; Eph. 5: 25–30), in which each preserves his/her own identity and delights in the other being different from oneself. In this kind of union self-seeking disappears into mutual commitment and devotion to the other. In such a relationship the performance of works to gain merit, Luther asserted, is lifeless and thus cannot glorify God; faith, as a personal relationship with him, gives him glory.[25]

This image of bride and bridegroom expresses a description of Christ's saving work that Luther labeled 'the joyous exchange'. He joined to it a parallel description branded 'the magnificent duel' between Christ and Satan for the allegiance of the sinner.[26] In this 'joyous exchange' the bridegroom took the sinner's place, assuming the sin, death, and hell afflicting his bride, making them his own. Through his suffering, death, and descent into hell he conquered them all, swallowed them up, through his righteousness, which is mightier than all these enemies.[27] In this way Luther presented Christ as the one who substituted himself for sinners and vanquished all

---

[24] *WA* 7: 51.12–52.19 (22.23–23.23), *LW* 31: 346–8.

[25] *WA* 7: 52.20–56.14 (23.24–26.31), *LW* 31: 348–53.   [26] See pp. 121–2 below.

[27] *WA* 7: 55.7–23 (25.34–26.12), *LW* 31: 352; see M. Lienhard, *Luther: Witness to Jesus Christ, Stages and Themes of the Reformer's Christology*, tr. E. Robertson, Minneapolis, Augsburg, 1982, 131–6; U. Rieske-Braun, *Duellum mirabile. Studien zum Kampfmotiv in Martin Luthers Theologie*, Göttingen, Vandenhoeck & Ruprecht, 1999, 159–60.

that imprisons them or keeps them from practicing their true humanity in trust toward God and the obedience that results from it.

Marriage to their king and high priest transforms sinners, through forgiveness of their sins, into children of God, kings and priests themselves. Being king means to be lord over all the sinner's enemies; none of them can harm Christ's people. Being priest means that 'we are worthy to appear before God to pray for others and to teach each other God's things'.[28] This does not mean that Luther was naive about the afflictions Christians encounter in life. God makes his power perfect in their weakness (2 Cor. 12: 9); therefore, even suffering and death contribute to the believer's welfare.[29]

God's gift of forgiveness and the restoration of a trusting relationship with him—the heart of humanity—frees believers from having to strive to win his favor and also frees them to love their neighbor. They demonstrate this love first by proclaiming Christ and then in other actions. Neither task has been reserved for clergy or monks. God's people never dare think that they need not struggle to discipline the body and strive to aid others. 'Works do not justify before God, but believers do works out of spontaneous love in obedience to God and, conscious of nothing except that God loves them, they wish to obey him most responsibly in every regard.'[30] Just as Adam and Eve freely performed God's will in Paradise, not to win God's favor but because they had confidence that he loved them, so believers distinguish their performance of good works for their own sake, to gain favor with God, from what they do for God's sake, out of trust and delight in him. The former kind of works is not truly good, for those who perform them worship their own efforts, not God.[31] Faith's works aim simply at serving and benefiting others, meeting their needs, promoting their advantage, following Christ's example (Phil. 1: 1–11), for Christ lives in them (Gal. 2: 20).

The Holy Spirit fills believers' hearts with the love that renders them free, joyful, almighty performers of good, who overcome all afflictions, serve their neighbors, and nevertheless remain lords of all things.[32] In such service those bound to their neighbor in love find true Christian freedom. Therefore, Luther can conclude that Christians live not in themselves but in Christ and in their neighbor, or they are not Christian: in Christ through faith, in the neighbor through love. This love expresses itself in the context of their callings or walks of life (Luther used the term 'profession' and

[28] *WA* 7: 56.35–58.3 (27.16–28.25), *LW* 31: 354–6.
[29] *WA* 7: 57.2–12 (27.23–28.5), *LW* 31: 354–5.
[30] *WA* 7: 58.12–60.29 (28.26–30.30), *LW* 31: 356–9.
[31] *WA* 7: 60.30–61.33 (30.31–32.34), *LW* 31: 359–61.
[32] *WA* 7: 64.13–66.18 (34.23–36.19), *LW* 31: 365–9.

'status' for the societal positions of all Christians although these terms had usually designated the calling of monks). Through faith they are taken above into God; through love they move down into the neighbor.[33] Therefore, reliance on works, including the ceremonial works of ritualistic religion, has no place in the Christian's life; those ceremonies serve to teach and guide, not as ways to earn God's favor.[34]

Although this treatise did not define God's justifying action in terms of the re-creative power effected by his word of promise, it made clear to readers what Luther meant by restoration to righteousness in God's sight by faith. Faith recognizes God as loving Lord and throws itself completely into his hands. Thus, this faith forms the orienting core of the human being as God originally created humanity. That faith, passive in receiving the identity God gives his people as his own, expresses itself inevitably in works of love.

Luther had made that point clearly five months earlier in *On Good Works*, a commentary on the Decalog in the medieval catechetical tradition.[35] Positing that only what God has commanded can be a good work—not those 'religious' works which humans invent—he stated, 'the first, highest, and most noble good work of all is faith in Christ,[36] as Christ said in John 6 (:29), "That is God's good work, that you believe in him whom he has sent." ' Faith is not one work among many, as the medieval list of virtues had claimed, subordinating it to love; all other works stem from faith and receive their goodness from it. Everything that is not done in faith, that is without Christ as the orienting core of life, is sin (Rom. 14: 23).[37] Faith fulfills the first commandment, but faith's very nature reveals that believers cannot create confidence in God's grace and favor but must receive it as a gift.[38] For human beings do not generate trust in their own hearts; the trustworthy person must elicit it and create it. The righteousness of faith simply recognizes God as God and receives his goodness.

His theology of the cross led Luther to observe that faith's finest art is to have sure confidence in God when suffering appears, especially under his wrath against sin. Spiritual struggles test but also display faith at this highest stage.[39] If righteousness in God's sight consists of God's gift of that righteousness in Christ and trusting his promise of that righteousness, then works are clearly the result of that faith, which constitutes the believer's

---

[33] *WA* 7: 69.12–18 (38.6–15), *LW* 31: 371.   [34] *WA* 7: 72.1–36, *LW* 31: 375–6.

[35] James M. Estes, *Peace, Order and the Glory of God: Secular Authority and the Church in the Thought of Luther and Melanchthon 1518–1559*, Leiden, Brill, 2005, 9–13.

[36] A definition he later disavowed, rejecting faith as a human work, 'Disputation concerning Justification', 1536, *WA* 39.1: 90.5–91.11, *LW* 34: 159–60.

[37] *WA* 6: 204.25–205.1, 206.8–23, *LW* 44: 23–4, 25–6.

[38] *WA* 6: 209.24–210.9, *LW* 44: 30.   [39] *WA* 6: 208.6–209.24, *LW* 44: 28–9.

righteousness.[40] 'Faith does not arise from works, nor do they create it. It must spring and flow from Christ's blood, wounds, and death. In him you see that God is kindly disposed toward you, that he gave his Son for you, and therefore your heart becomes tender and kindly disposed toward God. Thus, your confidence grows out of sheer treasuring and loving, him you and you him.'[41] Luther's exposition of the last nine commandments followed,[42] reminding readers of their violations of God's commands and offering specific instruction on how to carry out God's will in daily life.

By the end of 1521 Luther had prepared another major work on daily life, his *Judgment on Monastic Vows*. It rejected the medieval distinction between a superior, more God-pleasing realm of sacred, religious activities or 'callings' and a lesser (though not per se sinful) realm of profane, earth-bound activities. The former provided steeper but shorter paths to God. Luther had experienced this distinction especially in the monastery. He focused on monastic vows, criticizing them as contrary to God's commandments, undermining faith, destroying Christian freedom for proper service to God through meeting the neighbor's needs, thus undercutting true love for the neighbor, and contrary to reason and common sense.[43]

Luther based his analysis on his understanding of the goodness of God's creation and his structure for normal human life as the setting of God-pleasing living within family, political community, and church. This analysis also reflects explicitly his distinction between the two kinds of righteousness: he emphasized that neither vows nor sacred activities make people pleasing to God. Instead, God makes human creatures pleasing to himself by giving them trust in him, which produces truly good works in daily life.[44]

Fully as vital for Luther's theological structure as his view of the reconciliation of God and sinner was his view of how God's Word works as the instrument of that reconciliation. *The Babylonian Captivity of the Church* concluded its critique of medieval sacramental teaching without mentioning what would become the heart of his understanding of God's Word, that God's utterly reliable promise possesses re-creative power. He was coming to recognize the sacraments as forms of the re-creative Word even though he did not clearly, consistently, express this view here. Opponents such as

---

[40] WA 6: 211.1–36, LW 44: 31–3.   [41] WA 6: 216.29–34, LW 44: 38.

[42] WA 6: 217.1–276.30, LW 44: 39–114.

[43] WA 8: 573–669, LW 44: 252–355. Cf. *Babylonian Captivity*, WA 6: 538.24–542.38, LW 36: 74–81.

[44] R. Kolb, 'Die Zweidimensionalität des Mensch-Seins, Die zweierlei Gerechtigkeit in Luthers *De votis monasticis Judicium*', in C. Bultmann, V. Leppin, and A. Lindnor (eds.) *Luther und das monastische Erbe*, Tübingen, Mohr/Siebeck, 2007, 207–20.

Eck and Emser had realized what Luther's descriptions of God's action in the sacraments meant for their understanding of the way in which their religious system functioned through the human approach to God in sacred ritual. Their responses occasioned this treatise.[45]

Luther posited a new definition of the term 'sacrament': a form of Christ's promise of life and salvation, commanded by him, in which external means or signs carry that oral promise. Later his definition shifted away from the traditional language of 'sign' for the external means and explicitly identified the promise as a word of re-creative power. At the beginning of *Babylonian Captivity* he listed 'baptism, penance, and the bread' as sacraments; by its end he listed only 'baptism and the bread' because he viewed confession and absolution as an oral form of the Word, without external signs, and as a repetition of God's baptismal action within the life of daily repentance, which flows from new birth in baptism.[46] Luther therefore rejected confirmation, marriage, ordination, and extreme unction as sacraments, each for slightly different reasons, but all because they lacked Christ's command or did not convey forgiveness of sins according to a promise affixed by him. Critiques of ritual religion as an effort to gain God's favor through pious activities and performance accompanied each analysis.[47]

Because the mass had claimed the central role in parish practice in Luther's late medieval experience, he devoted much time to it, also in *Babylonian Captivity*. He objected first to withholding the cup from the laity, defying Christ's command that all who receive should receive both his body and his blood, and depriving the people of the blessing of the whole sacrament as Christ instituted it. This constituted in Luther's mind an act of tyranny by the priests.[48]

'The second captivity of this sacrament is less grievous' though enough to earn condemnation: the explanation of Christ's presence in bread and wine on the basis of what Luther regarded as the misapplication of Aristotle's physics to the question. Medieval teaching tried to clarify how Christ's body and blood could be present in the sacramental elements. 'Transubstantiation' posited the substitution of what Aristotle defined as the substance of the bread—what makes bread bread—for the substance of Christ's body, while the 'accidents'—the specific unique characteristics of this bread—remained externally. Luther rejected both this theory and the explanation of 'consubstantiation'—that the substances of both body

---

[45] *WA* 6: 497.24–499.7, *LW* 36: 12–14.

[46] *WA* 6: 572.10–12, *LW* 36: 124. The lists are found in *WA* 6: 501.33–8, 572.10–34, *LW* 36: 18, 124–5.

[47] *WA* 6: 549.20–571.34, *LW* 36: 91–123.   [48] *WA* 6: 502.1–507.33, *LW* 36: 19–28.

and bread lie under the external appearance of bread—because he believed Christ's presence to be a mystery, which human reason should not attempt to solve.[49] His doubts had been aroused by reading the French Ockhamist Pierre d'Ailly, who had died a century earlier. D'Ailly simply submitted to the church's authority; Luther submitted to Christ's words: 'If I cannot follow how the bread is Christ's body, I nonetheless take my reason captive to the obedience of Christ and cling simply to his words.'[50] Already in 1520, however, Luther supported his literal interpretation of Christ's 'this is my body' with a Christological parallel: his divine nature is contained under his human nature.[51] Later Luther argued for the possibility of the presence of Christ's human body and blood in the sacrament on the basis of the sharing of characteristics of the divine and human natures within Christ's one person. Here that argument is lacking, but the association he would later develop further is present.

'By far the most impious abuse of all', the third captivity of the sacrament, obscured its nature as God's promise by transforming it into mere ritual performance intended to win God's favor through human action. Luther insisted on recognizing the sacrament as Christ's 'testament', his bequest promising the inheritance of forgiveness of sins. Christ confirmed the promise with his death. Faith clings to God's promise; everything which diverts believers from God's promise to their own efforts wreaks havoc with the sacrament.[52]

Furthermore, Luther objected to understanding the mass as a sacrifice, a repetition and extension of Christ's sacrifice for sin. Some opponents protested that they did not teach this, though the opinion was not restricted to popular piety; it also could be found in some scholastic teachers. Luther was most concerned about clarifying the true nature of the sacrament as God's promise, not as a ritual by which the priest could offer God this sacrifice to appease his wrath. The sacrament therefore does not bestow grace automatically or magically, Luther insisted, rejecting it as an *opus operatum*, which accomplished its intent apart from the recipient's faith. Originally designed to assure the validity of the sacramental word on the basis of God's word, instead of human faith or the priest's worthiness, this term had come to signify for many that ritual attendance at mass, rather than trust in its promise, delivered grace.[53] Luther affirmed that this sacramental testament functions as God's Word that establishes and confirms the relationship of the conversing Father with his trusting children, a reflection of his pastoral concern for building his readers' faith.

---

[49] *WA* 6: 508.1–511.34, *LW* 36: 28–35.
[50] *WA* 6: 508.7–26, 511.13–21, *LW* 36: 28–31, 34.   [51] *WA* 6: 511.34–512.6, *LW* 36: 35.
[52] *WA* 6: 512.7–523.7, *LW* 36: 35–51.   [53] *WA* 6: 523.8–526.23, *LW* 36: 51–7.

Luther dedicated about the same number of words to baptism, not because it was equally important in medieval piety—he asserted that the devil had succeeded in quenching its power in adults by focusing attention on their performance rather than God's gift of new life through this sacrament—but because it was vital to his understanding of the Christian life. Baptism bestows God's promise of forgiveness of sins and nourishes trust in the promising God. Apart from faith it brings no benefit. Like the Lord's Supper it is not efficacious automatically or magically, Luther wrote, reacting against its ritualistic use. It is efficacious because it imparts God's favor to the believer. 'Baptism signifies two things—death and resurrection, that is full and complete justification' (Rom. 6: 3–11). He called this death and resurrection 'the new creation, regeneration, and spiritual birth', 'actual death and resurrection', but at the same time saw that death and resurrection as only gradually setting into the Christian's life. Luther favored this 'death and resurrection' definition of what baptism accomplishes over the also apt description of baptism as washing because it made it clear that sinners need to die to sin and be raised to new life. And in spite of his hesitation to affirm the absolute reality of God's regard for his reborn children as totally righteous, he affirmed that baptism is not a process in development but something that lasts, not only a spiritual or mental death but 'in reality (*revera*) we begin leaving this bodily life and receiving the life to come'.[54] Although he could not yet explicitly state that God's re-creative Word fashions a reality even stronger than the reality of the consciousness of continuing sinfulness, he was searching for the best way to address the mystery of continuing sin and evil in the believer's life.

He did so in part by making the baptismal pattern of God's action standard for the whole Christian life. Each day believers are to put to death their sinful desires and be raised up to serve God. That is the true significance of the sacrament of penance, which for Luther centered in confession of sins and reception of absolution from sin that sets believers free to trust in God and serve him.[55]

Challenges to infant baptism had not yet become critical in 1520, but Luther presumed that God acts through baptism in infants' behalf as well. All conversion to faith in Christ happens by God's power. He who can change godless adult hearts, which are just as unresponsive and helpless as infants, can transform, cleanse, and renew infants.[56] For God cultivates the faith that responds to his baptismal promise of life as his children grow older through absolution.

---

[54] *WA* 6: 526.34–534.39, *LW* 36: 57–69.   [55] *WA* 6: 535.1–538.3, *LW* 36: 69–73.
[56] *WA* 6: 538.4–18, *LW* 36: 73–4.

Luther wished to renew the sacramental use of penance, which had been transformed, he charged, into a means of encouraging the search for righteousness through human performance. Medieval practice had emphasized making satisfaction for sin's temporal punishment through the works priests assigned in confession. Luther's criticism of medieval practice claimed that it had perverted all three parts of penance: contrition, confession, and satisfaction. Contrition was regarded as a human effort that prepared the heart for approaching God, a human merit. Trusting in one's own contrition is a false faith. Confession of sins to the priest had become the occasion for priestly tyranny rather than the pronouncement of free forgiveness for Christ's sake. Satisfactions had diverted attention from the renewal of Christian obedience on the basis of faith in Christ, again directing faith toward human performance of the priest's prescriptions. This had led many to despair, Luther's pastoral heart alleged. He called for use of confession and absolution as a proclamation of life in Christ, an encouragement for faith in him that gives strength for living a new life in him.[57]

The Babylonian Captivity addressed the heart of medieval Christianity, its sacramental-sacerdotal system, and its presuppositions in a ritually determined context. Against this kind of religion Luther asserted his understanding of God's continuing conversation with his people through his Word in oral, written, and above all sacramental forms. That Word served as God's means for creating faith and thus for saving sinners.

SPREADING THE REFORMATION
THROUGH GOD'S WORD

Not only did God address sinners to restore them to himself through God's Word in sacramental form. His Word had come initially in oral form, through the proclamation he gave the Old Testament prophets and the apostles. God had had this proclamation recorded in written form to preserve it from inevitable adulteration when people pass it from one generation to another. Luther admonished his contemporaries to draw the gospel of Christ out of Scripture, in order to implement God's saving action in their time.[58] Luther was concerned to implement the spread of his message through both preaching and print. Mark Edwards argues that the Reformation was an oral event; preaching brought Luther's message to hearers across Germany, often before any of his tracts had become accessible to them.[59] Nonetheless, 'the printed word played a crucial role

---

[57] *WA* 6: 543.4–549.18, *LW* 36: 81–91.   [58] *WA* 10.1.1: 17.4–14, *LW* 35: 123.
[59] M. Edwards, *Printing, Propaganda, and Martin Luther*, Berkeley, University of California Press, 1994, 37, 11.

in the early Reformation, and when multiplied by the effects of preaching and conversation, can be said to be a major factor in spreading a relatively coherent message throughout the German-speaking lands'.[60] Printed works spread Luther's ideas with unprecedented speed and permitted him to influence leaders and common people from afar in unprecedented ways.[61]

Because Luther believed that Scripture provides access to God's Word as delivered to prophets and apostles in authoritative form, he wanted to have its words in the vernacular for the German people. By the time *On Monastic Vows* had appeared in early 1522, half a year after the imperial Edict issued after the Worms diet had made him an outlaw, he had been taken to Wartburg Castle in Elector Frederick's protective custody. With time on his hands he turned to translating the New Testament into German, using Erasmus's Greek text to check his reading of the Latin text, with which he was familiar as a monk, and some older German translations.[62] Luther went to the streets and shops of Wittenberg to determine how best to render some terms for German readers. He practiced the art of translation into dynamic equivalence, catching the necessity of adding 'alone', for instance, to the word 'faith' in Paul's writings to convey the sense of the text.[63]

At the same time he was concerned that pastors learn to preach, correctly conveying the gospel of Christ from Scripture's pages to their people's ears and hearts. He composed a postil, a medieval form of help for preachers. Postils contained model sermons for the pericopes, the appointed lessons for the Sundays of the church year. Eventually, under the editorial hand of students, sermons appeared from his pen for the entire church year, but his original effort, written at the Wartburg in late 1521, offered sermons for the several festival days from Christmas through Epiphany. By April 1522 sermons for the four Sundays of Advent had also appeared in print.[64] His later postils appeared in German, but initially he wrote for priests who could read Latin. The prefaces to this work and his New Testament translation[65] argued that all Scripture, also the Old Testament, focuses on Christ and delivers the message of salvation through him. Here he did not teach that God's Word is an instrument that actually effects the rescue and conversion of sinners into children of God.

[60] Ibid., 172.   [61] Ibid., 7.

[62] Heinz Bluhm, *Martin Luther, Creative Translator*, Saint Louis, Concordia, 1965; and *Luther, Translator of Paul: Studies in Romans and Galatians*, New York, Lang, 1984.

[63] See his *On Translating* (1530), WA 30.2: 632–46, LW 35: 181–202.

[64] WA 7: 466–537; 10.1.2: 1–208.

[65] WA 10.1.1: 8–18, LW 35: 117–24; WADB 7: 2–11, LW 35: 357–62.

THE WITTENBERG TEAM

Despite the acclaim of those who heralded him as a prophet, and his own styling himself as successor to the prophets or apostles—in contrast to his oft-stated acknowledgement of his own sins and weaknesses—Luther did not operate as a hero in isolation. His accomplishments reflect not only his own genius and imagination but also his ability to work with the team that assembled around him from 1516 on. It embraced those who stayed with him in Wittenberg for the last twenty-five years of his life and others who left 'on assignment' to spread Wittenberg reform elsewhere. Melanchthon was the most significant, gifted, and creative of his associates. He developed his own way of thinking out of what Luther gave him; Luther received from Philip not only philological help but also stimulation to advance his own thinking in new directions.[66]

When Melanchthon joined the faculty in 1518, Nikolaus von Amsdorf had already committed himself to Luther's cause. Staupitz's nephew and an arts instructor in Wittenberg, he struggled with Luther's new ideas but became convinced of them by 1516. In 1524 Amsdorf departed to head reform efforts in Magdeburg, but stayed in close touch with his Wittenberg colleagues. During this time Elector Frederick's secretary Georg Spalatin was also serving as Luther's partner in thinking through how to advance reform, and Luther's prize student, Johann Agricola, was becoming active in his cause. Agricola later brought grief to his mentor because, bright enough to capture the outline of Luther's thought, he failed to capture how it functioned, particularly how the dynamic of law and gospel meets the real-life situation of believers in the mysterious battle against continuing sin and evil in their lives.

In March 1521 Johannes Bugenhagen came to Wittenberg as a 35-year-old student, settled into Wittenberg as colleague in theology and parish pastor, and lent his exegetical and above all his organizational skills to advancing Luther's reform. By summer 1521 Justus Jonas had come from Erfurt to teach canon law at Wittenberg. He contributed some polemic and many translations, from German to Latin and Latin to German, of Luther's and Melanchthon's work, departing Wittenberg to reform the city of Halle in 1541. Others, students or former students, later joined the team, Caspar Cruciger and Georg Major as instructors in theology, Georg Rörer and Veit Dietrich as amanuenses and editors.[67] Lukas Cranach,

[66] T. Wengert, 'Luther neben Melanchthon, Melanchthon neben Luther', *LuJ* 66 (1999), 55–88; B. Lohse, 'Philipp Melanchthon in seinen Beziehungen zu Luther', in H. Junghans (ed.), *Leben und Werk Martin Luthers von 1526 bis 1546*, Göttingen, Vandenhoeck & Ruprecht, 1983, 1: 403–18.

[67] H.-G. Leder, 'Luthers Beziehungen zu seinen Wittenberger Freunden', in ibid., 1: 419–40.

Wittenberg pharmacist and sometime mayor, administered an artistic workshop that promoted Reformation theology through paintings, engravings, and woodcuts.[68] Luther, Cruciger, and Cruciger's wife, Elizabeth, spread the Wittenberg message through their hymns.[69]

These men shared insights and criticism, divided tasks, and wrote treatises and formal memoranda for princes and town councils. Luther dominated; Melanchthon's considerable influence helped shape the thinking of all, even as he absorbed Luther's insights and the counsel of others.

CONTINUING CONFLICT

The challenges of Luther's criticism and especially his alternative approach to the teaching and practice of the faith demanded response. The Roman Catholic hierarchy, often uncertain how to proceed, leery of too public a debate, did not give steady support to Luther's public critics. Nonetheless, several tried to rebut his stance. King Henry VIII of England entered the lists against him, with a ghost-written response to the *Babylonian Captivity*, to which Luther also responded. German theologians, including Heronymus Emser, Johann Cochlaeus, and Thomas Murner, also continued their counter-arguments in print, defending papal authority, the necessity of teaching some measure of the freedom of the human will in relating to God, and the ritualistic approach to God through sacraments, ceremonies, and pious practices.[70] Their tracts reduced the scholastic disputation to print. Their pointed barbs, untamed by confrontation in person in university exercises, turned to ever sharper rancor and recrimination.

Some critics made a special point of accusing Luther of neglecting or even forbidding good works.[71] In view of his repeated reaffirmation of the natural flow of good works from faith, it is easy to suspect them simply of bad faith in making this charge. As probable as that may be, it must also be remembered that they remained impervious to his argument simply because they did not grasp Luther's new paradigm, which centered the definition of humanity in God's unconditional creation of human beings, his gift of life that makes living according to his design possible. The deep concern of their age for public order, their intense fears of revolt and anarchy, deafened them to his new way of reading Scripture. What

[68] C. Christensen, *Art and the Reformation in Germany*, Athens, Ohio, and Detroit, Ohio and Wayne State University Presses, 1979, 110–63.

[69] M. Jenny, *Luthers geistliche Lieder und Kirchengesänge*, Cologne, Böhlau, 1985; M. Haemig, 'Elizabeth Cruciger (1500?–1535): The Case of the Disappearing Hymn Writer', *SCJ* 22 (2001), 21–44.

[70] Bagchi, *Earliest Opponents*, 93–180. [71] Ibid., 168–73.

Luther had actually written seemed less important than possible misinterpretations among the populace. His foes' disputation style legitimated their destruction of a falsely attributed position. In addition, they sensed how serious his attack on the institutions of the church, particularly on the monastic way of life, was for their entire concept of piety.

Most important for these defenders of the old faith was the issue of authority. Luther's challenge to the authority of popes and councils, implicit in his critique of indulgences, explicit at the Leipzig Debate, unsettled a fundamental principle in his adversaries' perception of God's order and structure for church and world. Their objections to his stance caused him to think more deeply about issues of authority. He picked up on medieval protests against the papacy that had labeled individual popes 'the Antichrist'. Scott Hendrix traces six stages in his rapidly developing conviction that the institution of the papacy itself was 'Antichrist'.[72] Evidence points to his serving the church initially as an obedient monk, not openly dissatisfied with papal lordship, although he wrote of doubts elicited by his reading criticisms of the Roman system by Pierre d'Ailly and Jean Gerson. His maturing view of how God works through his Word in the church loosened the papacy's hold on his conception of ecclesiastical authority. This 'ambivalence' turned to 'protest', Hendrix argues, by October 1517. His objection to papal abuse of indulgences and papal exploitation of the people the pope was called to shepherd became sharper in the debate that followed publication of the Ninety-five Theses. Though he couched this as an appeal to the pope to reform, German and Italian critics saw it as an undermining of papal authority. Their attacks produced more acute honing of Luther's assessment of the papacy, which turned to outright 'resistance' by mid-1518. Responding to Eck's criticism, Luther argued that the assertion of papal supremacy in the church's governance had arisen in the last four hundred years, against historical precedent, Scripture, and the council of Nicea.[73] He denied not the papal rule of the church but only its origin by divine right. He blamed the papacy for widespread abuses in pastoral care and oversight.

He carried this view into the Leipzig Debate with Eck, but it turned to even harsher 'opposition' by early 1520. His reading of the critiques of the papacy by John Hus and Lorenzo Valla fed his growing conviction that a dreadful papal tyranny was depriving God's people of good pastoral care. In *Open Letter to the German Nobility* and *The Papacy at Rome* he challenged the divine establishment of the institution. He rejected papal formulation of

[72] S. Hendrix, *Luther and the Papacy, Stages in a Reformation Conflict*, Philadelphia, Fortress, 1981, 1–143.
[73] WA 2: 161.35–8.

new articles of faith and papal condemnation of good Christians as heretics; he subjected the papacy to Scripture. Popes are called to weep and pray for his people as vicar of the crucified, not the glorified, Christ.[74] By December, when Luther received the papal bull excommunicating him, he had decided that the papacy embodied the Antichrist. This stage of solidifying this 'conviction' regarding the papacy lasted some two years.[75] 'Persistence' in this view marked Luther's ecclesiology the rest of his career.[76]

Johann Eck's publications helped crystallize Luther's views between 1518 and 1522. The Ingolstadt professor not only wrote against Luther; he actively campaigned on the political front against him, with a strategy dedicated to excommunicating and outlawing his foe in Wittenberg. His efforts resulted in moves toward excommunication in Rome by January 1520, with stepped-up pressure on Frederick the Wise to yield and surrender his recalcitrant Augustinian professor. In May Eck returned to Rome to sharpen the case against Luther; by September he had returned to Germany to circulate the bull giving Luther a final warning to submit to the church. He responded first with his *Freedom of a Christian* and then with his *Basis and Reason for all the Articles Wrongly Condemned by the Roman Bull*, issued in January (Latin) and March (German) 1521. Its explanation of forty-one theses condemned in the bull provides an apt, often extensive, summary of this thought at the time.[77]

Throughout 1520 diplomatic pressure mounted on Elector Frederick. He resisted; Luther remained defiant, burning the papal bull warning of excommunication with enthusiastic students around him in Wittenberg in December. These events took place with a new emperor on the German imperial throne. Maximilian I had died in January 1519. After considerable political maneuvering his deceased son's son, Charles, whose grandparents had included not only Maximilian of Austria but also Mary of Burgundy and Ferdinand of Aragon and Isabella of Castile, won election as emperor. Charles's upbringing made him a pious young man, dedicated to reforming church and society, but also pledged by oath of office to maintain tradition and order in church and empire. He decided to summon Luther to his first imperial diet in Worms, reversed the decision, then granted him immunity to plead his case before the assembled princes of church and state, nobles, and municipal representatives. His appearance at the diet on 17–18 April 1521 climaxed another cycle of intense negotiation between the Saxon government and Roman Catholic authorities. Hailed before the diet, Luther was asked simply to recant his many publications. He explained he could not, for they treated different subjects in differing ways. His conclusion,

[74] Hendrix, *Papacy*, 103–7.   [75] Ibid., 117–43.   [76] Ibid., 144–59.

[77] Brecht, *Luther*, 1: 389–415. *WA* 7: 94–151, 308–456, *LW* 32: 7–99.

Unless I am convinced by the testimony of the Scriptures or by clear rational argument (for I do not trust either in the pope or in councils alone, since it is well known that they have often erred and contradicted themselves), I am bound by the Scriptures I have quoted, and my conscience is captive to the Word of God. I cannot and will not retract anything since it is neither safe nor right to go against conscience. May God help me. Amen.[78]

Reports of the words 'here I stand' are disputed, but his supporters recognized his stand, hesitant in delivery, bold in intention, as a dramatic confession of faith.[79] It enhanced his status as God's special emissary and national hero. After formal adjournment of the diet, Charles gathered a rump session of his supporters to declare Luther an outlaw.

On his homeward way Luther was waylaid by agents of Elector Frederick and whisked away to protective custody at Wartburg Castle above Eisenach. From May 1521 to February 1522 he occupied himself with writing, completing his translation of the New Testament and the first edition of his German postil as well as other treatises, including rejoinders to Jacob Latomus at Louvain and Hieronymus Emser and a censure of Archbishop Albrecht of Mainz. A new examination of confession and absolution as well as his *Judgment on Monastic Vows* also flowed from his pen at the Wartburg.

In response to popular unrest pushing more rapid reforms in Wittenberg, fostered by his colleague Andreas Bodenstein von Karlstadt and his Augustinian brother Gabriel Zwilling, Luther composed *A Sincere Admonition to All Christians to Guard against Insurrection and Rebellion* and returned briefly to Wittenberg in December. In Invocavit week (March) 1522 he returned again, publicly calling from the pulpit for pastoral concern for the weak and doubting, that is, a dampening of the pace of reform.[80]

Eleven months later he resumed informal lectures, on Deuteronomy; in 1524 he resumed his formal university instruction, treating Hosea, then the rest of the minor prophets, into 1526.[81] Meanwhile, a number of activities filled his days. He worked further on his translation of Scripture, composed treatises on a number of topics relating to the encouragement of reform or the errors of his foes, and consulted personally or by letter with reformers across Germany and beyond as well as with Bohemian Hussite leaders. His revisions of liturgical services and his hymn-writing in this period opened a

[78] *WA* 7: 876.4–877.6, *LW* 32: 112–13.   [79] Brecht, *Luther*, 1: 415–70.

[80] Brecht, *Luther*, 2: 1–104.

[81] Hosea, *WA* 13: 2–66, *LW* 18: 3–76; Joel, *WA* 13: 68–122, *LW* 18: 79–123; Amos, *WA* 13: 124–206, *LW* 18: 127–90; Obadiah, *WA* 13: 208–23, *LW* 18: 193–204; Jonah, *WA* 13: 225–58, 19: 185–251, *LW* 19: 3–104; Micah, *WA* 13: 260–333, *LW* 18: 207–77; Nahum, *WA* 13: 345–94, *LW* 18: 281–315; Habakkuk, *WA* 13: 396–448, 19: 345–435, *LW* 19: 107–237; Zephaniah, *WA* 13: 450–509, *LW* 18: 319–64; Haggai, *WA* 13: 511–44, *LW* 18: 367–87; Zechariah, *WA* 13: 546–672, 23: 485–664, *LW* 20: 3–347; Malachi, *WA* 13: 676–703, *LW* 18: 391–419.

new avenue for bringing congregational life into line with his teaching. He sent notes of Melanchthon's lectures on Romans and 1 and 2 Corinthians to a printer, initiating what might be called 'the Wittenberg commentary', a series of biblical expositions written by several of his colleagues and himself to bring pastors a Wittenberg interpretation of the New Testament.[82]

These activities continued in varying forms for the rest of his career, but in 1525–8 five events served to demarcate a certain maturing of his thought. The attack on his views of the freedom of the will by the prince of the humanists, Desiderius Erasmus, elicited his continuing experimentation with his doctrines of God, the human creature, and the justification of sinners. Challenges to his understanding of the Lord's Supper by his colleague Karlstadt, the Zurich reformer Ulrich Zwingli, and the Basel reformer Johannes Oecolampadius and to his teaching on baptism by Anabaptists helped crystallize his view of how God's Word functions. The visitation of Saxon parishes that began in 1527 focused attention on his doctrine of the church and its practical implementation. His marriage and his writings on the Peasants Revolts of 1524–6 epitomized and concretized his understanding of God's structure of the world and how life proceeds in the earthly realm. Within this framework we proceed to survey the reformer's ever maturing theology over the final two decades of his life.

Those two decades often suffer benign neglect by biographers although they marked the time when Luther reflected on his earlier insights, developing and applying them to congregations and lives with some experience with his proclamation. His formulation of his teaching in his catechisms in 1529 introduced the classic definition of his reform for lay people over five centuries.[83] The Wittenberg team functioned as public teachers of the church not only through publications, however. Melanchthon's formulation of Wittenberg teaching for an ecumenical and a political audience at Augsburg in 1530, in the *Augsburg Confession*, and his *Apology* of that document in 1531, which he revised at Luther's behest,[84] won Luther's highest praise and support.[85] In 1537 Luther offered theological guidance to his followers in his own *Smalcald Articles*,[86] prepared as an agenda for the Evangelical estates to take to the papally called council but rejected as such by the princes of the Smalcald League. (They preferred using the

[82] Brecht, *Luther*, 2: 104–46; on the Wittenberg commentary: T. Wengert, *Philip Melanchthon's* Annotationes in Johannem *in Relation to its Predecessors and Contemporaries*, Geneva, Droz, 1987, 31–42.

[83] C. Arand, *That I May Be His Own: An Overview of Luther's Catechisms*, Saint Louis, Concordia, 2000; A. Peters, *Kommentar zu Luthers Katechismen*, 5 vols., ed. G. Seebaß, Göttingen, Vandenhoeck & Ruprecht, 1991.

[84] C. Peters, *Apologia Confessionis Augustanae*, Stuttgart, Calwer, 1997, 390–497.

[85] WA 30.3: 389.   [86] BSLK, 407–68; BC, 297–328.

Augsburg Confession for that purpose.) The document served, alongside his *Confession concerning the Lord's Supper* (1528), as his doctrinal last will and testament.

Conflict and illness marked these two decades for Luther. The threat of military force against his movement, in fact realized only after his death in the Smalcald War (1546–7), hung over his head from 1531 in renewed intensity. As his Reformation advanced in the late 1530s, attracting more rulers and municipal councils who followed large numbers of their subjects or citizens in embracing Wittenberg reform, hopes rose in Wittenberg, but the collapse of the first Regensburg Colloquy in 1541 deepened Emperor Charles's obvious intentions to suppress the Lutheran church by force of arms (as he demonstrated at the second Regensburg Colloquy in 1546[87]) and intensified Wittenberg efforts to defend the Reformation.

The last twenty years of Luther's life witnessed the natural unfolding of his thought as it developed and adapted to new challenges, changing situations, and the maturing beliefs of German parishioners. Institutionalization demanded specific applications of his insights to ever-changing concrete circumstances. Luther continued experiments in expressing his message, which can be assessed in five topics—what it means to be human, God's salvation of sinners, God's Word in practice, church and the end of time, and the Christian life—through the focal point of critical events in the years 1524–8. The following chapters give an overview of these developments.

---

[87] I. Dingel, 'Die Rolle Georg Majors auf dem Regensburger Religionsgespräch von 1546', in *idem* and G. Wartenberg (eds.), *Georg Major (1502–1574), Ein Theologe der Wittenberg Reformation*, Leipzig, Evangelische Verlagsanstalt, 2005, 189–206.

6

Fast Bound in Satan's Chains I Lay:
Luther's View of the Fallen Human Creature

Heiko Oberman viewed Luther's 'falling-out' with Erasmus as *the* internal crisis of the Reformation because it bitterly divided the Evangelical camp.[1] This seems an exaggeration in view of Martin Brecht's accurate observation that Luther's repudiation of Erasmus's attack on his anthropology did not alienate most younger humanists. Instead, it 'drew the spirits all the more vigorously in his path', yet with little impact on the populace and little mention in Luther's subsequent correspondence and treatises. It was indeed 'only a circumscribed episode for Luther'.[2] It was little different for Erasmus. He sought an easy way to make clear his break with Luther and appease Roman Catholic critics. He found it in the issue of the freedom of the human will, a topic he had largely ignored in his own writings.[3] Although he entitled his work a *diatribe*, a Greek term which humanist scholars used to denote an amiable exchange among scholars,[4] Erasmus chose the form of the scholastic disputation, at which he was unpracticed and somewhat inept.[5]

Initially, both these scholars had recognized their common concerns for reforming the church, but both quickly also perceived the significant breach between Erasmus's call for moral and institutional change and Luther's for a transformation of public teaching.[6] The two also defined central theological terms, including the human will, quite differently. Erasmus defined the will as a neutral ability to decide, which stands between the

---

[1] H. Oberman, *Luther: Man between God and the Devil*, trans. E. Waliser-Schwarzbart, New Haven and London, Yale University Press, 1989, 218.

[2] M. Brecht, *Martin Luther, 3 vols.*, tr. J. L. Schaaf, Philadelphia, Fortress, 1985–93, 2: 213; cf. R. Kolb, *Bound Choice, Election, and Wittenberg Theological Method From Martin Luther to the Formula of Concord*, Grand Rapids, Eerdmans, 2005, 11–15; B. Lohse, *Martin Luther's Theology*, tr. R. Harrisville, Minneapolis, Fortress, 1999, 160–8.

[3] Cf. E. Kohls, *Die Theologie des Erasmus*, 2 vols., Basel, Reinhardt, 1966.

[4] *De libero arbitrio ΔΙΑΤΡΙΒΗ; siue Collectae . . .*, Augsburg, Ruff/Grimm, 1524.

[5] J. Tracy, 'Two Erasmuses, Two Luthers: Erasmus' Strategy in Defense of *De libero arbitrio*', *ARG* 78 (1987), 37–60. Cf. K. Schwarzwäller, *Theologia crucis, Luthers Lehre von Prädestination nach De servo arbitrio*, 1525, Munich, Kaiser, 1970, 86–7, 108–10.

[6] Kolb, *Bound Choice*, 12–15.

judgment of reason and the actual decision. Luther understood it to be the inner orientation of human creatures which determines the entire direction of their lives and expresses—in the actions it causes—their very identity.[7] Thus, their exchange in the wake of the appearance of the *Diatribe* and Luther's belated reply in *Bound Choice* was limited to Erasmus's *Protector of the Diatribe* [*Hyperaspistes diatribae*][8] and Luther Ecclesiastes lectures (1526, published 1532).[9]

Scholars have debated the 'real' topic of Luther's *Bound Choice*. Erasmus chose to discuss 'freedom of the will', essentially an anthropological topic; Luther responded by analyzing 'bound choice', also anthropological but with primary focus on God's lordship over human life. Pastoral concerns moved both the prince of humanists and the German prophet; concern for public moral behavior and order drove Erasmus, concern for tender consciences unsure of their own salvation drove Luther. Therefore, some insist that *Bound Choice* is about the boundness of human choice in loving God;[10] others see it embracing a much broader spectrum of topics in Luther's body of doctrine. Given the very nature of his theology, with its interrelated elements, it is also true that it treats 'the majesty of God'[11] or the entire relationship between God and human creatures, in which each is integral to the definition of the other.[12]

LUTHER'S DOCTRINE OF THE HUMAN CREATURE AND ITS ANCHOR IN HIS DOCTRINE OF GOD

Luther employed several vantage points for viewing the relationship of God and humans, including the topics of the divine and the human wills, trust in the Creator as the core of humanity, and the two kinds of human righteousness. Luther's definition of God set aside consideration of the Hidden God and understood God as the Creator and continuing lord of human life; likewise, the human creature is above all created to fear, love, and trust

[7] B. Hägglund, 'Die Frage der Willensfreiheit in der Auseinandersetzung zwischen Erasmus und Luther', in August Buck (ed.), *Renaissance—Reformation. Gegensätze und Gemeinsamkeiten*, Wiesbaden, Harassowitz, 1984, 188–9, 193–4.

[8] *Hyperaspistes Diatribae Aduersus Seruum Arbitrium Martini Lutheri* . . . , Cologne, Quentel, 1526; *Hyperaspistae liber secundus* . . . , Nuremberg, Petreius, 1527.

[9] *Annotationes in Ecclesiasten*, WA 20: 7–203. See R. Rosin, *Reformers, the Preacher, and Skepticism: Luther, Brenz, Melanchthon, and Ecclesiastes*, Mainz, Zabern, 1997, 89–150.

[10] M. Doerne, 'Gottes Ehre am gebundenen Willen. Evangelische Grundlagen und theologische Spitzensätze in *De servo arbitrio*', *LuJ* 20 (1938), 46.

[11] Oberman, *Luther*, 212; cf. G. Krodel, 'Erasmus—Luther: One Theology, One Method, Two Results', *Concordia Theological Monthly* 41 (1970), 664.

[12] Hägglund, 'Willensfreiheit', 190, 193; cf. G. Forde, *The Captivation of the Will*, Grand Rapids, Eerdmans, 2005, esp. 31–45, 61–76; Schwarzwäller, *Theologia Crucis*, 45–63.

God above all his other creatures. Luther could treat the characteristics of humans within the context of Aristotelian psychology,[13] but his central definition centered on the human creature as 'creature of God, consisting of body and a living soul, made in the beginning according to God's image' and now freed for human living again by Jesus Christ.[14] *Bound Choice* focused on God's majesty and sovereignty, not as a figure indifferent to his human creatures but as the loving Creator who chose to make them in his own image, as his people, who can have absolute confidence in his love for them. Indeed, God's disappointment at their revolt against him evoked his wrath. Nonetheless, his love countered human sinfulness through his own incarnation, so that, as the thoroughly human Jesus Christ, the second person of the Godhead might restore their humanity through his death and resurrection. Therefore, despite the fact that this treatise omits discussion of Christ's saving work, Schwarzwäller correctly notes that it presumes, affirms, and implicitly centers on God's saving action in Christ alone.[15]

Nonetheless, *Bound Choice* comes as close as Luther came to speaking of God abstractly. That is because it was couched in the form of an academic disputation, a genre quite different from sermons or devotional pieces aimed for absorption in the very concrete world of everyday problems. Yet even here the Almighty Creator was no abstract concept but a concrete person, acting in relationship to his creatures even if his mode of operation remained mysterious and confusing at critical points in life. Human creatures are to 'let God be God', he asserted in his *Disputation on Scholastic Theology* (1517).[16] For Luther that meant to acknowledge fully that God cannot be subjected to any human judgment or measurement.[17] As his Ockhamist instructors had taught him, Luther asserted God's complete freedom and complete control of his creation, his total responsibility for all that happens within it. God has predestined and provides for all his creatures according to his decisions, conditioned by nothing else.[18] Nothing impedes or impairs the power of his will to make happen what he has decided.[19]

---

[13] e.g., in his 'Disputation on Man', 1536, WA 39.1: 175.1–176.4, LW 34: 137–8. G. Ebeling, *Lutherstudien*, vol. 2: Disputatio de Homine, 2: 1–469; P. Althaus, *The Theology of Martin Luther*, tr. R. Schultz, Philadelphia, Fortress, 1966, 9–11.

[14] WA 39.1: 176.5–177.14, LW 34: 138–40. O. Bayer, *Luther's Theology: A Contemporary Interpretation*, tr. T. Trapp, Grand Rapids, Eerdmanns, 2008, 150–72; Ebeling, *Lutherstudien*, 2.3: 1–622.

[15] Schwarzwäller, *Theologia crucis*, 199–200.

[16] WA 1: 225.1–2, LW 31: 10; his church postil (1527), WA 10.1.1: 24.4–11; cf. P. Watson, *Let God be God! An Interpretation of the Theology of Martin Luther*, Philadelphia, Muhlenberg, 1947.

[17] WA 18: 712.32–8, LW 33: 181.

[18] WA 18: 636.27–30, LW 33: 68; WA 18: 662.7–26, LW 33: 103; WA 18: 718.28–31, LW 33: 189. Cf. Hägglund, 'Willensfreiheit', 184, 191; Lohse, *Theology*, 165–6, 214–15, 242; Althaus, *Theology*, 274–86.

[19] WA 18: 615.33–616.6, LW 33: 38.

Preparing to treat human creatures as totally responsible within the sphere God gives them, Luther did not flinch before the logical necessity of the Almighty Creator's being totally responsible for all things. Luther was determined to hold these two total responsibilities in tension and not harmonize or homogenize them, as had his teachers. Therefore, he rejected their finely honed logical distinctions framing God's almighty power with the maneuvering room of contingency, which permitted human freedom. God's 'immutable, eternal, and infallible will' foresees, plans, and enacts all things that ensue in the course of creation. His foreknowledge is creative and determinative, not passively observing human actions and decisions but governing and affecting their thoughts and actions.[20]

God designed human creatures to be his creatures and do his will. Luther believed that part of the wonder of humanity involves the exercise of a good deal of freedom in the horizontal sphere of life. He did not believe they were free to do anything they pleased but rather anything that pleases God. In contrast to the sinful image into which Adam fell, the God-pleasing image of humanity that Christ presents reveals Adam's original image. To this image Christ restores God's people, an image of 'love, mercy, and grace, humility, patience, wisdom, light, and everything good, directing his entire person to serving others and harming no one'. To this image his death and resurrection returns his people when they are clothed in him, Luther told the Wittenberg congregation in preaching on Genesis in 1523.[21] 'It is absolutely certain that Adam was created upright and righteous, as is said, "Everything was good, pleasing to God, without any deficiencies." '[22] In these sermons there is no indication that Luther believed that human creatures were created to be improved or completed through subsequent development. Indeed, they were created for the development of certain characteristics and abilities. But they were totally God-pleasing as they lived out their lives in perfect harmony with him. In 1535 Luther told his students that even apart from sin Adam would have eventually left earthly living behind. Nonetheless, their spiritual life in Eden was the same relationship of total trust in God to which Christ restores believers in this life and transforms to full perfection in the eschaton.[23]

In his 1535 lectures on Genesis Luther warned against the patristic and scholastic definition of the image of God as mind, memory, will, and the like when the fathers contended that these remained unimpaired after the fall. At best, they have become 'utterly leprous and unclean'. 'The image of God is something far different, a unique work of God.' It meant that Adam

---

[20] *WA* 18: 615.11–14, *LW* 33: 37; *WA* 716.11–15, *LW* 33: 186.
[21] *WA* 24: 50.5–15, 21–33.   [22] *WA* 24: 74.15–20.
[23] *WA* 42: 42.21–43.11, *LW* 1: 56–7.

'not only knew God and believed that he was good but also lived a life that was completely godly, without the fear of death or any other danger; he was content with God's favor'. Faith restores the image of God and confirms believers in the certain hope of eternal life, at one with God (John 17: 21).[24] Luther later commented, 'original righteousness means that human creatures were righteous, truthful, and upright not only in body but especially in soul; [Adam] knew God, obeyed him with purest delight, and understood his works without prompting. . . . Adam loved God and his works with devoted and absolutely pure devotion;' he lived without fear of death and illness, without evil lusts.[25] Luther criticized the scholastic view that this 'original righteousness' was a gift added to fundamental human-ity: instead, it was integral to human nature to love, trust, and know God.[26]

NECESSITY, EVIL, AND THE FAITHFULNESS OF GOD

In *Bound Choice*, but never again thereafter, Luther developed a concept of the absolute necessity of all things happening according to God's will as an affirmation of God's total control and responsibility as Creator. His Ock-hamist instructors had acknowledged that Almighty God controls every-thing and that therefore some things take place according to a necessity of that which must result (*necessitas consequentis*) because God makes it so, and a necessity of consequence (*necessitas consequentiae*) that unfolds on the basis of the contingencies involved in human decision-making. Luther viewed this distinction as Ockhamism's gateway to placing the burden and responsibility for life on human beings, who must do their best to attain God's favor. He repeated his earlier rejection of this distinction[27] and affirmed his concept of absolute necessity.[28] That had aroused Erasmus's ire; he found it destructive of moral accountability. Luther believed it a necessary assurance that salvation depends on God alone. Only in this fashion could honest sinners be spared the agonizing doubts imposed by their own imperfect life.

Bound Choice concedes the difficulty that this confession of the Almighty Creator causes in the face of the existence of evil. Luther insisted that God is not responsible for evil even though he is responsible for all things and evil exists within his creation. Luther steadfastly refused to try to solve the problem on either the abstract or the concrete level. He was resisting the temptation to justify God, to defend the Almighty against the inevitable

---

[24] *WA* 42: 45.40–48.25, *LW* 1: 61–4; cf. *WA* 42: 68.31–69.22, *LW* 1: 90–1.

[25] *WA* 42: 86.1–16, *LW* 1: 113.   [26] *WA* 42: 123.38–124.21, *LW* 1: 164–5.

[27] *Defense and Explanation of All Articles*, 1521, *WA* 7: 450.8–451.7.

[28] *WA* 18: 614.27–620.37, *LW* 33: 36–44.

charge that if he really is omnipotent, he must be complicit in evil. Luther's 'theology of the cross' endeavored to crucify reason's inevitable insistence on searching for an explanation that will justify God. He could indeed contend that God hardened Pharaoh's heart, eschewing rationalizations that transformed God's action as mere permission in this case. However, he also affirmed that God does not create evil in human creatures *de novo*. He reasoned that God, who is at work in and through them, as he acts throughout creation, is also 'at work when evil takes place, but he is not at fault. The defect lies in us since we are by nature evil and he is good.' God 'does evil' because he continues to use the flawed, faulty instruments of sinful humanity and remains lord in spite of their sinfulness. But he is in no way responsible for their being evil.[29] Luther was answering questions about God, not about human responsibility, at this point. 'Do not imagine God to be like an evil-minded innkeeper, full of wickedness himself, who pours or mixes poison into a vessel that is not bad but does nothing but receive what is bad.' God continues to work with sinners inclined to evil, but he uses them for his good purposes according to his wisdom, to his glory and his people's salvation.[30]

In meeting Erasmus's objections to his earlier views of the bondage of human choice in relationship to God, Luther acknowledged that the critical question of how to justify the Creator who controls his creation totally, and yet who is not responsible for evil, defies human explanation. The offense of the fact that God wants all to be saved yet has chosen only some 'brought me to the very depth and abyss of despair, so that I wished I had never been created'.[31] At that point he decided to stop trying to master this element in the mystery of God's majesty. This aspect of God's hiddenness should not distract, however, from what God's Word reveals regarding his mercy. For in choosing his own for salvation, he 'must be honored and revered as supremely merciful toward those whom he justifies and saves, supremely unworthy as they are'. Reason cannot judge the incomprehensible, unsearchable ways and judgments of God.[32] Luther never ceased warning against the intrusion of human wisdom into God's mysterious majesty.[33]

This vision of God was not, however, of an inaccessible, immutable, remote, and aloof being. Luther spoke seldom of God's 'immutability'. His dynamic equivalent for the abstract 'immutable' was the concrete 'faithful' and 'truthful' person involved with his creation. Ian Siggins regrets that

---

[29] *WA* 18: 768.23–6, *LW* 33: 264.   [30] *WA* 18: 709.28–710.8, *LW* 33: 176–7.

[31] *WA* 18: 719.9–12, *LW* 33: 190.

[32] *WA* 18: 717.25–39, *LW* 33: 188; *WA* 18: 685.14–15, *LW* 33: 139; *WA* 18: 689.18–25, *LW* 33: 145; *WA* 18: 712.31–5, *LW* 33: 181.

[33] e.g., his Genesis lectures, *WA* 43: 458.35–459.15, *LW* 5: 43–4.

Luther did not affirm dogmatically that 'what we know of God's unchange-ability is determined by what we discover of it through faith in Christ. And this God is not the almighty, incomprehensible First Cause of the schools, but a God whose mercy is from everlasting to everlasting.'[34] But Siggins's own citations reveal that outside the arena of the disputation Luther repeat-edly told his audiences that God's fatherly voice, spoken through his Son and Holy Spirit, proclaims 'nothing but goodness, sweetness, and love. For that is what it means to be God.'[35] Certainly, elements of God's being and planning could not be subjected to human inspection; the distinction of God Hidden and God Revealed governed much of his exchange with Erasmus regarding the mystery of God's choosing his own from among the mass of sinners. Luther was singularly disinterested in the kind of speculation in which he had learned to indulge at the university regarding God's nature and the problems his governance of human history poses. It was for him a contradiction in terms to think that the creature could master and manage, appraise and assess the Creator.[36] Human creatures must rely totally on God's revelation of himself, as he had come through prophets and apostles and, ultimately, in person, as Jesus Christ, bearer and conveyor of God's promise of new life.

This understanding of God as a communicating, conversation-engaging person appeared as an unelaborated presupposition early on, a key to Luther's concept of God as Creator and of the human creature as con-versation partner with the Creator. God's promise brought assurance to those who confess their sins, a decisive development in Luther's way of thinking in 1518. His mature understanding of the parallel between his creative Word in Genesis 1 and the Word that conveys forgiveness of sins in preaching and in its sacramental forms took longer to articu-late. It became his fundamental presupposition for explaining how God makes new creatures of faith out of sinners (2 Cor. 4: 6).[37] By 1535 he compared God's act of creation in Genesis 1, where he had brought heaven and earth into being out of nothing, 'solely by the Word which he utters', to the new creation in conversion to faith in Christ, 'something which is also brought about by the Word—as a new work of creation' (2 Cor. 4: 6).[38]

Following his instructors, he found God's promises sure, also in *Bound Choice*.[39] Only from a God whose promise of salvation is unchanging, who himself is personally faithful and reliable, could believers find the comfort

---

[34] I. Siggins, *Martin Luther's Doctrine of Christ*, New Haven, Yale University Press, 1970, 240.

[35] WA 33: 149.36.

[36] WA 18: 689.18–23, LW 33: 145–6; WA 18: 784.9–13, LW 33: 290.

[37] Genesis lectures, 1535, WA 42: 13.31–14.22, LW 1: 16–17.

[38] WA 42: 13.31–14.22, LW 1: 16–17.   [39] WA 18: 619.3–21, LW 33: 42–3.

of assurance of their new identity as children of God. The heart of what God has to say about himself Luther found in Jesus Christ. All that is necessary to know about God Christ discloses. Apart from his revelation there exists only Satan, divine wrath, darkness, error, lies, and death (John 1: 18; 14: 6).[40] In Christ and the promise of the gospel the true nature of the hidden God becomes clear, Luther commented fifteen years later, in an effort to prevent misinterpretation of *Bound Choice*, lest people be driven to fruitless speculation over their own salvation.[41]

PREDESTINATION AS GOD'S GRACIOUS CHOICE OF HIS OWN

God's entire plan of salvation is comprehended in Christ, and Luther early acknowledged that the plan proceeded from God's counsel planned before the world. Luther naturally fell into the extensive discussion of 'predestination' of God's people that was seething in the 1510s,[42] but by 1525 he used the term only for God's providential care of creation in general—even though many scholars have contended that *Bound Choice* teaches not only the predestination of those chosen for salvation but also of the reprobate. That is not true although some passages defending God's complete control of his creation seem to imply or even state that.[43] He largely shied away from speaking of predestination for the last quarter-century of his career and even warned against speculation regarding whether believers should count themselves among the predestined. Instead, they should turn to God's Word, where he had revealed, in his baptismal promise, in preaching and absolution, in the Lord's Supper, that this individual believer belonged to him.[44]

Indeed, Luther did not totally ignore the sure ground believers have in knowing that behind that promise of new life in Christ lies God's intention formulated before the foundations of the world. In 1531, lecturing on Galatians 1: 17, he confessed that 'even before I was born, when I could not

[40] WA 18: 778.38–779.21, LW 33: 281–2; cf. Chapter 4 above, pp. 61–2.

[41] WA 43: 459.24–32, 460.26–35, LW 5: 45–6.

[42] K. Zickendraht, *Der Streit zwischen Erasmus und Luther über die Willensfreiheit*, Leipzig, Hinrichs, 1901, 1–3; cf. Kolb, *Bound Choice*, 294 n. 4.

[43] WA 18: 686.4–10, LW 33: 140; WA 18: 689.17–690.8, LW 33: 145–6; but cf. WA 18: 719.7–8, LW 33: 190; Bayer, *Theology*, 202–9. Althaus, *Theology*, 274–5, argues this view without treating Luther's position beyond 1522. Even in the passage from the preface to Romans Althaus mentions, Luther places belief and unbelief, ridding oneself of sin or not, in God's hands but explicitly states only that this means that salvation, but not damnation, is in God's hands alone, WADB 7: 23.26–34, LW 35: 378.

[44] WA 18: 619.3–21, LW 33: 42–3.

think, wish, or do anything good but was a shapeless embryo', God had predestined him to saving faith in Christ.[45] In 1542, he cautioned students against falling into presumption and despair with false thoughts regarding predestination and reminded them that God does not change (Mal. 3: 6). Therefore, his gifts and call are irrevocable (Rom. 11: 29); this coupled God's predestination to salvation with his promise in the several forms of the Word.[46] Yet, at table, he often forewarned students against speculation regarding God's predestination that did not properly divide law and gospel, therefore either giving a license to sin to those who believed their sins could not void their predestination or driving those who believed they were not predestined to despair.[47]

Luther regarded God's unconditional choosing of his own out of the mass of sinners as an expression of his mercy, his gospel. He regarded any mention of predestination that did not function as reassurance of the inviolability and utter reliability of Christ's unconditional, unearned promise of salvation as a false, deceptive use of God's predestination. He held God's omniscience and God's nature as one who chooses in tension with an affirmation that God wants all to be saved and come to a knowledge of the truth (1 Tim. 2: 4). He wants sinners to turn to him and live rather than die (Ezek. 18: 32).[48]

Luther never returned to treating these questions at the theoretical level he did in *Bound Choice*. He never resolved the tension between holding out God's promise to everyone and insisting that those who receive it are the people God chose for himself before the foundations of the world. Writing to despairing correspondents fifteen years later, he repeated that message, directing their focus away from speculation about God's plan, to which believers have access only through the promise in God's Word, to that Word itself and to Christ, whom it conveys.[49] He urged an anonymous 'prominent' person to 'remember that God the Almighty did not create, predestine, and choose us to perish but to be saved'.[50]

To comfort such doubting, despairing believers, Luther always strove to place all responsibility for rescue from sin and condemnation upon the shoulders of God, of the crucified Christ. However, he also held human beings totally responsible for the sphere of responsibility given them by God. He strove to hold God's responsibility in tension with human responsibility to preserve the integrity of God as Creator and the integrity of the human creature as this special creation, fashioned in God's image,

[45] *WA* 40.1: 130.31–140.17, *LW* 26: 71–2.

[46] *WA* 43: 457.33–40, 458: 31–5, *LW* 5: 42–3; cf. *WA* 42: 670.26–8, *LW* 26: 71–2.

[47] See *WATR* 5: 293–6, #5658a, and other passages; see Kolb, *Bound Choice*, 38–43.

[48] *WA* 18: 686.1–13, *LW* 33: 140; *WA* 18: 683.11–13, *LW* 33: 136.

[49] *WABr* 10: 492–4, #3956; 11: 165–6, #4144.   [50] *WABr* 10: 492.128–39.

who reflects something of God in the exercise of love and care for other creatures (Gen. 1: 26–30).

Luther never referred to humanity as such as a mystery, but his treatment of what it means to be human displayed ragged edges. He reflected his experience that neither the biblical description of human life in sin nor daily life itself can be fit together into a rationally satisfying system to answer all questions. As creatures, already before the advent of the mystery of sin in their lives, human beings are totally dependent on their Creator. Adam and Eve did not bestow identity upon themselves; they did not shape what being human is. They did not earn righteousness in God's sight with their performance of his will. Instead, they received their humanity as a free gift of the Creator, and, after the fall, as a free gift of his re-creating activity.[51] All human righteousness before God, not just righteousness restored after the fall into sin, is passive, God's gift. For 'before human creatures are created and become human, they do nothing, nor do they attempt to do anything toward becoming creatures. After they are created, they neither do nor try to do anything toward remaining creatures. These both are accomplished by the will of the omnipotent power and goodness of God alone, who creates and preserves apart from our assistance.'[52] God is the totally responsible Creator. These words precede directly, however, an affirmation of human responsibility. 'He does not work in us apart from us because this is why he has created and preserved us, that he might work in us and we might cooperate with him, whether outside his own realm in his general omnipotence or inside his own realm by the special power of this Spirit.'[53] God exercises his own responsibility in part through the exercise of human responsibility when his providence or the Holy Spirit move his creatures to serve his purposes.

HUMAN CREATURES BETWEEN GOD AND SATAN

Luther used metaphors to express human dependence on God. The picture of God's or Satan's riding and reining the human creature illustrated the subjection of the human will to either the Creator or the Deceiver.[54] The metaphors of potter and clay and of new birth in the Holy Spirit underscored God's giving of life, righteousness, and identity to human beings.[55] Erasmus had countered by depicting human beings as those on whom God had placed responsibility for all they do through the power of their

---

[51] Genesis lectures, 1535, *WA* 42: 13.31–14.22, *LW* 1: 16–17; Althaus, *Theology*, 119–29.
[52] *WA* 18: 754.1–4, *LW* 33: 242–3.   [53] *WA* 18: 754.4–12, *LW* 33: 243.
[54] *WA* 18: 635.7–22, *LW* 33: 6–66.
[55] *WA* 18: 727.3–729.19, *LW* 33: 203–6; *WA* 18: 740.19–749.19, *LW* 33: 222–9.

own free choice, according to Sirach 15: 14–17. Luther rejected interpreting God's demand for human performance as a condition for establishing the relationship that he has placed at the core of being human. He recalled his distinction of two kinds of righteousness, expressed in the language of 'realms'. Sirach referred to the realm 'beneath' human beings, in which God has granted them free use of and lordship over things, so that they may make choices of how to perform, as they cooperate with him. But in relationship to God they are bound. Their creatureliness binds them to their Creator; their rebellion against him has bound them to serve false gods until he rescues them from sin's and Satan's domination.[56] Free choice therefore cannot describe a human potential for establishing one's own identity in God's sight. Righteousness in that relationship depends totally on the action of the Creator, who re-creates sinners on the basis of Christ's death and resurrection apart from all human contribution or performance.[57] God knew that once alienated from him, human beings could not restore themselves to trusting and loving him, so he undertook a plan for forgiveness and life by sending Christ to draw them back to himself. God alone gives sinners the power to become his children (John 1: 12); he gives them the gift of trusting him again.[58]

Four years after writing *Bound Choice*, Luther expressed human dependence on the Creator in his *Small Catechism*'s explanation of the first article of the Creed. As Creator, God has 'made me and all creatures', given human creatures every blessing, and he did so 'purely out of fatherly, divine goodness and mercy, without any merit or worthiness in me'. Not only as sinner but as creature human beings bring nothing to God. They receive their identity, their continued existence, their righteousness from him, Almighty, Father, Creator.[59]

Yet, in the mystery of this humanity, God gave them their identity of righteousness in order that they might live out that identity in the performance of good works of love. These works serve as his instruments for sustaining his creation. This tension between human responsibility to perform and God's being in charge of that performance remained throughout Luther's preaching and teaching, sometimes with emphasis on God's responsibility, sometimes on human accountability for carrying out his commands. Human creatures are obliged to exercise responsibility. They do so with the will as a constituent part of their humanity. The will

---

[56] Erasmus, *Opera omnia*, Louvain, 1703–6, 9: 1220–1; *Collected Works*, Toronto, University of Toronto Press, 1974–, 76: 21–3; WA 18: 672.7–19, LW 33: 118–19.

[57] WA 18: 697.29–30, LW 33: 157.

[58] WA 18: 697.31–698.24, LW 33: 157–8; WA 18: 739.1–22, LW 33: 218; WA 18: 768.5–18, LW 33: 264.

[59] BSLK, 511; BC, 354–5.

(*voluntas*) itself is active even if, in regard to God, its ability to choose (*arbitrium*) is bound. 'Eating, drinking, begetting, ruling' lie within the creature's own responsibility or freedom of choice; properly done, they express righteousness among the neighbors without any thought to winning God's favor through them. Receiving that favor and loving the neighbor belong to different 'realms'.[60] Even though Almighty God controlled Judas's betrayal of Jesus, Judas's will acted to decide to betray his master; that is the mystery of humanity as creature of the omnipotent Creator.[61] Therefore, God's law, as the expression of his expectations for human performance once he had given human creatures their righteousness or identity in his sight, was not designed to teach sinners how to please God. It functions to reveal their inability to live the life he designed them to live and return them to dependence on him. God kills sinners in order to make them alive; he convicts of guilt to restore righteousness; he brings sinners to hell to exalt them to heaven. Therefore, Luther contended, the law, originally intended only to evaluate and teach human performance, functions to prepare people for the promise of new life in Christ, as fathers demonstrate their children's helplessness and dependence on them, as physicians diagnose what is wrong to heal, as victors show their foes' foolishness in resisting them by trampling on them. In this way the law reveals the wonders of God's mercy.[62]

CREATURES AS SINNERS

Alongside their creaturely dependence on their Creator, human beings since the fall have inherited a disposition of rebellion against God, denial of his Lordship, that springs from their doubt of his promise to be their God. Luther's Genesis lectures described fallen creatures 'ignorant of God, despising God, turned aside from him', practicing 'cruelty and lack of mercy toward our neighbor', 'love of self in all matters in relation both to God and human creatures'.[63] Without excusing sinners one whit for their sin, Luther did emphasize that the bound will is bound to false gods not only by human choice but also by Satan's captivity.[64] In lecturing on Genesis he depicted for his students how Satan had played with Adam

---

[60] *WA* 18: 752.7–8, *LW* 33: 240; *WA* 18: 771.38–49, *LW* 33: 270; *WA* 18: 694.17–20, *LW* 33: 153.

[61] *WA* 18: 715.20, *LW* 33: 185.

[62] *WA* 18: 733.9–12, *LW* 33: 62; *WA* 18: 673.34–8, *LW* 33: 121; *WA* 18: 684.26–32, *LW* 33: 138.

[63] *WA* 18: 762.30–763.4, *LW* 33: 255–6.

[64] *WA* 18: 635.7–22, *LW* 33: 65–6; Althaus, *Theology*, 161–8.

and Eve, closing their eyes to God and then opening them to their own disobedience in order to lead them to despair.[65]

Luther's entire discourse on justification arose out of his presuppositions regarding sin. His understanding of sin rested upon his belief that the relationship of trust with the true God stands at the heart of God's creation of humanity. Complete trust in God leads inevitably to obedience to his plan for human life; the failure to perform godly acts reveals the deeper sin beneath sinful actions. Breaking that trust and doubting God and his Word constituted for Luther the original sin (Gen. 3: 1–6).

Luther assumed the Augustinian concept 'original sin' from his instructors but deepened its meaning to a fundamental conception of human life in sin as the brokenness of the relationship with God that stands at the heart of humanity. In the *Smalcald Articles* he described this doubt as 'a deep, evil corruption of nature that reason does not comprehend; rather it must be believed on the basis of the revelation in Scripture'. Its permeating power remains after baptism—an unexplainable mystery. Those who do not recognize God as God cannot fathom how the absence of trust in him can be so determinative of human living; only believers can recognize it.[66] In Aristotelian terms it is 'a kind of continuous motion or entelechy, producing its own effects. It is not a quiescent quality but a restless evil which labors day and night.... It is a restless animal, a beast which cannot stand still... It moves human beings to avarice, disobedience, and other vices... It always tries to move us away from God.'[67] Luther adopted the medieval term 'original sin', in German most often 'inherited sin', and also 'root sin', to describe that permeating doubt and denial of God. As root and source of all acts of sinfulness, this original, foundational attitude toward God could also be called 'nature-sin' or 'person-sin'.[68]

The original sin in Genesis 3, he pointed out to the Wittenberg congregation in 1523 and to students in 1535, lay in rejecting God's Word and ceasing to trust him.[69] 'The intellect has become darkened, so that we do not trust God's mercy nor fear him, but confidently disregard his Word and will, following the desires and impulses of the flesh. Our conscience is no longer peaceful, but, thinking of God's judgment, despairs and seeks its own defenses and remedies.'[70] This sin transforms human beings from

---

[65] *WA* 42: 123.19–34, *LW* 1: 164.

[66] *Smalcald Articles* III.i.3; *BSLK*, 434; *BC*, 311; 'Disputation concerning Justification', 1536; *WA* 39.1: 82.12–30, *LW* 34: 154.

[67] *WA* 39.1: 112.15–113.9, *LW* 34: 182.

[68] Cf. *WA* 51: 354.20; 46: 39–40, *LW* 24: 341–2; *WA* 10.1: 508.20, *LW* 52: 151–2.

[69] *WA* 14: 135.32–3; 24: 91.11–13, 92.8–9, 27–32, 93.28–94.20. Cf. *WA* 42: 110.5–116.29; 122.4–123.34, *LW* 1: 146–54, 162–4; Bayer, *Theology*, 173–92; Lohse, *Theology*, 248–57.

[70] *WA* 42: 86.18–30, *LW* 1: 114.

God's friends into his bitterest, most obstinate enemies.[71] They flee in fear from his presence.[72] This refusal to trust God and his Word leads to every form of self-justification and acts of disobedience against God. This way of living is really existing in death, for the absence of the creator of life spells death for human beings created to be trusting in him.[73]

How vital Luther's conception of sin was for the body of his teaching emerged clearly in his engagement with Jacob Masson (Latomus) of Louvain in 1521. Luther's claim that even the saints did not live without sin, a conviction born of personal experience and reading the lives of the biblical saints, threatened Latomus's conviction that human performance can achieve righteousness when grace and proper human efforts combine. Luther's assertion that God's law demands what is impossible for sinners to perform lay outside Latomus's theological-anthropological framework. Luther insisted that the law, weakened by the sinful disposition of the fallen human being, could not accomplish the fulfillment of the righteousness demanded by the law; Christ had to intervene (Rom. 8: 3–4). Paul's judgment that the law of Moses could not justify meant that performance of its demands could never save sinners (Acts 15: 38–9). Confronted with Jesus's dictum regarding the difficulty of the rich entering the kingdom, the disciples' query, 'who can be saved?' elicted Jesus's reply, 'with God everything is possible' (Matt. 19: 25–6).[74]

Luther and Latomus also differed on whether sin remains after baptism. Luther presumed that the mystery of the continuation of sin in the baptized could not be solved. He simply lived with the tension between his recognition that God re-creates sinners into his totally righteous children in baptism yet even Paul continued to struggle against sinfulness within himself (Rom. 7: 7–25).[75] Isaiah 64: 5–12 affirmed that 'we have all become like one unclean, and all our righteous deeds are like filthy rags'. Like pots in the hands of a potter, creatures depend totally on their Creator, and sinners continue to offend their Creator by failing to place their lives completely in his hands (Eccl. 7: 20; Rom. 7: 7–25).[76] *Against Latomus* distinguished God's grace (which makes the righteous and faithful wholly pleasing to God) from God's gifts (which increasingly provide healing from sin and corruption).[77] As Luther explained in his preface to Romans, composed about this time, 'grace actually means God's favor, or the good will which in himself he bears toward us, by which he is disposed to give us Christ

---

[71] *WA* 42: 107.25–6, *LW* 1: 143.   [72] *WA* 42: 127.9–132.6, *LW* 1: 169–76.
[73] *WA* 42: 132.7–147.41, *LW* 1: 176–98.   [74] *WA* 8: 53.11–55.38, *LW* 32: 151–6.
[75] *WA* 8: 57.2–31, *LW* 32: 157–9.
[76] *WA* 8: 59.24–63.24, *LW* 32: 162–7; *WA* 8: 73.1–74.36, *LW* 32: 180–3; *WA* 8: 99.25–126.14, *LW* 32: 217–56.
[77] *WA* 8: 107.13–36, *LW* 32: 229.

and pour into us the Holy Spirit with his gifts. . . . The gifts and the Spirit increase in us every day, but they are not yet perfect since there remain in us the evil desires and sins that war against the Spirit.'[78] When later focusing on the real struggles with sinful inclinations that God's people experience, Luther did not try to explain sin's power away, yet he posited a difference: those who live by faith contain sin's power to determine their identity and their actions through that trust in God.

Luther believed that the more sin is underestimated, the smaller the significance of God's grace.[79] Therefore, this view of sin provided the necessary framework for speaking of God's restoration of humanity to sinners.

[78] *WADB* 7: 8.10–29/9.10–8.29/9.29; *LW* 35: 369–70.
[79] *WA* 42: 107.12–13, *LW* 1: 142.

7

Christ Jesus Holds the Field Victorious: Luther's Understanding of the Person of Christ, the Atonement, and Justification

JESUS CHRIST, THE INCARNATE SON OF GOD

One sure sign that Luther intended *Bound Choice* for a specialized, academic audience, in addition to its characteristics as an argument for formal disputation, lies in the paucity of its references to Christ's person and work. Indeed, Schwarzwäller accurately observes that its goal, even if largely tacit and implicit, is to fix the reader's gaze on Christ alone just as much as in Luther's other writings.[1] He is justified in saying that because, like all Luther's writings, *Bound Choice* must be read in the context of his other works. From the Psalms lectures a decade earlier, where his Christological interpretation guided students through the entire book,[2] and almost every other treatise from his pen, 'the Lord Jesus' formed the underlying organizing axiom of his thought. 'To have Christ is to have everything. If Christ remains mine, everything remains mine.'[3] Luther's confession of his Lord Jesus followed certain basic contours throughout the rest of his life.

His understanding of Jesus as true God and true human creature followed traditional lines, early on with certain Augustinian, certain Ockhamist characteristics, some of which remained, while others shifted. For instance, traces of Neoplatonic terminology diminish while Augustine's emphasis on the centrality of Christ's incarnation and saving work and his Christological interpretation of the Psalms remain.[4] Luther's early repetition of Ockham's description of the relationship of his human and divine natures as the former's being 'supported' or 'borne' by the latter yielded to a position that regarded them as being joined together in their

[1] K. Schwarzwäller, *Theologia crucis, Luthers Lehre von Prädestination nach* De servo arbitrio, 1525, Munich, Kaiser, 1970, 199–200.

[2] *WA* 3: 58.33–59.37, *LW* 10: 71–2; *WA* 4: 12.21–15.8, *LW* 11: 164–8.

[3] *WA* 23: 207.27, *LW* 37: 103; O. Bayer, *Martin Luther's Theology: A Contemporary Interpretation*, tr. T. Trapp, Grand Rapids, Eerdmans, 2008, 79–81.

[4] M. Lienhard, *Luther: Witness to Jesus Christ, Stages and Themes of the Reformer's Christology*, tr. E. Robertson, Minneapolis, Augsburg, 1982, 20, 33–4, 43–5, 76; I. Siggins, *Martin Luther's Doctrine of Christ*, New Haven, Yale University Press, 1970, 191–243.

distinct integrity in the 'hypostatic' or 'personal' union of the one person Jesus Christ. Like all Christian theologians, Luther used the term 'person' in two quite different senses when speaking of the Trinity, with its three 'persons', Father, Son, and Holy Spirit, and of Jesus, one 'person' in which are united two 'natures', divine and human, inseparable but totally distinct.

Ockhamist focus on Christ's humanity sometimes led to such discrete treatment that the union of the one person seemed de-emphasized, a position Luther reflected in annotations on Lombard in 1509 but avoided thereafter.[5] Althaus claims that no other theologian since New Testament times 'has so deeply and powerfully expressed the meaning and significance' of Christ's divinity,[6] but he never lost his fascination with the most human aspects of the human nature that Bernard bequeathed him: Christ suckling at his mother's breast, his agony on the cross, his sympathy with human suffering.[7] Luther preferred everyday common-sense portrayals of Christ's humanity to the elaborate argument practiced by Ockhamist thinkers: 'He let himself be seen, heard, touched; he ate, drank, slept, worked, suffered, and died as any other human being.' 'He had eyes, ears, mouth, nose, chest, stomach, hands, and feet, just as you and I have. He grasped his mother's breast, and she nursed him as any other child is nursed.'[8] Yet Christ, who came to die 'for us' because of human sinfulness, differed from sinful human creatures in one regard. He did not sin. Luther distinguished sin from humanity as God's good creation.[9] Jesus assumed the gift of that good, created human nature, in order to restore sinners to their original goodness.[10]

Luther's orientation toward Ockhamist views of God as the one who determines the laws that govern the universe may stand behind his argument that the two natures share characteristics, in the specific way in which he taught the 'communication of attributes'.[11] From the early 1520s on, he used this ancient Christological formula, teaching that the two natures of Christ share their own characteristics with each other while never losing their own uniqueness in essence. His development of his own definition of the formulation took shape under the influence of his opponents in controversy over the presence of Christ's body and blood in the Lord's Supper.

---

[5] M. Lienhard, *Luther: Witness to Jesus Christ, Stages and Themes of the Reformer's Christology*, tr. E. Robertson, Minneadpolis, Augsburg, 1982, 29–32, 328–31, 336–7, 389.

[6] P. Althaus, *The Theology of Martin Luther*, tr. R. Schultz, Philadelphia, Fortress, 1966, 181, 181–98.

[7] T. Bell, *Divus Bernhardus. Bernhard von Clairvaux in Martin Luthers Schriften*, Mainz, Zabern, 1993, 265–85, 307–13.

[8] WA 33: 115.26–116.25; 46: 69.28; 10.1.1: 243.6–22, 235.18–237.3; 46: 634.31; Siggins, *Christ*, 198–200.

[9] WA 42: 46.11–17, LW 1: 62–3.

[10] WA 47: 205.27–206.35; 21: 484.5; 17.2: 434.3–14; 46: 557.9–16.

[11] Lienhard, *Witness*, 226–7.

Luther's proclamation of Christ's incarnation served as much more than a description of the mysterious uniting of the second person of the Holy Trinity with the man Jesus of Nazareth, the Messiah promised for the delivery of sinners. The 'theology of the cross' focused here on God's supreme, final revelation of himself and his disposition toward humankind. It accentuated God's way of revealing himself by hiding himself under the opposite of human expectations. Luther made extensive use particularly of John's gospel to speak of Christ as 'truly God, begotten of the Father from eternity, not made. [John] wrote his gospel in order to proclaim this article of faith.'[12] To demonstrate that Christ is truly God, Luther cited, for instance, Romans 9: 5; Titus 2: 13; John 20: 28; Colossians 2: 9; Ephesians 1: 20; Isaiah 42: 8; and Psalm 2: 8.[13] Not only Scripture's assertions of Christ's divinity revealed it, however; also his life exhibited the characteristics that belong to God alone, Luther repeated in his sermons. All this led Luther to conclude that 'Christ is the sublime Majesty, equal with God; He is creator and preserver of all things; and he is eternally begotten of God.'[14] Yet at the same time Luther found both the biblical confession concerning his person and its report on his actions to be twofold, affirming sometimes that he is the one true God, sometimes that he is completely human.[15] He often repeated the simple formulations conveyed by the tradition stemming from the Council of Chalcedon (451), which synthesized the reactions of the church to various deviations from orthodox teaching regarding Christ's person: 'two natures united in one person', 'God and human creature in one person', 'essential, natural, true, complete God and human creature in one person, undivided and inseparable',[16] or, in the words of the *Small Catechism*, 'true God, begotten of the Father before all worlds, and true human creature, born of the Virgin Mary'.[17] He could reaffirm this belief in dramatically non-traditional expressions, too: 'Mary makes broth for God,' Mary suckles God with her breasts, bathes God, rocks and carries God, and Pilate and Herod crucified and killed God, 'the infant Christ, lying in the cradle, suckled by the Virgin Mary, created heaven and earth'.[18] For, Luther explained to his hearers repeatedly, God does and suffers what Christ does and suffers. Therefore, God's body lay in Mary's womb, as the Council of

[12] Sermons on John 3, 1538, WA 47: 112.3–30.

[13] Postil, WA 10.1.1: 57.5–14; Lectures on Psalm 2, 1532, WA 40.2: 260.25–269.30; 34.2: 57.7; 10.1.2: 295.9–30; 41: 89.29–102.21; 45: 244.24–39.

[14] Siggins, *Christ*, 192–7; Lienhard, *Witness*, 158–66, 318–26, 374–6.

[15] Siggins, *Christ*, 209–10.

[16] WA 33: 79.15–81.3; 46: 568.14–25; 47: 188.25; 33: 115.4–117.10; 43: 251.21–252.3; 47: 53.13–54.8.

[17] BSLK, 511, BC, 355.

[18] *On Councils and the Church*, 1539, WA 50: 587.6–588.11; 47: 199.29–201.13, 77.23–78.6, 86.17–87.32; 46: 633.2–634.36, 634.7–26.

Ephesus (431) had affirmed.[19] So intimate was the union of the two natures, so complete their uniting, in his view.

Before 1525 Luther had become accustomed to affirming that God is truly known only through his incarnation as Jesus Christ (John 1: 18).[20] God's accommodation to human weakness in entering human existence discloses his limitless love for humankind. It defines the very nature of his Godness: mercy, self-sacrifice, compassion. Critical for Luther's expression of this embracing love from the mid-1510s was his use of the preposition 'for' or 'in behalf of'—'for you', 'for me', 'for us' (*pro te, pro vobis, pro me, pro nobis*).[21]

Luther sought to elucidate the nature of the Trinity as he taught hearers about Jesus. He did not consistently follow Augustine in simply emphasizing the unity of the persons of the Godhead but often followed 'Eastern' fathers when he proclaimed that 'the Father is the first and original person in the Godhead', that the Son takes his being from the Father.[22] (Luther, of course, did not make a geographical but only a chronological distinction among patristic authorities; for him, it was significant that Cyrill of Alexandria and Augustine came from the same era.) However, this implied no denial of the equality and unity of these two persons, and the Holy Spirit, in the Trinity.

Indeed, the relationship of Father and Son involved more than the affirmation of their unity. The person of Christ brought human and divine natures together in God's unexplainable reconciliation of sinners to himself. Luther often used Philippians 2: 5–11 to speak of Christ's taking on human form. He did not regard the incarnation itself as humiliation but rather that which enabled him to be humbled through death on the cross, to bear human sin[23] and set aside the Father's wrath as it expended itself upon Christ. When Jesus expressed his abandonment by the Father on the cross (Matt. 27: 46), he descended into hell as he bore sinners' pains of conscience in this unfathomable mystery.[24] Breaking with tradition already in his 1519 lectures on the Psalms, Luther went beyond Gerson, Tauler, and others by attributing real temptations—the terrors of hell and the spiritual struggles accompanying his bearing sin—to Jesus himself (even though he did not succumb to them).[25] This meant that Christ embraced 'the highest joy and

[19] *WA* 20: 603.2–606.36; 28: 486.20–487.33; 41: 480.19–482.31; 10.1.1: 150.18–151.6.

[20] Wartburg Postil. *WA* 10.1.1: 208.6–209.7.

[21] Siggins, *Christ*, 297; Lienhard, *Witness*, 283–6; G. Kalme, 'Words Written in "Golden Letters"—a Lutheran Reading of The Ecumenical Creeds', Ph.D. dissertation, Concordia Seminary, Saint Louis, 2005, 54–138.

[22] *WA* 10.1: 151.7–155.24, 183.13–186.8.   [23] *WA* 2: 148.14.

[24] *WA* 2: 692.10–21; 5: 601.14–25, 607.11–12.

[25] *WA* 5: 463.23–35, 603.14–22, 611.33–612.19. Cf. Lienhard, *Witness*, 116–17.

the deepest sorrow, the most abject weakness and greatest strength, the highest glory and lowest shame, the greatest peace and deepest tribulation, the most exalted life and most miserable death'.[26]

This coincidence of opposites in God's cross-centered modus operandi pointed to the close association and continuing absolute distinction of his two 'natures' within his one 'person'. Ulrich Zwingli challenged Luther's concept of the presence of Christ in the Lord's Supper on the basis of the impossibility of human body and blood being in more than one place at one time. This issue became critical when Zwingli asserted that Christ's human body ascended into heaven, was seated at God's right hand, and there had the single place of its presence.[27] Luther reacted with further affirmation of the reliability of Christ's words of institution of the sacrament, 'this is my body', arguing that with God nothing is impossible. According to Luther's theology of the cross God reveals himself in ways contrary to human reason.[28] But to pose a possible framework for overcoming this objection, he argued that heaven is not a geographical location above the earth and that the Hebraic concept 'God's right hand' refers not to a place but to the position of power and glory. Luther furthermore contended that the 'communication of attributes' between the two natures established the ability of the two natures to share their characteristics, including the ability to be in more than one place at the same time in any form God chooses.[29]

Zwingli's response elicited Luther's elaboration of his argument in *That These Words 'This is my Body' Hold Fast Against the Ravers* (1527) and *Confession on Christ's Supper* (1528) with some refinements. He repeated his argument that the 'right hand of God' is his almighty, incomprehensible, immeasurable, creative power that had made creation and the incarnation possible; therefore, God could certainly accomplish the presence of Christ's body and blood in the sacrament.[30] His Ockhamist roots permitted Luther to assert that no general rules external to God govern his way of operating and therefore his implementation of that presence need not follow the universal patterns of other exercises of his providential power. God was able to make special arrangements for conveying the benefits of Christ to his people.

Zwingli's concern for the integrity of both the divine and the human in Christ led him to charge Luther with Docetism, the ancient heresy which denied the human nature, and with Eutychianism, the monophysitic view that the divine nature absorbed the human nature in Christ (condemned by the Council of Chalcedon). Luther feared losing sight of God's mysterious plan for reconciling sinners through becoming, in his second

[26] WA 5: 602.21–6.   [27] *Klare Unterrichtung vom Nachtmal*, 1526, CR 91: 773–862.
[28] *Sermon von dem Sakrament des Leibs und Bluts Christi*, 1526, WA 19: 485.6–11.
[29] Ibid., WA 19: 489.24–499.38.   [30] WA 23: 131.28–152.4.

person, human himself. He believed that Zwingli embraced Nestorianism, the ancient error which held the two natures separate from each other to the greatest extent possible without denying that Christ is one person. Both concerns had a valid basis though Zwingli affirmed that the two natures constituted Christ's person and Luther waxed eloquent on the humanness of Christ and the necessity of preserving the integrity of his human nature in teaching the faith. Luther sharply rejected the positions attributed to Nestorius and Eutyches but ascribed their errors to lack of theological acumen rather than ill-willed deceit of God's people.[31] In the twentieth century Regin Prenter also suggested that, like ancient articulations of the communication of attributes, Luther's statements contain a latent Docetism, an ancient denial of Christ's humanity.[32] In fact, Luther strove to use this formulation to maintain the integrity of both natures and especially the unity of the person of Christ.[33] For him this relates ultimately to God's way of restoring sinners to life and salvation. Salvation is given through Jesus Christ alone. This God-man reveals and effects God's presence and justifies re-creation among sinners.

Zwingli had construed the communication of attributes in another manner than Luther. He used the ancient Greek grammatical term 'alloeosis', literally 'change, alteration', to describe the relationship between the two natures as one in which Christians speak of one nature but mean the other; that is, he described the communication of attributes as purely rhetorical, taking place in the eye of the beholder rather than in fact, within the person of Christ. Luther sharply rejected this interpretation, especially because he saw this as a denial of the personal union of the two natures.[34] Zwingli was striving to defend the integrity of each nature, Luther the unity of Christ's person, as incarnate God.

Luther believed he had preserved the integrity of both natures through his refinement of the doctrine of the 'communication of attributes'. He taught that each of Christ's natures preserves its own authenticity and integrity, the human nature never becoming the divine, the divine remaining always God. But he envisioned the hypostatic (personal) union of the two natures as so absolute that the two share characteristics, the human nature able to exercise some traits of the divine nature (though not all), the divine nature bearing some characteristics of the human. Most theologians had affirmed a general communication of attributes between the natures though some had insisted that this was a 'verbal', not a 'real' or 'ontological' sharing of characteristics. Luther insisted on its reality. Whether he in fact taught that Christ's human body is 'ubiquitous', as

[31] *On the Councils*, WA 50: 586.9–34, 589.15–20, 594.3–595.34, LW 41: 98–102, 107–9.

[32] R. Prenter, *Creation and Redemption*, tr. T. Jensen, Philadelphia, Fortress, 1967, 345; Lienhard, *Witness*, 344–6.

[33] WA 45: 297.14–324.17.   [34] WA 26: 317.19–327.32, LW 37: 206–15.

some contemporary foes and modern scholars assert, is problematic. Some statements suggest this, others differentiate. His instructor von Usingen had followed Ockham and Biel in teaching that God, who stands above all law and constituted laws as his covenant with humankind, could have indeed so set up his world.[35] But Luther also grounded this view in his understanding of God's modus operandi, revealing what he accomplished through the whole person of Christ in humble hiding within his humanity that is inseparable from his divine nature.

Marc Lienhard finds that integral to Luther's theology of the cross is his belief that God's presence and revelation of himself are real for believers in the Word Made Flesh (John 1: 14), Jesus, and in the proclamation in oral and sacramental forms. It also stresses the cross on which the God-man Christ died a genuine human death. That is God's address to faith. Zwingli's faith, Lienhard posits, 'did not demand to the same extent as Luther's the presence of this humanity'. Zwingli saw Luther 'threaten[ing] the spiritual nature of the object of faith'.[36] Their differing presuppositions regarding God's use of selected elements of the created order, including the human flesh of Christ and the sacramental elements, made it impossible for the two to understand each other.

Zwingli did not disappear from Luther's agenda in his last fifteen years,[37] but questions concerning the person of Christ emerged largely in his attempts to affirm the catholicity of the Wittenberg confession and to oppose ideas advanced by an errant adherent turned foe, Caspar von Schwenkfeld. He did so especially in formal disputations, restored as tools for examination and promotions to academic degrees in Wittenberg (1533). They offered occasions for Luther to return to scholastic questions regarding the relationship of the persons of the Trinity and the natures of Christ. In general, he remained faithful to the catholic tradition, discussing its terminology carefully,[38] though with some freedom to formulate appropriate explanations.[39] But he also dismissed some scholastic speculation and rendered metaphysical approaches to the incarnation inoperative.[40] Hesitant to rely on human logic to solve questions not posed by Scripture, Luther contended that the Holy Spirit has his own language. It often veils God's modus operandi from human mastery, expressing something that is indescribable.[41] Luther freely conceded that such assertions do not

---

[35] Lienhard, *Witness*, 226.   [36] Ibid., 222–3.
[37] e.g. *WA* 50: 591.9–21, *LW* 41: 105.   [38] *WA* 39.2: 30.10, 305.17.
[39] *WA* 39.2: 305.15–26.   [40] *WA* 39.2: 94.7–26; Lienhard, *Witness*, 343–6.
[41] Ibid., 320–6; cf. *WA* 39.2: 19.7–12, 17–19; 10.28–35, 116.25–118.4, 308.3–5, 293.3–26; M. Tolpingrud, 'Luther's Disputation Concerning the Divinity and the Humanity of Christ', *LQ* 10 (1996), 155.

measure up to human logic but argued that, just as in grammar nouns vary in declension and some verbs are irregular, so in theology some ideas do not conform to standards applicable in philosophy. Indeed, 'in Christ, every noun takes on a new meaning regarding the very thing which is signified' even though Scripture does explain itself in ways that all can understand.[42]

Schwenkfeld, a Silesian nobleman, exiled for his propagation of reform, denied that the human Christ is a creature, with human flesh like that of other human beings. The fourth-century heresy of Arius, who denied Christ's full divinity in part by affirming his creatureliness, cast its shadow over any usage of that term. Luther's Ockhamist instructors had debated whether Christ can be called a creature, conceding that with proper safeguards this could be said. Luther eschewed the logical constructions of his school while asserting against Schwenkfeld, in theses prepared in 1540, that Christ is indeed truly human and thus truly a creature in his human nature. This is true not because of logical argument but because God had revealed it in Scripture and God's plan for reconciling sinners demanded that his humanity be truly human.[43] Luther insisted that Christ is 'creature' in a unique way, since he is united with the Creator in one person. What is said about the joining of the second person of the Trinity with Jesus of Nazareth pertains only to the concrete instance of the incarnation, not to divinity and humanity as abstract concepts. Within Christ's person, however, 'those things that are attributed to the human being may rightly be asserted with respect to God; and on the other hand, those things that are attributed to God may rightly be asserted with respect to the human being. So it is true to say: this human being created the world and this God has suffered, died, was buried, etc.'[44]

New issues arose with the emergence of anti-trinitarian thought in writings by the former Wittenberg student Johann Campanus and the Spanish physician Michael Servetus, which reinforced Luther's commitment to the Trinitarian tradition.

The 'communication of attributes' remained key to Luther's Christology, for Christ's person, divine and human natures inseparable yet distinct in one person, provides the foundation for understanding his work of the salvation of sinners.[45] That formed the heart of Luther's call for reform of public teaching.

---

[42] *WA* 39.2: 94.17–18, 103.1–11; Tolpingrud, 'Disputation', 153, 162.

[43] Lienhard, *Witness*, 330–4; *WA* 39.2: 107.4–13, 114.12–21.

[44] *WA* 39.2: 93.1–94.8, 100.25–102.27; Tolpingrud, 'Disputation', 152–3, 160–1.

[45] K. Nielsen, *Simul, Das Miteinander von Göttlichem und Menschlichem in Luthers Theologie*, Göttingen, Vandenhoeck & Ruprecht, 1966, esp. 228.

CHRIST WAS SACRIFICED FOR OUR SIN AND RAISED FOR OUR JUSTIFICATION

'No side of Luther's theology has been more summarily treated or more grossly misinterpreted than his teaching on the Atonement,' stated the Swedish theologian Gustaf Aulén in 1930.[46] Aulén launched one of the most intensive discussions of how and why Christ's work accomplishes salvation with his proposal that theologians have held three views of Christ's atoning work: the classical or dramatic, which emphasized his powerful conquering of evil, the 'Anselmic' emphasis on his vicarious or substitutionary satisfaction for guilty sinners, and Abelard's teaching that he shows the way for sinners to perform their way out of sin by obedience to the law. Often misinterpreted as adhering to the second, Luther, Aulén argued, actually taught the first, focusing above all on Christ's victory that overcomes sin, death, the devil, the law's accusation, and God's wrath.[47] Siggins counters, 'Luther has no theory of the atonement', in the sense of a 'coherent explanatory discourse about how the atonement works'. Instead his writings 'abound' with renderings of what Christ accomplished for sinners, without ever stipulating how and why God constructed this plan of salvation.[48] The atonement occasioned no controversies in the sixteenth century, and, therefore, elicited less than exact work on its formulation. Luther's concentration on the controversial teaching of how the benefits of the atonement transform sinners into God's children, the doctrine of justification, absorbed his attention.

This left his reflective powers free to experiment throughout his life with how best to portray what God did in history as the foundation for his justification of sinners. God acts through his re-creative Word of forgiveness in believers' lives to complete what historically Jesus initiated in his incarnation, obedient life, suffering, death, and resurrection. Reading Luther in context reveals that he highlighted precisely those images of Christ's work that spoke most directly to the pastoral problem which specific sermons, treatises, or lectures were addressing. His rich palette of depictions of Christ's life, death, and resurrection provided carefully focused applications to distinct dilemmas suffered by sinners under the various impacts of evil. The common thread lies in all pointing to what Christ did 'for you', 'for us'.[49]

---

[46] *Christus Victor: An Historical Study of the Three Main Types of the Idea of Atonement*, tr. A. Hebert, New York, Macmillan, 1961, 101. Cf. Althaus, *Theology*, 218–23; Bayer, *Theology*, 210–34.

[47] Aulén, *Christus*, 101–22; H. M. Barth, *Der Teufel und Jesus Christus in der Theologie Martin Luthers*, Göttingen, Vandenhoeck & Ruprecht, 1967, 35–82.

[48] Siggins, *Christ*, 109, 108–43.   [49] Ibid., esp. 108–43, 244–66, 110–11.

Luther did not systematically break apart Christ's birth, living of the godly life, agonies leading to death, death, and resurrection, but often regarded them all as part of his saving action. Yet he did come to focus on his death 'for sin' and resurrection 'for restoration of righteousness' (Rom. 4: 25). The Holy Spirit delivered the benefits of Christ's death and resurrection through baptismal burying of sinners and the resurrection of God's own children (Rom. 6: 3–11) as the basis of God's reconciling sinners to himself in Christ.

Among the first of the organizing principles for many of his innumerable depictions was his description of Christ as 'sacrament and example' (*sacramentum et exemplum*).[50] As late as 1540 he employed the pair.[51] Focusing on what Christ reveals about humanity, 'example' permitted Luther to take seriously the necessity of following Jesus in doing good works. Fundamentally recasting the medieval 'imitation of Christ' he had learned in the Brethren of the Common Life circles, he taught that following Christ's example embraces the killing of fleshly desires and dying to sin as well as deeds of love. Lienhard finds that after 1529 Luther's preaching on Christ's humanity emphasized his delivery of God's favor to his people over his serving as their example.[52] Nonetheless, he continued to use Jesus's life to describe what it means to be human, as a model of trust and devotion to the Father and a pattern for their own performance of God's will.

The fundamental focus for Luther's proclamation of Christ remained the pronouncement of forgiveness of sins on the basis of his death and resurrection as the God-man, from 1518 on. Luther never succumbed to any temptation to draft systematic explanations of how God abolishes sin and gives new life through Christ. He never tried to solve the mystery of why God did not justify by the fiat of his Word or why he became incarnate when the resurrection of a totally human Christ might have sufficed to pave the way for salvation. Against Zwingli's contention that Christ's presence in the sacrament is not necessary, Luther replied, 'God knows well how it shall be and why it must be thus. If he says that it is necessary, then all creatures should be silent.'[53]

Luther used a number of biblical forms of expressing this foundational truth in his thought, however. One complex of such portrayals of the Savior focused on elements of sacrifice and reconciliation through substitution even though Aulén discounted their importance for Luther. Luther never abandoned the language of Christ's substitutionary satisfaction of the law's sentence of death for sinners. He proclaimed Christ as the mediator or priest, who stands between God and sinners to reconcile them

---

[50] See Chapter 4 above. [51] *WA* 43: 273.20–274.12, *LW* 4: 190–2.
[52] Lienhard, *Witness*, 252–5. [53] *WA* 19: 496.13–26, *LW* 36: 344–5.

by eradicating sinners' sin, their identity as sinners. This priest served as sacrifice as well, providing the propitiation that cleanses sinners from their sins. Luther did not venture more deeply into how propitiation functions, but it is clear that it eliminates sin and buries sinners by suffering the law's judgment and God's wrath in their place.[54] At other times he spoke of Christ as Messiah, deliverer, redeemer, who liberates his people from their captivity to Satan, sin, and death and gives them life as God's children.[55]

One of Luther's abiding images of God's conveying to hearers the benefits of Christ's dying and rising was the 'joyous exchange' (*fröhlicher Wechsel*). In his Romans lectures he stated, 'He has made his righteousness my righteousness and my sin his sin' through his death.[56] Sometimes employing the imagery of bride and bridegroom, 'the joyous exchange' placed the sinner's offence against God upon Christ and Christ's standing before God upon the sinner—in the manner of the Germanic common-law contract that established brides' and bridegrooms' sharing of what they had in common. Luther did not use this image to speak of believers' sharing Christ's obedience to the law with them as an empowerment to perform good works. These works stem from hearkening to God. The ability to hear him is God's gift, the result of their new identity as God's children.[57] Luther spoke of this joyous exchange with Christ to show how God's wrath against the sinner is taken away through Christ's dying for sin and guilt. Christ's death and resurrection provide the basis for the fundamental change of identity that the Holy Spirit works through the Word of the gospel.

His lecture on Galatians 3: 13 of 1531 associates sinners with the Crucified by clothing and wrapping Christ in the sins of the entire world, abolishing this sinfulness and bestowing righteousness. Luther asserted that Christ is 'the greatest thief, murderer, adulterer, robber, desecrator, blasphemer, etc. there has ever been anywhere in the world'. Here Christ 'is not acting in his own person. Now he is not the Son of God born of the Virgin but a sinner, who has and bears the sins of Paul, the former blasphemer, persecutor, and assaulter; of Peter, who denied Christ; of David, who was an adulterer and a murderer, and who caused the Gentiles to blaspheme the name of the Lord.'[58] Luther created a dialog in which the Father tells Christ, 'Be Peter the denier; Paul the persecutor, blasphemer, and assaulter;

---

[54] U. Rieske-Braun, *Duellum Mirabile. Studien zum Kampfmotiv in Martin Luthers Theologie*, Göttingen, Vandenhoeck & Ruprecht, 1999, 171–201; Siggins, *Christ*, 113–22, 128–37; Lienhard, *Witness*, 282–5.

[55] Siggins, *Christ*, 122–8, 137–43, 164–90; Lienhard, *Witness*, 281–2, 285–6.

[56] WA 56: 204.18–19, LW 25: 188.

[57] *Freedom of a Christian*, WA 7: 25.26–26.12, LW 31: 351–2.

[58] WA 40.1: 433.26–31, LW 26: 277. Siggins, *Christ*, 144–56.

David the adulterer; the sinner who ate the apple in Paradise; the thief on the cross. . . . the one who has committed the sins of all people. . . . See to it that you pay and make satisfaction for these sins.' The law attacked and killed Christ,[59] for 'he has and bears all the sins of all people in his body—not in the sense that he has committed them but in the sense that he took these sins, committed by us, upon his own body, in order to make satisfaction for them with his own blood'.[60]

Such words show clearly that Luther taught substitutionary or vicarious satisfaction, but not, as he had written in his *Small Catechism*, as a payment of gold or silver, a tit-for-tat recompense for actual sins.[61] He noted: the term 'satisfaction' is 'too weak to fully express Christ's grace and does not adequately honor his suffering'.[62] The law evaluates sinners as guilty and condemns them to death. Only execution satisfies the law's demand that sinners die.[63] Thus, sinners are so closely drawn into Christ's crucifixion that they die with him.[64] Luther regarded Christ's fulfilling of the law in his perfect obedience as an important presupposition for being the perfect sacrifice for sin. But his concept of passive righteousness meant that his perfect human performance of obedience did not atone for sin since the law demands only death, not good works to make up for bad works. Even before the Fall perfect obedience was the product, not the cause, of righteousness in God's sight.

Alongside Christ's 'joyous exchange' Luther often places an image called 'the magnificent duel', in which Christ conquers all enemies of the believer. From 1517 on, he presented Christ's work as a battle won against the believer's foes.[65] Luther told his students in 1531, Christ's 'victory is a victory over the Law, sin, our flesh, the world, the devil, death, hell, and all evils; and this victory of his he has given to us. Even though these tyrants, our enemies, accuse us and terrify us, they cannot drive us into despair or condemn us. For Christ, whom God the Father raised from the dead, is Victor over them, and he is our righteousness.'[66] The *Large Catechism* depicts this victory: 'Before this I had no lord or king but was captive under the power of the devil. I was condemned to death and entangled in sin and blindness. . . . we lay under God's wrath and displeasure, sentenced to eternal damnation, as we had merited it and deserved it. There was no source of help, no comfort for us until the only, eternal Son of God, in his

---

[59] *WA* 40.1: 437.23–7, 438.12–13, *LW* 26: 280.

[60] *WA* 40.1: 433.33, 434.12, *LW* 26: 277.   [61] *BSLK*, 511, *BC*, 355.

[62] 'Summer Postil', 1544, *WA* 21: 264.21–35; Althaus, *Theology*, 202.

[63] *WA* 40.1: 434.19–20, *LW* 26: 278.

[64] See below, pp. 138–40; *WA* 40.1: 280.3–281.20, *LW* 26: 165.

[65] Rieske-Braun, *Duellum*, 139–47.

[66] *WA* 40.1: 65.12–17, *LW* 26: 21–2; Rieske-Braun, *Duellum*, 66–100.

unfathomable goodness, had mercy on us. . . . Those tyrants and jailers have now been routed, and their place has been taken by Jesus Christ . . . He has snatched us, poor lost creatures, from the jaws of hell, won us, made us free, and restored us to the Father's favor and grace.'[67] Rescue results in liberation. The transfer of lordship to Christ replaces an identity as slave of Satan with that of child of God.

Not only Satan's hostility and tyranny fell to Christ's victory. In Luther's preaching and devotional/catechetical works Satan, sin, and death appeared as the enemies; in lecturing to students, Luther's emphasis fell on God's wrath against sin and the hostile condemnation of his law.[68] The law died, along with its sentence of death for sinners, because Christ came on their behalf. Paul claimed to die to the law through the law (Gal. 2: 19). Defining 'law' as the accusing and condemning voice of God, Luther 'baptized' the law into a new identity and ended its capability for terrorizing and tyrannizing repentant believers: it 'has now been baptized with a new name because it is no longer alive but is dead and damned' (echoing Romans 6: 3–4). Paul presented the law as a captive, 'bound hand and foot, shorn of all power, so that it cannot exert its tyranny, that is, accuse and condemn'. When oppressed by guilt and fear of judgment, God's people have 'the courage to insult the law with a certain holy pride and to say: "I am a sinner. If you can do anything against me, Law, go ahead and do it!" That is how far the law now is from frightening the believer.'[69] This conversation takes place because 'if we are dead to the law, then the law has no jurisdiction over us, as it has no jurisdiction over Christ, who has liberated us from the law in order that in this way we may live to God'. To die to the law means to live freely according to God's pattern for human living, not to do one's own will departing from God's plan for life.[70] Apart from this death to the law, human creatures cannot have life with God: 'to live to the law is to die to God and to die to the law is to live to God'.[71]

This death to the law took place in Christ, Luther insisted: 'Only Christ takes away the law, kills my sin, destroys my death in his body, and in this way empties hell, judges the devil, crucifies him, and throws him down into hell. In other words, everything that once used to torment and oppress me Christ has set aside; he has disarmed it and made a public example of it triumphing over it in himself' (Col. 2: 15).[72] He has liberated the sinner's conscience. Against the voice of the law that lingers, directing attention to past sins, believers should say, 'I am deaf and do not hear you. . . . I am dead to you; I now live to Christ, where I am under another Law, the

[67] *BSLK*, 651–2, *BC*, 434; Rieske-Braun, *Duellum*, 233–5.

[68] Rieske-Braun, *Duellum*, 133, 74–81; Bayer, *Theology*, 192–202.

[69] *WA* 40.1: 277.18–29, *LW* 26: 162–3.

[70] *WA* 40.1: 268.20–2, 270.14–15, *LW* 26: 156–7.   [71] *WA* 40.1: 271.32–3, *LW* 26: 159.

[72] *WA* 40.1: 274.28–33, *LW* 26: 160–1.

law of grace, which rules over sin and the law.'[73] The liberated conscience therefore knows that Christ has decisively confronted the accusation of the law. 'The accusing law now hears this law [of liberty in Christ] say: "You shall not bind this person, hold him captive, or make him guilty. But I will hold you captive and tie your hands, lest you hurt him who now lives to Christ and is dead to you." This knocks out the teeth of the law, blunts its sting and all its weapons, and utterly disables it.' It remains a condemning law for the wicked but not for those with whom Christ has effected the joyous exchange.[74] This is, for Luther, the re-creative act of God which prepares his children for good works.

Luther sketched the battle scene in his Galatians commentary on the basis of Romans 7: 23. Christ becomes a law that condemns the law for condemning those whom Christ has made innocent through his death and resurrection. 'Law, if you are able to bite, bind, and plague me, I will put another law above you, that is another tyrant and tormentor, who will turn the tables and accuse, bind, and oppress you. You are indeed my tormentor, but you have another tormentor, Christ. He will torment you to the utmost.' Thus the sinner becomes free to enjoy a new identity as God's child.[75] This image serves to reveal the believer's relationship not only to the law but also to sin. It is 'a powerful and cruel tyrant, dominating and ruling the entire world, capturing and enslaving all people . . . a great and powerful god who devours the whole human race'. Sin attacks Christ, but in dueling against it, Christ conquers and kills sin, so that righteousness prevails and lives.[76]

When he addressed the guilt or shame of his hearers, Luther presented Christ's substitutionary sacrifice, which took away the penalty of death which the law lays upon sinners, through a variety of descriptions. When he addressed their fears and terrors, he emphasized Christ's power and presence in their situations through his mighty deliverance in his resurrection. The resurrection also insured the death of Satan's power over believers even though they and the Holy Spirit engage in a continuing struggle against him. The devil played an important role in Luther's understanding of the Christian life although Satan's place in Luther's consciousness should not be exaggerated. He felt himself caught between God, on one side, and the condemnation of the law and his own sinfulness, on the other, as well as between God and the devil. He did not ignore Satan's active efforts to subvert his trust in God, but he remained ever confident of Christ's victory over the Evil One.[77]

---

[73] WA 40.1: 271.25–30, LW 26: 158.   [74] WA 40.1: 275.33–4, LW 26: 161–2.
[75] WA 40.1: 278.30–279.29, LW 26: 164.   [76] WA 40.1: 439.17–27, LW 26: 281.
[77] Barth, *Teufel*, passim; cf., H. Oberman, *Luther: Man between God and the Devil*, tr. E. Waliser-Schwarzbart, New Haven and London, Yale University Press, 1989.

Luther certainly did not restrict his treatment of Christ's work to the atonement even though it stood at the heart of his proclamation. Vital as well was Christ's revelation of God—inseparable from the atonement but distinct in its own focus. Although Luther did not adopt the medieval schema of prophet, priest, and king to organize his presentation of Jesus's work and significance, he did treat him as the royal priest after the order of Melchizedek, and he also taught that Jesus was called by the Father to the assignment of prophet or preacher, who revealed God. This assignment was his occupational vocation—his 'office' (*officium, Amt*) on earth.[78] The Father sent Christ into this world as savior and as messenger or witness, the one who unveiled the fullness of God's revelation of himself and his plan to restore fallen humanity to himself. Christ fulfilled the assignment borne by this office, which all preachers of the Word have, in a unique way, as prophesied in Deuteronomy 18: 15–18. Jesus carried out this assignment by performing a work that did not properly belong to him, the 'alien' work (*opus alienum*) of the law's condemnation of sin, so that he could perform the task appropriate to him, the 'proper' work (*opus proprium*) of giving life through the gospel of forgiveness.[79] In doing this task he taught sinners who God is and how he restores the relationship between their Creator and themselves through his death and resurrection.

RIGHTEOUSNESS RESTORED BY GOD'S GRACIOUS FAVOR THROUGH TRUST IN CHRIST

Luther's own search for his identity as God-pleasing, combined with his encounters with God's demand for human righteousness in the Scripture texts on which he was lecturing, drove him to find the center of the biblical message in God's 'justification' of sinners. This search for the restoration of perfect humanity, in the face of the sin that divided sinners from God, had commanded much attention in late medieval scholastic teaching, but not so vital a role there as in Luther's teaching. He described the critical turn in his own thinking as his beginning 'to understand God's righteousness as that through which, as through God's gift, the righteous person lives, namely on the basis of faith, and that it means the passive [righteousness] through which the merciful God makes us righteous through faith' (Hab. 2: 4).[80] Wilfried Härle points out that this justifying action seems to have two subjects: God and human trust in him.[81] This reflects the nature of Luther's

---

[78] Siggins, *Christ*, 48–64.   [79] Ibid., 64–78; Lienhard, *Witness*, 274–80.

[80] *WA* 54: 186.5–8, *LW* 34: 337.

[81] 'Die Entfaltung der Rechtfertigungslehre Luthers in den Disputationen von 1535 bis 1537', *LuJ* 71 (2004), 227–8.

definition of God and what it means to be human. Whereas most medieval thinkers conceived of human 'righteousness' in terms of performance or activity, Luther believed that the concept rested on a deeper foundation. Righteousness is being what the person or thing is supposed to be. That identity issues naturally into action. Härle establishes that the Old Testament concept of what both God and human creature are—are supposed to be—consists in 'communal faithfulness' (צדקה, *Gemeinschaftstreue*).[82] Relationship, for Luther, constituted a vital part of reality because God, as the first and fundamental reality, is a person. The reality of God as he has revealed himself to humanity cannot be defined apart from his disposition toward and interaction with human beings; the reality of humanity cannot be defined apart from the creature's reliance upon the Creator. Faithfulness to each other define both God and the human creature.

Because medieval theologians taught that human worth and identity rested upon performance of God's law, they contended that justification— literally 'making righteous'—happens in the way in which personal identity is created by a person's action. Some theologians emphasized the help sinners needed from God's grace more than others. From Biel's students Luther had learned the necessity of sinners performing good works and thereby earning merit. Luther found this belief inadequate because it fully recognized neither the viciousness and deep-rooted entrenchment of sin in fallen human creatures nor the overwhelming majesty of God's mercy in Christ.

Luther explored both the noun 'righteousness' and the verb 'to make righteous' or 'justify' in biblical contexts, concluding that God acts to restore the human righteousness he had created in the first place by speaking the 'new creature' (Gal. 6: 15) into existence through forgiveness of sins. Paul spoke of the conversion of the wicked, 'which happens through the Word', 'a new work of creation', in 2 Corinthians 4: 6, Luther told students in 1535.[83] This word-act that restores sinners to righteousness accomplishes its task through the mystery of God's becoming human in Jesus, his dying to satisfy the law's demand for the sinner's death, and his rising from death to give new life to his people. That new life begins with the fundamental orientation of human life, trusting in God, a trust that accepts the gift of identity as child of God and hearkens to God's will for an obedient life of good works.

Luther often used the medieval term 'imputation' to describe how God delivers the benefits of Christ's work to sinners. Relatively seldom used

---

[82] Ibid., 217–19.
[83] WA 42: 14.12–22, LW 1: 17; B. Lohse, *Martin Luther's Theology*, tr. R. Harrisville, Minneapolis, Fortress, 1999, 258–66.

in late medieval scholasticism, it meant an accusation or, more generally, a way of viewing things, a pronouncement of evaluation.[84] For Luther, God's regard, his pronouncement, created and sustained fundamental reality. God's imputation could not be merely a legal fiction. His imputing fashioned actuality. Luther did not deny the reality of sin, but its reality could not trump God's reality. The mystery of sin remained, but the fact of God's gift of righteousness through his regard and his Word constituted the dominant truth of the sinner's state. When addressing those deeply convicted of their continuing struggle against sin, he emphasized that God's view of human creatures, his regard for the sinner, determines the future and promises life without sin despite its presence in the believer's experience now. Here he depicted justification as the verdict of the judge who determines guilt or innocence by what he says. When highlighting the fundamental reality of what God has accomplished, he employed the language of re-creation, of death and new life.

He based this on both Greek and German usage. *Rechtfertigen*—'justify' or 'render righteous'—meant 'to do justice to: that is to inflict punishment, "judicially" on the basis of a conviction, and thus to execute the law's demands',[85] or 'to conduct a legal process as an activity of a judge', 'to execute, to kill'.[86] From early on, Luther spoke of God's killing and making alive as he described justification, for he presumed that sinners must die (Rom. 6: 23a) and be resurrected to life in Christ. In his Romans lectures (1515–16) he associated justification with baptism as Paul described it in Romans 6: 3–11 in far less than its mature expression of its motif of the burial of the sinful identity and the resurrection of a new identity in Christ. There he interpreted this passage in terms of the ongoing struggle to put the desires of the flesh to death in the never-ending struggle against sin; he did not speak of God's decisive restoration of righteousness through his Word of forgiveness.[87] In *The Holy and Blessed Sacrament of Baptism* of 1519 Luther favored baptism by immersion because baptism 'signifies that the old man and the sinful birth of flesh and blood are to be wholly drowned by the grace of God. . . . the significance of baptism is a blessed dying unto sin and a resurrection in the grace of God, so that the old man, conceived and born in sin, is there drowned, and a new man, born in grace, comes forth and rises. . . . Through this spiritual birth [the baptized person] is a child of grace and a justified person.'[88] This motif continued in his presentation of

---

[84] J. Niermeyer, *Mediae Latinitatis Lexicon minus*, Leiden, Brill, 1976, 516.

[85] Werner Elert, 'Deutschrechtliche Züge in Luthers Rechtfertigungslehre', in M. Keller-Hüschemenger (ed.), *Ein Lehrer der Kirche, Kirchlich-theologische Aufsätze und Vorträge von Werner Elert*, Berlin, Lutherisches Verlagshaus, 1967, 23–31.

[86] J. and W. Grimm (eds.) *Deutsches Wörterbuch*, Leipzig, Herzel et al., 1854–1960, 8: 412–13.

[87] WA 56: 320.10–328.26, LW 25: 308–16.

[88] WA 2: 727.10–19, LW 35: 29; WA 2: 727.30–728.9, LW 35: 30.

justification throughout his life.[89] However, Luther could also use language which placed the burden of preserving the baptismal covenant upon the baptized: 'So long as you keep your pledge to God, he in turn gives you his grace,'[90] the law's call to faithful hearkening to God.

Luther's discourse on justification arose out of his presuppositions regarding sin. Luther defined sin as doubt of, and offense against, the Almighty Creator and loving Father, failing to hearken to his Word. Therefore, God's law, the expression of his plan for human life—the Creator's definition of what it means to be human—condemned sinners to death (Rom. 6: 23a). God, however, promised life as a free gift to his people (Rom. 6: 23b), and he bestowed that promise and the life it gives through his Word, first of all in baptismal form (Rom. 6: 1–18). By 1520 Luther found the words of absolution in the sacrament of penance an absolute assurance of forgiveness.[91]

Justification is also an act of new creation. In a doctoral promotion disputation of 1535 on faith and law, composed in the midst of papal initiatives for a general council, at which Luther wanted justification to be a topic, he wrote: 'justification is in reality a kind of rebirth in newness' (John 1: 12–13; 1 John 5: 1), 'a washing of regeneration and renewal' (Titus 3: 5), new birth (John 3: 3); the Holy Spirit calls God's people 'righteous, a new creature of God and the first fruits of God's creatures, who, according to his will brought us forth by his Word (2 Cor. 5: 17; Jas. 1: 18)'. 'It is as blasphemous to say that human creatures are justified by their own works as to say that they are their own gods, creators, makers.'[92]

Many twentieth-century scholars missed Luther's underlying understanding of God's Word as his creative agent for determining reality. Therefore, they debated fruitlessly whether Luther's doctrine of justification was 'effective'—God's 'actual' rendering sinners righteous in deed—or 'forensic'—God's 'merely' saying that they are righteous. First the 'Holl school'[93] and recently the 'Finnish' school of Tuomo Mannermaa challenged the so-called 'forensic' interpretation of Luther's doctrine of justification. Holl recognized that Luther had emphasized the performance of good works and tried to tie the sanctified life to the act of justification. Mannermaa associates Luther's view with the Eastern Orthodox concept

[89] e.g. Galatians commentary, 1535, *WA* 40.1, 539.17; 26: 348. R. Kolb, 'God Kills to Make Alive: Romans 6 and Luther's Understanding of Justification (1535)', *LQ* 12 (1998), 33–56.

[90] *WA* 2: 731.3–4, *LW* 35: 34.

[91] O. Bayer, *Promissio. Geschichte der reformatorischen Wende in Luthers Theologie*, Göttingen, Vandenhoeck & Ruprecht, 1971, 254–73.

[92] *WA* 39.1: 48.10–30, *LW* 34: 113–14.

[93] J. Stayer, *Martin Luther, German Saviour: German Evangelical Theological Factions and the Interpretation of Luther, 1917–1933*, Montreal and Kingston, McGill-Queens University Press, 2000, 20–39; K. Holl, *Gesammelte Aufsätze zur Kirchengeschichte*, Tübingen, Mohr/Siebeck, 1928–32, 1: 1–287; 3: 527–41, 558–67.

of *theosis* or divinization, in arguing that justification is more real than 'merely' a divine verbal observation.[94] Both interpretations wish to avoid regarding justification as the creation of a legal fiction—believers remain really sinners but God simply refuses to consider them as such. Gerhard Forde rightly recognized that such attempts are both historically inaccurate and theologically unnecessary when he observed that the more 'forensic' Luther's teaching becomes, the more 'effective' it is, because nothing can be more real than that which God's Word declares. Furthermore, Luther's distinguishing God's restoration of human righteousness and the effect it has on human performance of new obedience dare not be confused with a separation of the two, as though there were no moral consequences of receiving new identity and new dignity as God's child.

Always conscious of the continuing mystery of sin and evil in the lives of the baptized, Luther nonetheless distinguished the question of human moral performance from the identification of the source of the believer's righteousness in God's sight and the believer's trust. Mannermaa argues that faith in Christ brings believers to full participation in the person of Christ. 'Because faith means a real union with Christ, and because in Christ the Logos is of the same essence as God the Father, therefore the believer's participation in the essence of God is also real.'[95] This view ignores the nature of the 'union' of bride and bridegroom that Luther employed so frequently (in which the two participants in the union do not become 'one essence' but retain their distinctiveness), and his understanding of the preposition 'in' when Luther uses the Hebraic concept of two distinct entities being 'in' each other (that is, in a close association which does not merge them but brings them together in intimate relationship). It also ignores Luther's strong doctrine of Creator and creation, which emphasized the distinction of the Creator and the human creature and the goodness of being human as God's creature. Luther viewed 'divinization' as the vain wish of the first sinners, not God's goal in shaping the human creature. Luther believed not that 'faith communicates divine attributes' to believers[96] but rather that Christ's word of forgiveness restores the perfect attributes of God's human creation. Schwarzwäller succinctly and aptly summarizes the flaws in this new interpretation of Luther's doctrine of justification on the basis of its inadequate methodology, its flawed reading of Luther's texts in historical context, its faulty logic in equating several distinct terms, its insufficient theological understanding of Luther's doctrine of creation, God's Word, and related teachings, and its linguistic

---

[94] *Christ Present in Faith, Luther's View of Justification*, Minneapolis, Fortress, 2005, 55–6; cf. idem, *Der im Glauben gegenwärtige Christus. Rechtfertigung und Vergottung. Zum ökumenischen Dialog*, Hanover, Lutherisches Verlagshaus, 1989, and S. Peura, *Mehr als Mensch? Die Vergöttlichung als Thema der Theologie Martin Luthers von 1513 bis 1519*, Mainz, Zabern, 1994.

[95] Mannermaa, *Christ Present*, 19, 16–22.   [96] Ibid., 22.

misinterpretation of much of Luther's key terminology.[97] Indeed, Luther very occasionally uses the medieval mystical term 'divinization', but he always clearly distinguished Creator from creature. He defined trust, not an indwelling presence of the divine, as the central human characteristic that brings all else in human life into harmony with the Father who created his people and rescued them from evil through Christ's death and resurrection.

FAITH OR TRUST AS THE HEART OF HUMANITY

The nature of God's re-creative Word as a promise demands the response of trust in that promise. Trust defines the human side of this relationship which God restores. The relationship is based upon the work of Christ, which actually effects the end of the sinner's identity as sinner and the assumption of the new identity as child of God. In his disputation on justification (1535) Luther repeated his long-time insistence that saving faith is not 'historic faith', the acknowledgement of the facts of Jesus's story. 'It grasps Christ, who died for our sins and arose again for our justification' (Rom. 4: 25) and 'understands the love of God the Father, who wants to redeem and save you through Christ'. It recognizes that Christ died and rose 'for me'. The Holy Spirit creates and preserves this faith. It 'joyfully embraces the Son of God given for it with arms outstretched joyfully, saying, "He is my beloved, and I am his." ' Good works flow from this faith, not under compulsion but voluntarily, as a good tree naturally and freely produces good fruits (Matt. 7: 16).[98]

This trust directs itself to the absolute reliability of what God says to sinners about their identity, both because what he says has accomplished the re-creation that restores their identity as his children and because he will not lie. That assurance of God's utter reliability lay behind Luther's insistence in *Bound Choice* that God does not change, or, better said, is utterly faithful to his promise. Luther taught that assurance rests on the basis of God's plan fashioned before creation. But election or predestination could arouse either arrogance in those who took from this teaching a license to sin, or despair in those who thought that weakness of faith or obedience indicated that they were not elect. Therefore, Luther also rested assurance on the work of Christ, who was given for the whole world (John 3: 16). Individual Christians could know that they were included among

---

[97] K. Schwarzwäller, 'Verantwortung des Glaubens. Freiheit und Liebe nach der Dekalogauslegung Martin Luthers', in D. Bielfeldt and K. Schwarzwäller (eds.), *Freiheit als Liebe bei/Freedom as Love in Martin Luther*, Frankfurt am Main, Lang, 1995, 146–8.

[98] WA 39.1: 45.11–46.10, LW 34: 109–11.

those for whom Christ died and rose on the basis of the promise in his Word, in oral, written, and sacramental forms.

The promise is reliable; it establishes the true description of God's chosen children. But for some unknown reason sin and evil continue in the lives of the baptized. They remain fully righteous in God's sight, and yet at the same time the sinfulness that abides in them permeates their lives. Luther designed his expression 'sinful and righteous at the same time' (*simul justus et peccator*) to bring comfort to those believers who focused, as he often did, on their sins and tilted toward despair over their faith. This expression enabled them to take comfort in God's promise despite the all-too-obvious sin that beset them. At the same time it reminded believers that their sin is also real, even if it contradicts the promise. Therefore, they had to recognize that the entire life of the Christian is a life of repentance.[99]

Repentance takes place as God's words of law and gospel address the sinner within the believer. Each day the law kills anew fresh sins and new false gods, eradicating them as that which determines the believer's identity; the gospel restores trust in Christ and his word that renews the new identity of the child of God, created in justification. The Holy Spirit's speaking his Word creates faith. Therefore, Luther emphasized the use of the Word of God in all its forms, oral, written, and sacramental.

---

[99] Althaus, *Theology*, 242–5.

8

One Little Word Can Slay Him: God's Power and Presence in the Oral, Written, and Sacramental Forms of His Word

The religious atmosphere in which Luther grew up centered on the mass. According to popular belief at that time human relationships with God and all other supernatural powers took concrete form primarily in rituals of various kinds. The most important of them brought Christ's body and blood to the village altar through the priest's consecratory words. This gave him unique power in village life. The mass became a prime target of criticism by popular reform movements in the half-millennium before Luther. These movements proposed a moralistic rather than ritualistic approach to God, relying on Scripture rather than ecclesiastical traditions and authorities. Because the mass served as center for ritualistic practice of Christianity, they were anti-sacramental and therefore anti-clerical; they also expected Christ to return soon to support their cause.[1]

Both in official religious practice and thought and in this sort of reform proposal, Luther found a focus on human performance, either of moral or of ritual actions. Both obscured the biblical depiction of God the Creator as the initiator and activator of all relationships between himself and his human creatures, as a person who engaged his people in conversation through his Word in its several forms. God communicates with human beings and draws them into the relationship of trust in him and care for their neighbors for which he had originally designed them. Therefore, Luther believed that God is present in the various forms of his Word and that he exercises his power to claim and restore sinners through these forms, oral, written, and sacramental. This conception of how God works with human creatures differed from predominant medieval views, both official and reforming.

Although Luther and his circle seldom used the term prominent in later Lutheran dogmatics, 'means of grace', for the word in oral and sacramental

---

[1] N. Cohn, *The Pursuit of the Millennium*, 3rd edn., Oxford, Oxford University Press, 1970.

forms, they believed that God has selected certain elements of his created order not merely to signify or point to heavenly realities, such as God's disposition toward sinners, nor to effect them in what reformers regarded as a magical way. His Word in all its forms actually conveys and performs his saving will. God designed his Word in these forms as instruments of his re-creating power which accomplish what they announce. More than performative speech, they are creative speech, parallel to God's speaking in Genesis 1.

Luther reacted to what he regarded as his colleague Karlstadt's betrayal of the gospel in rejecting 'God's outward order in the material sign of baptism and the oral proclamation of God's Word' as the Spirit's way of 'coming to you', and instead seeking 'how you come to the Spirit'. Luther held that the Holy Spirit works inwardly, creating faith and giving other gifts, 'through the oral word of the gospel and through material signs, that is baptism and the sacrament of the altar. . . . The inward experience follows and is effected by the outward. God has determined to give the inward to no one except through the external [Word]' (Luke 16: 29; Titus 3: 5, Rom. 1: 16).[2]

While Karlstadt was advancing his rapid, radical program for reform in 1521/2, and Luther remained at the Wartburg, a small group of anti-sacramental, moralistic millenarians from Zwickau visited Wittenberg. They urged Melanchthon and Amsdorf to abandon their reform program and embrace the special, non-biblical revelations these 'Zwickau prophets' claimed to have. This further confirmed Luther in his uncompromising conviction that only in the proclamation of God's Word in Scripture and sacramental practice anchored in Scripture could God's saving purposes be accomplished.[3] Karlstadt broke with Luther over this and related issues, leaving Wittenberg in 1523.[4]

Luther believed that God approaches sinners through conversation expressed in human means of communication, words but also sacramental expressions in material form as well. In 1536 he spoke of the 'gospel which gives resources and help against sin in more than one way' (what he occasionally labeled 'means of grace') as 'the spoken word, in which the forgiveness of sins is preached to the whole world', baptism, the sacrament of the altar, and the power of the keys, or absolution, 'and also through the mutual conversation and consolation' of Christians with one

[2] *Against the Heavenly Prophets* (1524), WA 18: 136.9–137.4, LW 40: 146, 147; R. Kolb and C. Arand, *The Genius of Luther's Theology: A Wittenberg Way of Thinking for the Contemporary Church*, Grand Rapids, Baker, 2008, 128–211.

[3] M. Edwards, *Luther and the False Brethren*, Stanford, Stanford University Press, 1975, 6–33.

[4] Ibid., 34–59, 73–81; B. Lohse, *Martin Luther's Theology*, tr. R. Harrisville, Minneapolis, Fortress, 1999, 144–50; R. Sider, *Andreas Bodenstein von Karlstadt: The Development of His Thought*, Leiden, Brill, 1974.

another, which he understood as the implementation of Christ's command in Matthew 18: 15–20.[5]

ORAL FORMS OF GOD'S WORD

As a medieval churchman, Luther initially believed that God's Word impacts believers' lives first of all in sacramental form. But he quickly came to treasure the value of the proclaimed Word, reflecting his view of God as a speaking Creator. His postils addressed the task of preaching in practice but also contained theoretical observations about the nature of that task. Proclamation delivers Christ in the interplay between oral and written forms of God's Word. 'The preaching of the gospel is nothing else than Christ coming to us or our being brought to him.' This gospel is at its root not 'something written but a spoken word which brought forth the Scriptures . . . good news or proclamation spread not by pen but by word of mouth', but which is now dependent on Scripture: when the church abandoned Scripture, God abandoned it to human deception.[6]

Because penance occupied, alongside the mass, a central place in medieval piety, Luther strove early in his public career to reform it and reinforce its role in pastoral care, in the consolation of troubled consciences. His criticism of the medieval practice of penance never ceased since it took away rather than gave consolation to terrified consciences. In 1530 he composed a treatise on 'the keys to heaven', an analysis of papal abuses of the power to open or close heaven, as Christ described this power he gave his disciples, and thus the whole church, in Matthew 18: 15–20. Luther rejected interpreting this power in any other way than for the forgiveness of sins. The power to 'close heaven' was not the pope's or bishops' right to impose mandatory regulations on Christians.[7] 'With this binding Christ attempts nothing else but to free and rid sinners' conscience of sins' by calling them to repentance. Christ's blood, death, and resurrection 'must lie hidden in the keys of Christ'.[8] Loosing sinners from their sins does not depend on the worthiness of their repentance but on Christ alone.[9]

This reflects the *Large Catechism*'s 'Brief Exhortation to Confession' written a year earlier. Luther wished to free confession from 'the pope's tyranny', specifically the use of the confessional to 'burden and torture consciences', through the required enumeration of all mortal sins and

---

[5] *Smalcald Articles* III. iv, *BSLK*, 449, *BC*, 339.

[6] Wartburg Postil, dedicatory epistle, *WA* 10.1.1: 17.15–20, *LW* 35: 123.

[7] *WA* 30.2: 487.25–492.20, *LW* 40: 353–9.

[8] *WA* 30.2: 467.23–468.2, 497.1–501.9, *LW* 40: 328, 364–9.

[9] *WA* 30.2: 477.7–480.2, *LW* 40: 339–44.

the satisfactions, largely ritual works, that theoretically won release from the temporal punishments for sins, the eternal guilt of which had been abolished in the priest's absolution.[10]

In his *Sermon on the Sacrament of Penance* (1519) Luther had come to view the Word of God, not the priest's office, as key to what God accomplishes in the sacrament of penance. He did not deny the priest's role in forgiving sins on God's behalf, but he emphasized that God's Word, not the priestly office, conveyed forgiveness to those who trusted this Word. In conversation with his people God forgives their sins; they receive this gift in faith, which finds peace, comfort, and joy in God's absolution.[11] 'In the New Testament every Christian has this authority to forgive sins, whether priest or not.'[12] This Word from God through human agents such as the priest 'genuinely forgives sin and guilt' to those to whom God gives faith. The words 'I absolve you' give the faithful assurance of absolution before God on the basis of Christ's commission (Matt. 16: 19; 18: 18).[13] This position, repeated in *Babylonian Captivity*,[14] elaborated in other writings throughout Luther's career, became ever clearer in explicitly assigning to the Word in human language God's power to save (Rom. 1: 17). Initially concerned about combating the hierarchical views of the medieval church, Luther later focused more on insuring that God's work goes on through pastors, designated to act for God and in behalf of the priesthood of the baptized in the public ministry of the church. This is true in regard to confession and absolution. While he urged that Christians forgive each other sins in mutual conversation and consolation, he also urged them to enjoy the absolution pronounced by pastors publicly and privately.

Christians may confess sins and receive forgiveness in prayer to God alone or in conversation with other Christians. But Luther also advised secret or private confession. For 'Christ himself has placed absolution in the mouths of his Christian community and commanded us to absolve one another from sins.' Confession consists of the human act of lamenting sin and desiring comfort and restoration and God's act of forgiving sins 'through the Word placed on the lips of another person'.[15] The *Small Catechism* taught readers to believe firmly that through absolution 'our sins are forgiven before God in heaven'. Luther encouraged believers to 'reflect on your walk of life in the light of the Ten Commandments', combining God's structure for life in the callings of daily life and his commands to practice virtue as a means of reviewing life. Appropriate Bible verses for

---

[10]   *BSLK*, 725–7; *BC*, 476–7.   [11]   *WA* 2: 714.1–716.35, *LW* 35: 9–13.

[12]   *WA* 2: 722.36–723.6; 716.36–717.5, *LW* 35: 22, 13.

[13]   *WA* 2: 722.28–34, 717.6–20, *LW* 35: 22, 13–14.   [14]   See Chapter 5 above.

[15]   *BSLK*, 725–33; *BC*, 476–80.

the distress of this particular person should supplement the simple formula 'I forgive you in the name of the Father, Son, and Holy Spirit.'[16]

Luther resituated the power of penance—precisely, its absolution—from the priest to God's Word itself. He often admonished his congregation to practice the mutual forgiveness of sins in the family and community in which they lived. In 1537, preaching on Matthew 18: 15–18, he stated that God pours out his forgiveness

in every corner, so that they not only find the forgiveness of sins in the congregation but also at home in their houses, in the fields and gardens, wherever one of them comes to another in search of comfort and deliverance. It shall be at my disposal when I am troubled and sorry, in tribulation and vulnerable, when I need something, at whatever hour and time it may be. There is not always a sermon being given publicly in the church, so when my brother or neighbor comes to me, I am to lay my troubles before my neighbor and ask for comfort. ... Again I should comfort others, and say 'dear friend, dear brother, why don't you lay aside your burdens. It is certainly not God's will that you experience this suffering. God had his Son die for you so that you do not sorrow but rejoice.'[17]

He told his students in 1542, 'If you want to be absolved from your sins in this manner, go to your pastor, or to your brother or neighbor if your pastor cannot hear you; [the neighbor] has the command to absolve you and comfort you.'[18]

Luther never abandoned this emphasis on pastoral care and the consolation of troubled consciences, expressed by 1520, for example in *On How Confession Should Be Made*. Confession and absolution center in God's promise of mercy and new life in Christ and in faith, the trust that clings to the promise. At the same time he admonished those confessing that they truly repent and intend to break off their sinful deeds. In the midst of sinners' struggles over their sincerity, however, Luther counseled 'pouring out your hearts before him' (Ps. 62: 8), praying for good intention, but then, citing Jean Gerson, he even advised that believers occasionally receive the Lord's Supper with a scruple, so that they could throw themselves completely on God's mercy and despair of the purity of their own contrition.[19]

GOD'S SACRAMENTAL WORD IN BAPTISM

God's goodness in showering his Word upon his people took form also in connection with what Luther initially called the 'signs' of baptism and

[16] *BSLK*, 517–19; *BC*, 360–2.
[17] 'Sermons on Matthew 18–24', *WA* 47: 297.36–298.14.
[18] *WA* 44: 95.41–96.1, *LW* 6: 128. Cf. *WA* 44: 712.33–6, *LW* 8: 183.
[19] *WA* 6: 158.4–161.5, 166.1–30, *LW* 39: 28–32, 40–1.

the Lord's Supper. He included absolution among these 'sacraments' at times, in accord with his definition of 'sacrament' as those forms of Christ's promise of forgiveness that he commanded and connected with external signs.[20] His 1519 *Sermon on the Holy, Blessed Sacrament of Baptism* demonstrated an interest in baptism that exceeded that of his contemporaries, he claimed.[21] His enduring emphasis on baptism's effecting the death of sinners and their resurrection as people of Christ began early, although in 1519/20 the sacrament remained a sign. It did not bestow that new identity as God's child but only began the fight to attain its perfection at physical death. 'Spiritual baptism, the drowning of sin which it signifies, lasts throughout life and is completed only in death, when a person is completely immersed in baptism and what baptism signifies comes to pass.' Spiritual resurrection, begun in baptism, is completed on the Last Day. Baptism's comfort rests on its assurance that God's mercy is driving out sin through many trials.[22]

Anabaptist denial of baptismal regeneration and their contention that the sacrament was a symbolic act of human commitment to God helped drive Luther away from Augustinian language of 'sign' by the early 1530s.[23] Even later, however, he argued that God has always communicated through various physical signs.[24] This baptismal sign pronounces upon God's people the forgiveness of sins and gives assurance that he wishes to preserve them, as he preserved Noah and his family (1 Pet. 3: 20).[25] Luther treasured God's sensitivity to the human condition by delivering his Word together with such material signs. In 1538 he exulted that God graciously addresses the five human senses. Through the hand and tongue of the minister of the gospel God is at work.[26] 'In baptism there is an oral word and a pourer, in the sacrament an oral word and a feeder, in preaching an oral word and a speaker, as in absolution.' If God had sent justification through angels instead of through those who pour, feed, and speak, he would not have done it any other way. The angels, too, would have had to pour, feed, and speak. For God himself is pouring, feeding, and absolving.[27] God has so structured his world that the reality of salvation which his Word

---

[20] WA 6: 571.35–572.22, LW 36: 124; Peters, *Kommentar*, 4: 11–67.

[21] *Babylonian Captivity*, WA 6: 526.35–527.22, LW 36: 57–8; see A. Peters, *Kommentar zu Luthers Katechismen*, 5 vols., ed. G. Seebaß, Göttingen, Vandenhoeck & Ruprecht, 1991, 4: 71–126.

[22] WA 2: 727.4–729.5, 731.18–37, LW 35: 29–31, 34–5.

[23] WA 27: 55.24–56.10. See J. Trigg, *Baptism in the Theology of Martin Luther*, Leiden, Brill, 1994, esp. 1; Lorenz Grönvik, *Die Taufe in der Theologie Martin Luthers*, Åbo, Åbo Akademi, 1968, 101–26 on Luther's concept of *signum* as he used it in connection with baptism.

[24] WA 27: 60.9–21.   [25] WA 27: 59.10–12.   [26] WA 46: 148.16–21.

[27] WA 46: 149.23–150.30.

effects is delivered and brought into being through selected elements of the created order.

Luther continued to preach catechetical sermons on baptism throughout his career, sometimes reflecting more frequent reports of Anabaptist activity in central Germany,[28] always aimed at edifying his hearers. These sermons taught the congregation how baptism, as God's decisive intervention in the believer's daily life, shaped that life and produced daily return from sin to trusting Christ. 'In Baptism every Christian has enough to study and practice throughout life. Christians always have enough to do to believe firmly what Baptism promises and brings—victory over death and the devil, forgiveness of sin, God's grace, the entire Christ, and the Holy Spirit with his gifts. In short, the blessings of Baptism are so boundless that if our timid nature considers them, it may well doubt whether they could all be true.' 'We must...put it to use in such a way that we may draw strength and comfort from it when our sins or conscience oppress us and say: "But I am baptized! And if I have been baptized, I have the promise that I shall be saved and have eternal life, both in soul and body." '[29]

God set this resource for Christian living in place. 'Christ ordained this baptism. God and the Holy Spirit confirmed it. God gave his testimony with his voice, the Holy Spirit his with his presence. . . . If we do not listen to him, we will be in want. If we listen to him, the Father will be pleased with us and we will have his favor, his heart, and everything that he has.'[30] God's command to baptize, the very gift of life itself, placed the sacrament at the heart of his accomplishment of human salvation. This command prevented abuse of baptism as a magical ritual, for it could only be practiced for his purposes according to his command.[31]

God not only commanded and instituted baptism. He acts through it. Baptism is only a handful of water, he observed, and therefore is the object of contempt. All the acts of medieval monastic piety had been preferred to it. But God had placed the promise of salvation in baptism.[32] Luther's sermons drew the parallel between God's creative action in baptism and his creation of the universe through his Word.[33] This re-creative power permeates the water, like fire's heat permeating an iron rod or sugar and spices transforming water into relief for the ill.[34] 'Baptism is not a human work, but it is God's work. . . . The divine majesty ordained it. It is his command, commandment, and word', and thus a powerful weapon against

[28] e.g., in 1528, when he also wrote *On Rebaptism, to Two Pastors*, WA 26: 144–74.

[29] *Large Catechism*, Baptism, 41–4, *BSLK*, 699–700, *BC*, 461–2.

[30] WA 46: 185.12–29, cf. 194.15–195.9, 194.22–196.31; and 37: 270–3.

[31] WA 47: 648.12–649.3, 648.31–650.24; 37: 638.1–10.

[32] WA 46: 179.6–8; the entire thought is developed, pp. 179–83.

[33] WA 37: 278.15–22.   [34] WA 37: 642.22–34.

Satan.[35] Pastors or midwives[36] serve as God's agents when baptizing: 'the priest who baptizes is an instrument which carries out the baptism. He lends God his hands and tongue, but the words are God's, not the person's. "I baptize you" is not said by the one who is performing the baptism but by the Trinity. The Trinity is baptizing through this tool.'[37]

Luther defined baptism with increasing emphasis on its delivery of new life, new birth, as God's re-creative act, commanded by God, bearing his promise of forgiveness and new life. In 1539 he wrote, 'Baptism is the water of regeneration through the Holy Spirit in this life for life eternal.'[38] Yet God reveals his will and delivers new life with the method of the theology of the cross—under the appearance of opposites. 'The word may not look like much, and the water either, but let nothing else sway you, but rather look to him who is giving the command,'[39] namely God, Luther proclaimed in 1538. The validity of this promise does not depend on human faith. God means what he says and is faithful to his pledge. In a 1528 sermon Luther argued, 'Choose whether you wish to risk being saved on the basis of God's Word and institution or on your faith! I say, "certainly I believe today, but I do not know what tomorrow will bring." God's truth is more certain than my heart, and his Word is more certain than my faith.'[40] Children, he believed, become the faithful children of God through God's action, but he did not treat the faith of children at this point. Soon thereafter he defended the concept of infant faith, in his *Large Catechism*. Comfort nonetheless must rest upon God's action, not human reaction. To argue that I did not have faith when I was baptized, and therefore must be rebaptized, is to hand myself into Satan's hand, Luther avowed, for Satan will always make my heart uncertain about whether I did and do believe properly. 'Faith does not establish baptism nor enhance it, and unbelief does not diminish or reduce it. God's Word establishes it. It is the factor that makes baptism work,' Luther affirmed in 1538.[41] Therefore, although baptized infants must later enter into the conversation God has initiated in

---

[35] WA 27: 33.3–14. Cf. WA 36: 102.21–103.23, 117.18–22 and 30–4. Cf. the treatment of Matthew 3 in the fifth sermon of 1534, WA 37: 289.4–293.14, 264.34–265.5; see also the sermon of 1535, WA 47: 646–51 on the confirmation and assurance connected to the sacrament of baptism by the baptism of Jesus. Cf. Trigg, *Baptism*, 32–7.

[36] Because God's Word was acting in baptism, Luther permitted lay people, particularly midwives, to baptize in emergencies, WA 47: 649.3–4.

[37] WA 46: 148.36–149.27. Luther repeated the point in 1539, WA 47: 648.2–3, 23–5. Therefore, the Donatist denial of the validity of the sacrament, if the priest was unworthy, had to be rejected, WA 46: 151.15–154.34. Cf. a similar discussion in 1534, WA 37: 278.27–280.5.

[38] WA 47: 653.21–22.

[39] WA 46: 168.5–6. Cf. WA 37: 258.12–1, and Trigg, *Baptism*, 67–75.

[40] WA 27: 44.29–45.11. Cf. the sermons of 1538, WA 46: 152.37–154.34, on faith, WA 46: 152–5.

[41] WA 46: 155.30–2.

their baptism, when psychologically appropriate, and trust him, believers take comfort in the fact that God acts in baptism. Because God is the one at work, his people retain the promise; even if they lose its use for a while, they will return to it.[42] Jonathan Trigg concludes that Luther's understanding of justification is 'intimately related to—indeed even predicated upon—Luther's understanding of the abiding covenant of Baptism'.[43]

Because baptism is God's work, and because infants born as sinners need God's grace, Luther had no qualms about practicing and defending infant baptism. With his baptismal Word God takes charge of human life. Just as it remains valid for those who are sleeping, and as God's Word aroused John the Baptist in his mother's womb (Luke 1: 44), God's promise in baptism does its work also on infants.[44] God establishes the relationship between himself and his children, apart from their conscious faith, even though at the proper time, as children grow in consciousness, that faith is a necessary consequence and completion of what God began, by promising to be Father to his people in baptism. Here, as throughout his preaching and teaching, Luther emphasized the psychological aspects of faith as conscious trust in God but always subordinated the human side of the relationship to God's initiative and power.[45]

After 1528 Luther increasingly used the motif of new creation, or dying and rising, from Romans 6: 3–11, Colossians 2: 11–15, and Titus 3: 3–8, as a description of the reality accomplished by God's baptismal word. 'This flow of water, as God ordained, holds a mirror before our eyes' but is in fact 'the power and might which washes sins away and creates a new birth, draws us from the old [way of living] which we have from our parents and gives us a new birth into eternal life, adorning us with innocence and life.'[46] It is a 'bath which makes us young again [*Jungelbad*], purges us from sin and plants us into eternal life. Sin is washed away, as is God's wrath—these are the works of God.'[47] Baptism brings these newborn believers 'out of sin into righteousness, out of guilt and condemnation to innocence and grace, out of death into eternal life'.[48] Luther also spoke of Christ's blood as chrism, noting that the fathers had said that all the sacraments—'baptism, chalice, absolution'—flow from Christ's blood and that this bath was instituted for us as an ablution when we are born again and renewed (Titus 3: 5) as 'from another mother'. For being washed in Christ's blood means 'the presence

---

[42] WA 46: 173.13–15. P. Althaus, *The Theology of Martin Luther*, tr. R. Shultz, Philadelphia, Fortress, 1966, 348–74.

[43] Trigg, *Baptism*, 2. [44] WA 27: 49.12–50.3.

[45] BSLK, 700–7, BC, 462–7; Trigg, *Baptism*, 99–107; Peters, *Kommentar*, 4: 114–17.

[46] WA 46: 174.17–22; Trigg, *Baptism*, 92–9; Grönvik, *Taufe*, 208–29.

[47] WA 46: 175.1–2; Luther had already used the term '*Ju[e]ngel Bad*' in 1534, WA 37: 645.15.

[48] WA 37: 645.17–18; cf. 46: 175.14–18, 175.31–7.

of the mortification of sin and death as well as the gift of righteousness and life'. All this is effected by the Trinity, as was confirmed at Christ's own baptism.[49]

Baptism frees believers from death. The poison which kills believers first afflicted Adam, but healing has come through the Son of God, who was promised to Adam. Christ promises resurrection to the baptized.[50] God liberates and extracts his people 'from the old generation, from their corrupt and diabolical skin, and transplants them into original innocence'. They are 'freed from the old filth and received into grace, so that God's wrath, sin, death, and eternal damnation may be destroyed. These are works of God, not human works.'[51] The connection between baptism and the forgiveness of sins became a particularly important motif in the last of the reformer's baptismal homilies (1539). There he included the forgiveness as the goal of bringing water and Word together. Baptism creates a child of God, freed from the power of the devil, sin, death, and the law, from God's wrath and judgment, through the forgiveness of sins. It therefore forms the basis for a life of new obedience in trust, for the daily repentance that produces good works that meet God's design and expectations for human life.[52]

What God has done in baptism provokes the opposition and attacks of Satan. Luther observed in his 1523 liturgy for baptism that baptizing a child makes a lasting enemy for that baby.[53] 'The devil does not stay asleep but is always getting up to make people forget the fruits of their baptisms.' That is why Paul warned against such deceit that 'seduces us away from Christ our head, whose members we are' (Col. 2: 8).

Luther's Ockhamist instructors had spoken of God's pledge to sinners with the term 'covenant', interpreting it to mean that human performance upholding the human side of the covenant played a role in salvation. So Luther largely avoided the term. An exception was his treatment of baptism. This sacrament demonstrates that covenants are made at the initiative of their makers and are dependent upon them. Luther reaffirmed the objective nature of God's performative promise through it: 'No one can say [of baptism], "I did this myself." This covenant proceeds from God without our input.'[54] Corresponding to God's covenant with the Jews through circumcision, his baptismal covenant between himself and the faithful promises that he will be their God and that he takes the infant who was circumcised or who is baptized into his people as his own child. 'Baptism is an eternal covenant which does not lapse when we fall; it raises us up again. If we fall out of the ship, God helps us on board once again. When Christians fall, they always remain in their baptisms, and God

---

[49] WA 46: 176.1–12, 36–7.   [50] WA 46: 145.10–16, 28–32.   [51] WA 46: 175.25–9.

[52] Trigg, *Baptism*, 151–73.

[53] In his 1523 order for baptism, WA 12: 47.11–20, LW 53: 102.   [54] WA 27: 33.27–9.

binds himself to them so that he will help them when the baptized call upon him.' No satisfaction merits baptism before or after the sacrament is administered. There is only the lamb of God. He has the power to initiate life and to bring sinners into death.[55]

Abuse of baptism by baptized people who persist in sin does not render baptism invalid: officeholders' abuse of office does not abolish the calling of their posts, nor does marriage with the intention of simply stealing the dowry render the marriage invalid.[56] Luther did not try to solve the mystery of why the baptized continue to sin. Instead, he preached law, calling such people to repentance so that they could again receive the gospel assurance baptism gives. He distinguished the issue of the validity of God's baptismal promise simply because it is his Word from the mystery of the baptized's ability to live apart from the new life promised in baptism, or from the necessity of baptized people trusting God and growing in faith. Enjoying baptism's benefits does depend on trusting the promise since baptism's word is part of God's conversation with his chosen people, and he intends for them to respond with trust. Luther closely connected God's action in baptism and the faith relationship with God that it generates.

Baptism was not only a sign of God's grace, however; it was also to serve as a *signum* among Christians as well, according to the reformer. Not only love (John 13: 35) but also the sacrament provide a means for Christians to identify one another as it binds them together.[57] For new birth as God's child places the believer into God's human family. That family is sustained by hearing the Word in oral form, reading it in written form, and feasting together at the Father's supper.

GOD'S SACRAMENTAL WORD IN THE LORD'S SUPPER

As the focal point of medieval religiosity the Lord's Supper commanded Luther's attention in his initial efforts to cultivate the faith of the populace. He developed his criticism of popular sacramental piety and related scholastic teaching along three lines. He rejected the use of Aristotle's theory of substance in explaining Christ's presence in the sacrament as 'transubstantiation'; the distribution of the sacrament in only one 'kind', Christ's body—the withholding of Christ's blood from lay people; and the understanding of the sacrament as a re-sacrifice of Christ, an offering of his body and blood by the priest for the congregation as a propitiatory

---

[55] *WA* 46: 172.29–35, 12–17; cf. *WA* 46: 195–9; 36: 107.11–14, 22–30; Trigg, *Baptism*, 39–47.
[56] *WA* 27: 34.28–38.22.   [57] *WA* 27: 57.30–58.1.

oblation. The lines between Luther and his Roman opponents on these issues were set by 1520.[58]

Luther's *Sermon on the Blessed Sacrament of the Holy, True Body of Christ* (December 1519) simply presumes much of medieval teaching regarding the Lord's Supper. It emphasizes the sacrament's creation of the communion of Christ's people with one another and with Christ, topics seldom highlighted in medieval writing. He defined it in terms of the significance of its signs, which demonstrate that all saints share what Christ gives, as all citizens share in their town's possessions. The community brings comfort to the conscience burdened with sin, terrified by death, through participation in the sacrament. However, participation in the sacrament obligates all members to share Christ's dishonor and the misery of fellow-believers.[59] This sacrament pledges, grants, and bestows all of Christ's possessions, for his people's comfort and strengthening. Luther's expression of what the Lord's Supper actually gives is still relatively weak in 1518: it serves as a 'ford, bridge, door, ship, or stretcher, by and in which we pass from this world into eternal life', through faith,[60] but not yet as the Word which gives life and salvation.

Six months later, a transition was taking place in his view of the sacrament as a form of God's Word. His *Sermon on the New Testament* more clearly exhibited Luther's conviction that God's Word in sacramental form accomplishes what it promises. He emphasized faith and the assurance the Word offers but also clearly delineated the Supper as Christ's testament, with the power to effect its promise. It confers forgiveness and life. Christ is the testator, Christians the heirs. Christ's words 'given for you, shed for you' are the testament. The bread and wine, 'under which are his true body and blood,' are the seal or token of the testament, which actually bestows remission of sins and eternal life. The sacraments are dead, nothing at all, apart from God's words and promises, which faith receives in this special form of conversation with God.[61] The sermon criticized several practices of medieval eucharistic piety and the magical view of the sacrament that, Luther believed, regarded faith as unnecessary because the sacrament worked as an *opus operatum*. Luther attacked treatment of the mass as a ritual good work of human devising. It is a not a 'benefit accepted [by God] but one given', for 'we give nothing to Christ but only receive from him'. It is no sacrifice but a testament, a weapon against Satan, the world, and

---

[58] See pp. 68–71, 82–6; H. Sasse, *This is My Body*, Minneapolis, Augsburg, 1959, 13–77; Lohse, *Theology*, 127–36.

[59] *WA* 2: 742.5–747.3, *LW* 35: 49–56.

[60] *WA* 2: 749.23–753.38, *LW* 35: 60–7; Sasse, *This is My Body*, 78–115.

[61] *WA* 6: 357.10–364.13, *LW* 35: 84–93; see Peters, *Kommentar*, 4: 129–89.

sinful, fleshly desires.[62] Luther objected to refusing the laity Christ's blood and the commercialization of the sacrament, including masses for the dead, since these destroyed the comfort Christ gives in his body and blood, the forgiveness of sins and God's grace.[63] Luther was not the only reformer who objected to medieval views of the Lord's Supper and related practices. His senior colleague Andreas von Karlstadt caught Luther's enthusiasm for reform. He did not, however, understand the world in the Ockhamist terms that permitted Luther to believe that God could construct his plan of salvation according to his own wishes, without limitations from a Platonic view of reality that barred 'the spiritual' from intimate relationship with the material, created order. Karlstadt adopted much of the medieval model of reform that took anti-sacramental, anti-clerical positions.

Similarly, during 1524 the Zurich pastor Ulrich Zwingli turned from ardent excitement over Luther's prophetic call for reform[64] to criticism of Luther's view of Christ's bodily presence in the Supper. In March 1525 Zwingli published his letter to Matthäus Alber, pastor in Reutlingen, calling him to convert to a spiritualizing view of Christ's presence in the Supper, opening a sharp controversy between himself and Luther. Luther responded first by letter,[65] then in prefaces to two editions of the Swabian reformer Johann Brenz's *Syngramma* (January/September 1526).[66] Brenz, pastor in Schwäbisch Hall, highly respected by pastors throughout southwest Germany and Switzerland, opposed Zwingli's spiritualizing view of the sacrament, especially as represented by Johannes Oecolampadius, reformer in Basel, a Luther enthusiast at that time.[67] Oecolampadius had absorbed Erasmus's approach to piety while assisting him in preparing his Greek New Testament. Zwingli's humanistic training at Vienna and Basel had reinforced his 'Realist' conviction that 'the finite cannot convey the infinite'.[68] Therefore, he concluded that the bread and wine of the sacrament can only represent, not convey, Christ's body and blood. Zwingli borrowed arguments from the contemporary work of the Dutch humanist Cornelius

---

[62] WA 2: 751.18–752.24, LW 35: 63–5; WA 6: 364.14–373.8, LW 35: 93–106. Luther repeated this critique often, cf. *The Misuse of the Mass*, 1521, WA 8: 506–37, LW 36: 162–98, and *The Adoration of the Sacrament*, 1523, WA 11: 431–56, LW 36: 275–305.

[63] WA 6: 373.9–377.18, LW 35: 106–10.   [64] See p. 38 above.

[65] 4 January 1526, WA 19: 118–25; on their dispute, see W. Köhler, *Zwingli und Luther*, 2 vols., Leipzig, Heinsius, 1924, Gütersloh, Bertelsmann, 1953, vol. 1; Sasse, *This is My Body*, 116–86.

[66] WA 19: 457–61, 529–30.

[67] M. Brecht, *Die frühe Theologie des Johannes Brenz*, Tübingen, Mohr/Siebeck, 1966, 64–111; Köhler, *Zwingli und Luther*, 1: 206–8, 283–326.

[68] D. Bolliger, *Infiniti contemplatio: Grundzüge der Scotus- und Scotismusrezeption im Werk Huldrych Zwinglis*, Leiden: Brill, 2003.

Hoen, contending that Christ's saying 'This is my body' meant 'this bread represents my body', that the Supper is only a visible reminder of Christ's passion that calls for a 'spiritual' eating and drinking of Christ.[69] Toward the end of his life Zwingli spoke of Christ's 'spiritual presence' in the sacrament but still maintained an insurmountable cleft between material creation and the spiritual that did not permit the sacraments to be seen as conveying God's presence and power to those who received them.

Luther's public treatment of the contrary position on the Lord's Supper began by responding to utterances sympathetic to Karlstadt from two leading reformers and supporters of Luther in Strasbourg, Martin Bucer and Wolfgang Capito. Luther rejected several of Karlstadt's positions in his two-part work, *Against the Heavenly Prophets on Images and Sacraments* (December 1524, January 1525).[70] After an eighteen-month pause, *The Sacrament of Christ's Body and Blood, Against the Ravers*[71] appeared, probably edited by another member of the Wittenberg team from sermons Luther had preached late in March 1526, adding a term Luther devised for his sacramentarian critics, *Schwärmer*, to its title. *Schwärmer* or 'ravers' referred to what he regarded as speaking without scriptural basis, using human reason or sentiment.[72]

Zwingli and Luther were both skilled at public disputation, and their treatises reflected the sharp exchange of such disputations. Both believed that the heart of the faith was at stake in their differences. Zwingli feared Luther taught an 'automatic, magical' understanding of how the Supper works that kept believers trapped in the superstitions of medieval piety; Luther feared Zwingli's denial of God's use of selected elements of his created order to accomplish his salvation of sinners since it deprives believers of the assurance given by God's promise in human language, delivered also in sacramental form. Zwingli replied in a series of works,[73] against which Luther wrote *That These Words of Christ, 'This Is My Body,' etc. Still stand Firm Against the Ravers* (1527)[74] and *Confession Concerning Christ's Supper* (1528), his 'last word on the subject'.[75]

This exchange with Zwingli and Oecolampadius sharpened his view and deepened his conviction regarding Christ's presence in the sacrament. In *The Sacrament of Christ's Body* Luther stated that believers must above all

---

[69] Köhler, *Zwingli und Luther*, 61–75.   [70] *WA* 18: 62–125, 134–214, *LW* 40: 79–223.

[71] *WA* 19: 482–523, *LW* 36: 335–61.   [72] *Deutsches Wörterbuch*, 9: 2290–1.

[73] Köhler, *Zwingli und Luther*, 1: 619–729; cf. Zwingli's *Amica Exegesis*, 1527, CR 92: 548–758; *Klare Unterricht*, 1526, CR91: 773–862; *Das diese Worte*, 1527, CR92: 795–977.

[74] *WA* 23: 46–283, *LW* 37: 13–150.

[75] *WA* 26: 261–509, *LW* 37: 162, 161–372. Edwards, *Brethren*, 82–111; Althaus, *Theology*, 375–403; Lohse, *Theology*, 169–77.

know what Christ accomplishes through his presence in the Supper, for Satan was using the Ravers to 'bore a hole in the nut and empty it of its flesh', that is, was obliterating God's action accomplished through the Word of forgiveness and the presence of Christ's body and blood. The Supper is no human work but God's gift of life through the proclamation and memory of Christ's death for the forgiveness of sins 'for you'. Luther loved the personal application of the gospel in the distribution of the sacrament: in distribution 'I designate it for the individual receiving it, giving that person Christ's body and blood for the forgiveness of sins.' Believers come to the Supper 'because I am in sin, captive to death and the devil, because I feel weak in faith and in love, wayward, impatient, envious, with sin clinging to me foreward and backward; therefore I come where I find and hear Christ's word that I shall receive the gift of forgiveness of sins'.[76] Such reception demands understanding that comes from previous instruction, he maintained; God here speaks and gives to the trust that receives. Apart from faith the Supper's benefits cannot be apprehended.[77] The sacrament produces the fruits of trust in Christ's atoning work and in love for the neighbor, following his example. It produces Christian communion among God's people.[78] Like other forms of God's Word, it integrates God's gifts and human responses.

What the Supper accomplishes depends on understanding that Christ's body and blood are present and bestow upon believers the benefits of his death and resurrection, Luther argued. He did not presume that human reason could grasp this; his theology of the cross echoed in his reminder that God's wisdom is foolishness to sinners (1 Cor. 1: 21–3). Against Zwingli's argument that it is unfitting and unnecessary for Christ to offer his body and blood in bread and wine, Luther contended that Christ's words indicate such is the case, and God determines what and how he accomplishes salvation. Human reason does not.[79] The incarnation itself offends reason, as do other articles of faith that Scripture reveals. Christ's true presence in the sacrament is no more impossible to believe than they. He pointed out that his opponents had differing objections to his interpretation of Christ's words instituting the Supper: Zwingli said 'is' means 'represents'; Karlstadt maintained that 'this' does not refer to the bread; Oecolampadius that these words should be interpreted as 'a figure of my body'. Luther preferred the simple literal sense.[80]

[76] *WA* 19: 499–512, *LW* 36: 346–52.
[77] *WA* 19: 482.15–483.19, 506.16–25, *LW* 36: 335, 349.
[78] *WA* 19: 511.11–512.28, *LW* 36: 352–4.   [79] *WA* 23: 264.3–268.18, *LW* 37: 137–41.
[80] *WA* 19: 484.13–499.38, *LW* 36: 336–46; *WA* 26: 263.19–292.23, *LW* 37: 164–90.

His later replies to Zwingli reinforced this argument on the basis of unstated presuppositions Luther had learned from his Ockhamist instructors: God, bound by no rules, could arrange his world in any way he decided, according to his almighty power; God, as Creator of the material world, places at his own disposal all of creation. 'What God says, he can do' (Rom. 4: 21); 'with God no word [*sic*] is impossible' (Luke 1: 37).[81] He had indeed chosen selected elements of that world to serve as instruments of his saving power.[82] Certainly, God uses language figuratively and metaphorically, but not arbitrarily, Luther asserted, and found Christ's language in the words of institution of the sacrament straightforward, clear. The only grounds for not accepting these words literally were based on human reason and the principles it constructed. Belief in God's almighty power demanded recognizing that God could work in this way. Doubting Christ's words is the devil's effort to undermine all Scripture.[83]

In defending his literal interpretation of the words of institution Luther dealt extensively with the grammatical and syntactical questions raised by each alternative explanation to his own.[84] Against the argument raised by Karlstadt and Zwingli that John 6: 63, 'The flesh is of no avail', means that Christ's body in the sacrament is of no avail, Luther countered that the flesh as reliance on created objects and Christ's flesh in his body are two very different things. Spiritual eating and drinking, of which Christ speaks in John 6, Luther believed, refers not to the absence of anything created but to the presence of the Holy Spirit, who cultivates faith in God through words that proclaim Christ in metaphorical form as well as those that accompany the true presence of his body and blood in the sacramental form of the Word.[85] That Christ became incarnate certainly avails much, for through his becoming human he saved his people, so it is clear that in John 6 he is not referring to the body he gives in the Supper. However, Luther averred, Christ's flesh in the sacrament is poison and death if partaken apart from faith and God's Word.[86] God designed the sacrament to be part of his conversation with his people.

Luther's defense included evidence from the Fathers, especially Augustine, Tertullian, Irenaeus, Hilary, and Cyprian, to demonstrate that, rightly read, in their context, they supported the true presence of Christ's body

---

[81] WA 23: 117.27, 120.26–121.21, LW 37: 47, 49.   [82] WA 23: 260.5–36, LW 37: 135–6.
[83] WA 23: 65.1–70.16, LW 37: 13–17.
[84] WA 18: 144.16–163.22, LW 40: 154–73; WA 23: 89.32–114.13, LW 37: 30–45; WA 26: 298.32–313.32, 383.14–498.13, LW 37: 195–202, 254–360. A. Buchholz, *Schrift Gottes in Lehrstreit. Luthers Schriftverständnis und Schriftauslegung in seinen drei großen Lehrstreitigkeiten der Jahre 1521–28*, Fraukfurt am Main, Lang, 1993, 139–249.
[85] WA 18: 192.1–195.22, LW 40: 202–5; WA 23: 167.27–204.31, LW 37: 78–101; WA 26: 353.18–377.31, LW 37: 237–51.
[86] WA 26: 353.27–354.8, LW 37: 238.

and blood in the bread and wine, against Oecolampadius's contrary contention.[87] But his chief foundation for his position remained the biblical text, supported by his exegesis of passages relating to the Lord's Supper.[88] Luther also combined exegetical critique with a doctrinal assessment of the metaphysical framework for his opponents' views. His *Confession* set down four presuppositions for his relying on the literal meaning of the words of institution. In addition to the reliability of God's Word, he argued that Christ is 'essential, natural, true, complete God and human creature in one person, individual and inseparable', that the right hand of God, as the locus of God's power, is everywhere; and that God is present in several modes.[89]

Against the contention that Christ's human body cannot be in more than one place at a time and that his ascension into heaven, to sit at the Father's right hand, restricted him to heaven, Luther mounted two arguments. He showed that 'right hand' referred in Scripture not to a place but to God's power.[90] He used the ancient teaching of the communication of attributes to explain how Christ's human nature, his body and blood included, share the divine characteristic of being able to be present wherever God wills in whatever form God wills.[91] He buttressed this line of reasoning with careful discussions of God's omnipotence and his presence.[92] Presence can be described locally, in a circumscribed manner, with the space and object occupying it corresponding exactly. It can also be described 'definitively', that is, with the object not palpably graspable, for example the presence of angels, or Christ's presence when he came through the door on Easter night (Matt. 28: 2). There is also a repletitive presence, by which God is truly present everywhere. Christ's sacramental presence is a fourth kind of presence, a mystery, into which human reason cannot pierce.[93] Finally, Luther averred, all talk of Christ's presence in the sacrament must serve to assure the faithful that God works through the sacrament to give them eternal life, for 'the forgiveness of sins, consolation of souls, and strengthening of faith'.[94]

Landgrave Philip of Hesse was striving to defend the position of the reforming princes and cities of the Empire; he wanted Luther and Zwingli and their adherents to reconcile. Probably at the suggestion of Martin Bucer, he invited them to his castle in Marburg for conversation. A delegation from Zurich, Basel, and Strasbourg met with Luther, Melanchthon,

---

[87] WA 23: 209.28–243.23, LW 37: 104–24. [88] WA 26: 445.19–498.31, LW 37: 303–60.
[89] WA 26: 326.29–327.32, LW 37: 214–15. [90] WA 23: 131.7–145.32, LW 37: 55–64.
[91] See pp. 114–17 above. [92] WA 23: 133.19–155.31, LW 37: 57–71.
[93] WA 26: 326.29–349.28, LW 37: 214–32.
[94] WA 23: 155.31–158.19, LW 37: 71–3; WA 23: 207.18–28, LW 37: 102–3; WA 23: 255.30–256.11, LW 37: 132; WA 26: 293.20–298.23, LW 37: 191–4.

other Wittenberg colleagues, and adherents from Nuremberg, Schwäbisch-Hall, and Augsburg, on 1–3 October 1529. Alternating between friendly exchange and bitter recrimination, they repeated much the same arguments they had been presenting in their writings. At one point Oecolampadius asserted that Christ's human body was able only to suffer and die and thus could not be profitable. Luther responded, 'eating Christ's body is profitable because it is connected with the promise of the forgiveness of sins. Because every promise requires faith, faith is spiritual knowledge. Therefore, the bodily eating itself, taking place in faith, must become spiritual.'[95]

They came to agreement on a series of articles of faith which Luther composed, including their common rejection of distribution of the sacrament in one kind and the sacrifice of the mass. They affirmed that it is 'a sacrament of the true body and blood of Jesus Christ, that the spiritual partaking of this body and blood is especially necessary for every Christian', and that God gives the sacrament to arouse weak consciences to faith. They failed to agree on 'whether the true body and blood of Christ are bodily present in the bread and wine'.[96] Luther believed that the very foundation of God's dealing with human creatures through the communication of his Word, particularly in its sacramental form, was at stake, while Zwingli regarded the Lord's Supper as a significant but not vital part of biblical teaching. The two sides did not address their differences on this level effectively. Nonetheless, polemic between the two sides receded. Zwingli's death on the battlefield against Roman Catholic forces in October 1531 brought Heinrich Bullinger to leadership in the Zurich Reformation; he continued to represent Zwingli's position.

Some among those south Germans and Swiss who held a spiritualizing view of the Supper rejoiced in late 1530, when Luther published an *Admonition to [receive] the Sacrament*, composed at Coburg during the diet of Augsburg. It emphasized the Supper as a 'remembrance', a 'proclamation' of Christ's death, and a 'sacrifice of thanksgiving', without an explicit defence of the bodily presence of Christ in the bread and wine. An admonition to pastors, to urge their congregations to receive the sacrament, it affirmed that the Supper stimulates and strengthens faith by pointing to Christ's death 'for you' and then moves believers to love for neighbor and all good works.[97] Luther was trying to encourage sacramental piety and did not return to polemic in this treatise.

[95] WA 30.3: 133.21–7, LW 38: 46–7. On the Colloquy, see Köhler, *Zwingli und Luther*, vol. 2, and Sasse, *This is My Body*, 187–294.
[96] WA 30.3: 169.3–170.35, LW 38: 88–9.
[97] WA 30.2: 601.23–39, 609.30–610.26, 617.14–33, LW 38: 105, 116–17, 126.

Any doubts that he was compromising his earlier position disappeared with his reaction to the dismissal of a Lutheran pastor in Frankfurt am Main, Johann Cellarius, in 1532. His *Open Letter to Those in Frankfurt* attacked those who say that Christ's body and blood are truly present in the sacrament but conceal their understanding of his presence as a spiritual presence.[98]

Among the supporters of Cellarius's foes in Frankfurt was the Strasbourg pastor Martin Bucer. In 1527 Luther had denounced Bucer's attempts to parade spiritualizing views of the Supper under his and Bugenhagen's names, and to claim Melanchthon for his own position despite what Melanchthon had clearly written to the contrary.[99] Nonetheless, at Marburg in 1529 Bucer told Luther's follower Andreas Osiander of Nuremberg that he and Johannes Brenz of Schwäbisch-Hall had 'brought Bucer to the point where he admitted that Christ's body was in the Lord's Supper and was given to believers in and with the bread' though he refused to believe that unbelievers could receive it.[100] While working together with Bucer in several ecclesiastical-diplomatic efforts in the early 1530s, Melanchthon tried to find common ground with the Strasbourg reformer. In May 1536 Bucer led a delegation to Wittenberg, when Luther's sickness prevented him from traveling to meet the South Germans. Luther overcame his previous suspicions, and the Strasbourg and Saxon negotiators confessed together in the 'Wittenberg Concord' that 'with the bread and wine the body and blood of Christ are truly and essentially present, distributed, and received. . . . through the sacramental union the bread is the body of Christ.'[101]

'Sacramental union' of bread and body, wine and blood, was Luther's way of confessing the reality of the presence of Christ's body and blood in the Supper without defining the mode of presence in terms of Aristotelian or any other physics. Another key element in Luther's securing of his understanding of Christ's presence was his affirmation that the faith of the recipient (or lack of it) does not determine the presence but rather God's creative Word in Christ's words of institution does. He distinguished the benefits of Christ's death and resurrection, which faith receives from the sacramental form of God's Word, from the presence of his body and blood. Also unbelievers receive the body and blood through the miracle that God effects in his Supper. Luther wished to prevent a kind of subjectivity that would create doubt about their reception of the promise for those who

---

[98] *WA* 30.3: 558–71; J. Vieker (tr.), 'An Open Letter to Those in Frankfurt on the Main, 1533. By Martin Luther', *Concordia Journal* 16 (1990), 334–47.

[99] *WA* 23: 279.1–283.23, *LW* 37: 147–50.   [100] *WA* 30.3: 150.28–36, *LW* 38: 71.

[101] *CR* 3: 75–81; Edwards, *Brethren*, 127–55.

believed their faith was weak. He could do so in this way because he believed that Christ's Word created reality. Bucer could not accept that wording, so the Concord confessed that the 'power of the sacrament' does not rest upon the worthiness or unworthiness of the minister who distributes it nor of the recipient (1 Cor. 11: 27–32) as Christians celebrate the sacrament together, implying for Bucer that people of faith can become unworthy of the Supper through their behavior.[102]

That Luther held to his view is clear from the text he prepared in the *Smalcald Articles* seven months later. There he stated simply, 'The bread and wine in the Supper are the true body and blood of Christ and they are not only offered to and received by upright Christians but also by evil ones.'[103] Despite reservations on both sides the Swiss and Luther expressed hopes for accord in 1538.[104] But in 1544 an attack by the spiritualist lay theologian Caspar von Schwenkfeld, and rumors that a former Wittenberg student, the Hungarian Matthias Birò Dévay, had accepted Zwinglian views of the sacrament, provoked Luther to prepare his *Brief Confession on the Holy Sacrament*. It expressed his horror at Zwingli's claim that unbelievers who were noble people might be saved.[105] Luther rejected Zwingli's reaffirmation of his former sacramental doctrine, which, according to Luther's recollection Zwingli was abandoning in Marburg.[106] Luther stated his resentment at Zwinglians' labeling his followers 'cannibals' and 'blood-drinkers'. He reiterated that his opponents could not agree with each other in interpreting the words of institution, then recalled parts of their exchange in Marburg, but did not elaborate on his own position, apparently presuming that readers knew well what he taught.[107]

Luther's understanding of 'the means of grace' as God's active instrument for accomplishing his saving will formed an integral part of his teaching on God's justification of sinners. God's Word of life in Christ, delivered through oral, written, and sacramental forms of his Word, completed God's intervention against sin and evil. What the Father had planned from eternity, for which the Son had laid foundations in his incarnation, death, and resurrection, came to fruition in the Holy Spirit's new creation of trusting children of God through these forms of the Word and in his

---

[102] CR 3: 75–81.   [103] *Smalcald Articles* III.vi, *BSLK*, 450–1; *BC*, 320–1.

[104] Heinrich Bullinger to Luther, March 1538, *WABr* 8: 207–8, #3222; Luther to Albrecht of Preussia, a report on progress, especially with those at Basel, Strasbourg, Augsburg, and Bern, *WABr* 8: 215, #3225.

[105] *Fidei expositio*, written in 1531, published in 1536 posthumously, CR 93: 131–2.

[106] WA 54: 142.27–144.15, *LW* 38: 289–91; cf. Zwingli's position, CR 93: 75–108. Edwards, *Brethren*, 180–96.

[107] WA 54: 144.16–145.15, *LW* 38: 291–9.

renewal of God's life-bestowing promise in the rhythm of daily repentance. With his law and gospel God encounters his people, trapped in the mystery of continuing sin and evil in their lives. As the Holy Spirit creates faith, he not only calls, enlightens, and bestows holiness or righteousness upon God's chosen children.[108] He also gathers them, for mutual support and consolation, into his church.

---

[108] *Small Catechism*, Creed, *BSLK*, 511–12; *BC*, 355–6.

9

Lambs Listening to their Shepherd: Christ's Church and its Struggles

Some suggest that Luther had little concern for the doctrine of the church and the institutional, organizational forms of ecclesiastical life. His teaching on the church does take a different shape from that of medieval theologians; it reflects a different foundation and other concerns. These concerns engaged him as soon as tensions with church authorities emerged. Aspects of the doctrine of the church and church life continued to command his attention throughout his career.

Protracted, passionate debates in the fifteenth century regarding the respective roles of pope and council in church governance left papal defenders in control and placed the doctrine of papal authority at the center of the church's doctrinal enterprise. Luther thrust it from that position, placing every believer's relationship with God at that center. His understanding that trusting Christ constitutes human righteousness before God replaced confidence in the pope's guarantee of sacraments and salvation as the driving force for teaching the faith. Nonetheless, Luther was concerned about authority. On the level of the universal church, he challenged any ultimate authority apart from God's Word in Scripture. On the level of individual use of God's Word, he challenged the concept of divinely ordained power vested in the office of priest, understood as a special office with special powers bestowed through ordination. As issues around him changed, Luther modified the accents of his teaching on the church, but his insistence on both the 'priestly' status and responsibilities of all baptized believers and the key role played in God's economy by the pastoral office remained, even though the former received more attention earlier, the latter later in his career.

The church catholic and its form of government won his attention before 1525; thereafter these topics shared his consideration with the 'community of saints' in the local congregation. Both the larger institution and the local parish, however, provided the actual setting for his experiments with formulating the topic 'church'. He could occasionally use the terms 'visible' and 'invisible' with 'church' but always dealt with the church in its concrete forms. Carl-Axel Aurelius observes that Luther recognized the church as the vessel or instrument of God's gracious dealing with believers. However, he concentrated his attention on the church as the embodiment of that action, its incomplete and hidden product, as God's kingdom or rule that grows and struggles on this earth, as perceptible to faith and experienced by God's people.[1]

Luther's concept of the 'invisible church' served the purpose of comforting those who were unsure of their membership in Christ's body, either because of condemnation by the official church or because of their own sinfulness. The gospel assures believers that no matter what their external associations or entailments, God has chosen them. Nonetheless, the church always takes meaningful form in the concrete, perceptible community.[2] Because God's Word was the instrument whereby the Holy Spirit created and sustained both congregation and church universal, Luther rather defined the church as audible and tangible, but above all, he used 'church' to refer to the faithful people of God. They are hidden, in that sense 'invisible', under the crosses of suffering and persecution, often at odds with ecclesiastical powers.[3] The faithful continue to struggle against their own sinfulness; within the church the unfaithful remain in contact with the Word that can convert them. Luther did not attempt to explain why unfaithful 'tares' find places among those gathered around Word and sacrament. Within the mystery of continuing sin and evil the church cannot be other than a mixed assembly of wheat and tares.[4]

WHAT THE CHURCH IS

In October 1525, five months after Elector Frederick's death brought his brother John to the throne, Luther launched an initiative to tend to institutional aspects of church life in a serious way. Luther's relationship to Frederick had been indirect, Frederick's support for Luther's reform firm but muted. His relationship to John was personal, cordial, collaborative. John turned to him for advice on practical organizational problems; Luther urged, among other measures, a visitation of parishes modeled after medieval episcopal inspections of local churches and priests. Planning stretched over more than a year. Initial visits were poorly organized

---

[1] C.-A. Aurelius, *Verborgene Kirche. Luthers Kirchenverständnis aufgrund seiner Streitschriften und Exegese 1519–1521*, Hanover, Lutherisches Verlagshaus, 1983, 119–21; P. Althaus, *The Theology of Martin Luther*, tr. R. Shulz, Philadelphia, Fortress, 1966, 287–313.

[2] J. Headley, *Luther's View of Church History*, New Haven, Yale University Press, 1963, 29–41.

[3] *Bound Choice*, 1525, WA 18: 652.23–653.12, LW 33: 39; Genesis Lectures, 1542, WA 44: 110.3–111.14, LW 6: 147–9; S. Hendrix, *Ecclesia in Via*, Leiden, Brill, 1974, 162–4.

[4] WA 43: 36.18–31, LW 3: 225; WA 44: 23.18–28, LW 6: 32; Aurelius, *Kirchenverständnis*, 96–102.

and executed. Finally, Melanchthon composed an 'instruction for visitors', probably with Luther's input and with his preface.

Published in January 1528, this *Instruction* aided electoral visitors in evaluating parishes; it offered a digest of what the Wittenberg colleagues viewed as essential for congregational life. After summarizing the teaching expected to inform the faith of believers, focusing on repentance and the forgiveness of sins, a brief catechism—a functional synopsis of the Creed, instructions on how to teach the ten commandments and prayer—followed. 'Prayer' presented the good works that proceed from praying. Luther's own experience dictated that a treatment of 'tribulation' or *Anfechtung* follow. Then instruction was given on baptism and the Lord's Supper, penance and confession, liturgical festivals and daily worship schedules, marriage, free will, Christian freedom, the authority of secular government, and schools, with some detail on curriculum.[5] Luther and Melanchthon planned practical measures for reforming parishes on the cusp of becoming 'Lutheran'.

They did so on the basis of a definite understanding of what constitutes Christ's church on earth, a view that departed sharply from most medieval views. Luther's *Smalcald Articles* defined the church succinctly: 'holy believers and "the little sheep who hear the voice of their shepherd" (John 10: 3)'.[6] His *Large Catechism* confessed the church as 'a holy little flock and community of pure saints under one head, Christ. It is called together by the Holy Spirit in one faith, mind, and understanding' with a variety of gifts, yet united in love without division. 'Of this community I am also a part and member, participant and co-partner in all the blessings it possesses.' The Holy Spirit incorporates sinners into this holy community through God's Word and preserves it through the Word until the Last Day. He causes it to grow and produce the fruits of faith.[7] The church does not consist simply of God's Word in oral, written, and sacramental forms, but this Word does create the assembly of the faithful, an idea present in Luther's earliest lectures.[8] God's Word also governs church life. In 1521 Luther stated succinctly, 'a real Christian knows that the church never ordains or institutes anything apart from God's Word' (John 10: 5, 27).[9]

This focus on God's Word as the creative agent which brings the church into being and sustains it revealed itself often in Luther's writings, from 1518 on,[10] most explicitly in 1539, when, as part of exchanges aiming toward the papal council, Luther wrote *On the Councils and the Church.*

[5] *WA* 26: 195–240, *LW* 40: 269–320.
[6] *BSLK*, 459; *BC*, 324–5; B. Lohse, *Martin Luther's Theology*, tr. R. Harrisville, Minneapolis, Fortress, 1999, 277–83.
[7] *BSLK*, 657–8; *BC*, 437–8.　　　　[8] Hendrix, *Ecclesia*, 155–215.
[9] *The Misuse of the Mass*, *WA* 8: 491.28–492.11, *LW* 36: 144–5.
[10] Aurelius, *Kirchenverständnis*, 47–51.

Luther took a medieval concept of 'signs' or 'marks' of the church to designate the essential characteristics of what takes place in the assembly of believers. His lists always included the Word in preached and sacramental form.[11] The third part of *On the Councils and the Church* turned from discussion of the authority of councils to repeating his catechisms' characterization of the church as the locale of the Holy Spirit's activity in creating faith, forgiving sins, and producing faith's fruits in believers. The Spirit 'bestows strength and comforts timid, despondent, weak consciences', imparting true fear and love of God, as well as praise, thanks, and honor in believers' lives. He also sanctifies them, inducing them to a peace-filled and productive life of virtue in family and society.[12] Passively, the church receives its holiness or righteousness from the Spirit's use of the gospel; actively, the church serves and praises God in suffering and love. Luther then delineated eight attributes which identify where Christ's true church is found.

'First, the holy Christian people are recognized by their possession of God's holy Word.' The primary characteristic of the church, its use of God's Word, informs all the other characteristics on this list. Some Christians have the Word in purer form, but even when weakened by false teaching, it bestows righteousness and anoints the faithful to eternal life. Even when the number of hearers remains small, the Word does not return without doing its work (Isa. 55: 11), Luther assured readers. Already in the Psalms lectures twenty-five years earlier, Luther had begun to think of true church as the faithful synagogue, a struggling remnant (Ps. 88: 40);[13] his clashes with Rome intensified this view as persecution of his followers mounted. Neither numbers of adherents nor trappings of authority determine the church's presence; the truthful, faithful proclamation of God's Word does, he taught.[14]

Baptism, the Lord's Supper, and the public exercise of the office of the keys are also 'public signs' that the church is present. The 'office' or 'use' of the keys can be public or 'particular'. Some have consciences 'so tender and despairing that even if they have not been publicly condemned, they cannot find comfort until they have been individually absolved by the pastor'. Others stubbornly resist confession and avoid absolution. Luther gave advice on good pastoral care, an integral part of church life, as he told how to recognize the church. For the fifth characteristic of the

---

[11] O. Bayer, *Martin Luther's Theology: A Contemporary Interpretation*, tr. T. Trapp, Grand Rapids, Eerdmans, 2008, 251–277; Lohse, *Theology*, 283–5; T. Wengert, 'The Marks of the Church in the Later Luther', in G. Lathrop and T. Wengert, *Christian Assembly, Marks of the Church in a Pluralistic Age*, Minneapolis, Fortress, 2004, 81–112.

[12] WA 50: 625.33–628.28, LW 41: 145–8.

[13] WA 4: 49.3–9, 346.15–29, LW 11: 193, 471–2; Hendrix, *Ecclesia*, 243–83.

[14] WA 50: 628.29–630.20, LW 41: 148–51.

church is its public pastoral office; pastors are called to proper use of God's Word.[15]

God's Word creates the church by assembling the faithful; the faithful, God's conversation partners by divine design, respond. The sixth 'external' indication of the existence of the true church turns from God's bestowing passive righteousness in the vertical dimension of life to active righteousness, expressed in 'prayer, public praise, and thanksgiving to God' and in instruction in the faith. The 'sacred cross', endurance of persecution, trials, and evil assaults from the devil, the world, and the flesh, 'by sadness, timidity, fear from within and outside, poverty, contempt, illness, and weakness', constitute the seventh external sign of the church. Historically and even at that time all Christians stood prepared to endure torture and death for the sake of the church.[16] Yet, as John Headley notes, Luther held that 'faith, not blood, constitutes the church'.[17] This cross of suffering falls on people not only through physical or spiritual persecution but through everything that kills selfishness and sinful desire in the practice of love in daily life. (Sometimes Luther called the suffering of illness and misfortune 'cross', but usually he labeled specific afflictions incurred through one's callings in daily life as crosses.)[18]

The eighth 'public sign', the good works of love which the Holy Spirit produces in sanctified lives, cannot be counted as a reliable indicator of the church's presence since, according to Luther's understanding of the civic righteousness of those outside the faith, non-Christians produce such works, too.[19] Nonetheless, in other such lists he defined the church as 'people loving the Word and confessing it before others'[20] and the place 'where Christians believe in Christ, are saved by faith, and humbly give themselves to one another'.[21] In the context of their participation in the church, believers practice their callings from God in the rest of creation.

Luther did not regard this list of indicators of the church's presence as dogmatically fixed. Two years later he sketched another list in answering polemic published in the name of the ardent defender of the Roman party, Duke Heinrich of Braunschweig-Wolfenbüttel. Luther 'proved' his followers to be true faithful followers of the ancient church by citing indications of its presence among them. Baptism, the Lord's Supper, proper binding and loosing of sins, preaching of the Word of God, confession of the Apostles,

---

[15] WA 50: 630.21–633.11, LW 41: 152–4.

[16] WA 50: 513.1–16, 641.20–643.5, LW 41: 12, 164–6.

[17] Headley, *Church History*, 161.

[18] G. Wingren, *Luther on Vocation*, tr. C. Rasmussen, Philadelphia, Muhlenberg, 1957, 50–63.

[19] WA 50: 643.6–37, LW 41: 166–7.

[20] Lectures on Psalm 90, 1534, WA 40.3: 506.7–31, LW 13: 90.

[21] Maunday Thursday sermon, 1538, WA 46: 285.7–10.

Creed, and use of the Lord's Prayer all reveal the church's presence. So do honoring the temporal authorities as gifts of God, honoring marriage as his ordinance, suffering persecution itself, and not persecuting others, traits that denied the churchly nature of the papal party, a deft polemic in this context.[22] The church, as the instrument of God's Word and the assembly of Christ's people, is always locked in struggle against the forces of Satan.

THE PRIESTHOOD OF THE BAPTIZED AND THE MINISTRY OF PASTORS

In the last quarter-century of his life, Luther held fast to two principles through several shifts of agenda which elicited different accents in his teaching on the relationship between all baptized believers and those charged with pastoral leadership. He never ceased insisting that baptism grants all believers full access to God and the responsibilities of proclaiming the gospel to others. He increasingly urged the necessity of pastoral care and leadership which God established for the proper conduct of the church's life.

In 1521, reacting against abuses connected with the medieval priesthood, he emphasized the priesthood 'held in common by all Christians, through which we are all priests with Christ, children of Christ, the high priest; we need no priest or mediator other than Christ' (Heb. 5: 1). This common priesthood imposed obligations to pray for others and share his Word with them (Rom. 5: 2; Isa. 65: 24, 13; Jer. 31: 34; Isa. 11: 9; John 6: 45).[23] Two practical problems somewhat dampened Luther's early enthusiasm for the priesthood of all believers. First, he discovered that the savvy and wisdom of peasants regarding weather, crops, livestock, and other matters did not mean that they understood the biblical message, and they had no way of attaining sufficient knowledge for congregational leadership. He remained somewhat confident that parents could raise children and servants in the knowledge and fear of the Lord, as reflected in his design of his *Small Catechism*.[24] But they needed pastors to mine the biblical text for regular proclamation. Second, he discovered that dedication to learning God's Word and living the Christian life was rarer, and Christian maturity harder to cultivate, than he had initially anticipated when he began proclaiming the gospel. Nonetheless, even after his discouraging experiences during the Peasants Revolt, he dreamed of the day when readers would abandon 'unfaithfulness, hatred, envy, wrath, and unbelief', and 'at last become again a group of Christians, whereas at present we are almost

---

[22] *WA* 51: 479.20–486.22, *LW* 41: 194–8.   [23] *WA* 8: 486.18–487.14, *LW* 36: 138–9.
[24] C. Arand, *That I May Be His Own: An Overview of Luther's Catechisms*, Saint Louis, Concordia, 2000, 91–109.

completely pagan and only Christian in name'.[25] He suggested that 'those who want to be serious Christians and profess the gospel demonstrably' should meet in homes to worship and encourage each other in Christian living, an idea with foundations in his Psalms lectures.[26] Nonetheless, he never entertained the idea of abandoning the pastoral office, for he believed that God had designed human life in an orderly fashion with leadership positions to facilitate each walk of life.

Luther began his presentation of the priesthood of believers in the vertical realm of life. Their status as God's priests gives believers full and free access to him. But God also sends them with his Word, the locus of his power placed in human mouths, for use among other human beings. God calls every Christian to specific places of service in life's horizontal realm. There he placed the vocation of pastor, who had one special kind of service to others, specifically the public exercise of God's Word on behalf of the congregation. However, Luther made clear in writing to the Bohemian followers of Jan Hus in 1523 that he regarded the various 'offices' of the Word as the common 'right' and 'property' of all Christians. They bestow upon selected individuals the responsibilities of the office of pastor, which Christ instituted and which the Holy Spirit governs through human agencies of various forms.[27] The German word *Amt* and the Latin *officium* bore the meaning of both function and public position in Luther's time. This, alongside his wealth of terms for the pastoral office and his continuing experimentation over the years with formulations to meet the changing fronts he was addressing in regard to the church's public ministry, causes confusion among scholars.[28]

In various writings Luther criticized the medieval concept and practice of priesthood which made priests into agents who controlled God's grace through the sacrifice of the mass, fostered works-righteousness, and claimed superiority before God by virtue of their office. This led to their failure to fulfill God's design for pastoral care of the people.[29] His *On the Ministry* (1523) listed six 'functions' of the pastor. The first is 'the ministry of the Word, common to all Christians—all are royal priests (1 Pet. 2: 9)— the second baptizing, likewise permitted to all'. The third, administration of the Lord's Supper, belongs to all believers but is publicly celebrated by the pastor, Luther later made clear. All may exercise the other functions,

[25] *Both Kinds in the Sacrament*, 1522, WA 10.2: 39.9–11, LW 36: 264.

[26] *German Mass*, 1526, WA 19: 75.3–30, LW 53: 63–4; Hendrix, *Ecclesia*, 187–98.

[27] Althaus, *Theology*, 323–32; Lohse, *Theology*, 286–97.

[28] R. Kolb, 'Ministry in Martin Luther and the Lutheran Confessions', in T. Nichol and M. Kolden (eds.), *Called and Ordained*, Minneapolis, Fortress, 1990, 52.

[29] H. Lieberg, *Amt und Ordination bei Luther und Melanchthon*, Göttingen, Vandenhoeck & Ruprecht, 1962, 24–39.

however: 'binding and loosing from sin', the sacrifice of praise and thanksgiving, praying, and judging and deciding public teaching.[30]

Nonetheless, Luther insisted that some serve the congregation by implementing these functions publicly. Those in this walk of life should not be called priests but, according to the New Testament, 'ministers, deacons, bishops, stewards, presbyters'. Paul's use of the Greek word denoting service for pastors 'emphasizes that it is not the estate, order, or any authority or dignity that he wants to uphold, but only the office and function'.[31] Pastors perform their service apart from any special powers lodged in their office itself; the power they exercise arises only from the power inherent in the gospel. That is why all Christians share the same power, but not the right to exercise it in the public sphere.[32]

In the 1520s Luther assigned the right to call its pastor to the congregation,[33] but he did not insist on that mode of governance. As princes and town councils devised their own way of placing pastors in office, Luther simply accepted this process. He believed that God acts through the various human agents that order church life and recognized that the Holy Spirit had placed pastors in office through different methods throughout church history.[34]

Congregational life took place, according to Luther, in the use of God's Word. Therefore, he gave priority to creating or revising measures and instruments that encouraged evangelical practice in the Word by fostering good preaching (his postils), liturgy (hymns and liturgical services), devotional life (prayer books and other meditative treatises), instruction of the young (catechisms), and pastoral care (topical treatises). He himself did not compose new governing plans (*Kirchenordnungen*) for territorial churches, but his colleagues, particularly Johannes Bugenhagen, did.[35]

His preaching reflected his pastoral concerns for the repentance of those caught in sin and the comfort of those burdened by troubled consciences. His postils sought to cultivate the ability to proclaim law and gospel and to give instruction in how to live the Christian life. His proposals for liturgical worship fit together with this paradigm for preaching.[36] His transformation of ritual, in both the Sunday morning services and occasional services

---

[30] *WA* 12: 179.33–188.19, *LW* 40: 21–32.   [31] *WA* 12: 190.19–23, *LW* 40: 35.

[32] V. Vajta, *Luther on Worship*, Philadelphia, Muhlenberg, 1958, 109–21.

[33] *That a Christian Congregation Has the Right to . . . Call . . . Teachers*, 1523, *WA* 11: 408–16, *LW* 39: 305–14.

[34] *WA* 40.1: 58.12–60.14, *LW* 26: 17–18.

[35] J. Jaynes, ' "Ordo et Libertas," Church Discipline and the makers of Church Order in Sixteenth-Century North Germany', Ph.D. dissertation, Ohio State University, 1993.

[36] See pp. 86–7 above.

for baptism, marriages, and ordinations,[37] reflected his convictions that God restores human righteousness through his Word in oral and sacramental forms on the basis of Christ's death and resurrection. He objected to the 'silencing of God's Word' and the recourse to 'un-Christian fables and lies, legends', and rituals that did not convey the gospel. In addition, the liturgy had been performed as a work to gain God's favor.[38] In both preaching and the sacraments God reveals his presence and his power; the liturgy presents God's redemption of sinners as a gift to his people. The sermon, already in the fifteenth century becoming more frequent in late medieval towns, took on significance as an instrument of salvation. The sacraments were explained as vehicles for conveying forgiveness and new life in Jesus, shifting the focus from the participation of the priest and the laity attending the liturgy to God's effective promise concluded in Christ's self-sacrifice and resurrection. Human ritual performance was viewed as a response made possible by the power of the Holy Spirit, a fulfillment of the first three commandments arising from trust in Christ. The liturgy became the scene of God's action bestowing salvation upon the congregation, eliciting the adoration of his faithful people, the natural reaction of creatures to their Creator.[39]

Luther honored and treasured much of the ritual with which he had grown up even though he strove to eradicate those elements in it which reinforced the belief that human performance of either ritual or ethical good works contributes to believers winning God's grace. He allowed a good deal of freedom in liturgical decisions[40] and never prescribed specific forms for standard worship even though he composed two treatises that offered liturgical orders. Both, intended for use in Wittenberg, preserved the outline of the traditional Western liturgy, including introits, the Kyrie, the collect, the pericopes, the gradual, the Nicene Creed, and the consecration of the Lord's Supper.[41]

Worship should flow from church into small groups of dedicated believers, gathered for meditation, mutual encouragement, and prayer,[42] or into households, where parents teach children and servants the fundamentals of the faith. Luther fostered this catechetical cultivation of trust in Christ through his *Small Catechism*, which treated each of its sections 'in a simple way in which the head of a household is to present it to the household'.[43]

---

[37] *WA* 12: 51–2, *LW* 53: 96–103; *WA* 30.3: 74–80, *LW* 53: 110–18; *WA* 38: 423–31, *LW* 53: 124–6.

[38] *On the Order of Public Worship*, 1523, *WA* 12: 35.10–18, *LW* 53: 11.

[39] Vajta, *Worship*, 3–107.   [40] *German Mass*, 1526, *WA* 19: 72.3–73.31, *LW* 53: 61–2.

[41] *Order of the Mass*, 1523, *WA* 12: 206.15–214.13, *LW* 53: 20–30; *German Mass*, 69–90.

[42] *WA* 19: 75.3–30, *LW* 53: 63–4.   [43] *BSLK*, 507–23; *BC*, 351–64.

The catechisms complemented other works aimed at cultivating devotional life and good pastoral care.

Luther's concern for the faith of common Christians moved him to continue to criticize medieval religion and its program for Christian living. After 1522 his view of the papacy changed little; his foes' vitriolic attacks sharpened his own polemic's tone but did not alter its substance. His feeling of betrayal at the hands of ecclesiastical officials, especially the pope (whom he initially believed to be entrusted by God with the care of all Christians, but who instead fostered false teaching, indeed a false form of ritualized religion), only increased as Roman Catholic persecution of his followers grew. He relentlessly warned against the perfidy and irresponsibility of papal leadership.[44] The bishop of Rome claimed to be head of all Christendom by divine right, making claims to authority and power in the church that effectively dethroned Christ and denied his gift of redemption. That qualified him as the Antichrist of the end times, the one who 'sets himself over God and against God' (2 Thess. 2: 4). He did so by diverting the faithful from Christ's atoning work to their own ritual and ethical works, particularly in the sacrifice of the mass, and in tyrannizing God's people by creation of a priestly order that effectively abolished the priesthood of all believers.[45] The medieval tradition of criticizing individual popes as 'Antichrist', long practiced by reformers with various concerns and objections regarding papal immorality and abuse of power, gave way to Luther's identifying the institution of the papacy as a tool of Satan which actively undermined and suppressed the biblical message.[46] Not only the papacy received Luther's harsh critique. Also papal supporters, princely adversaries like Duke George of Saxony or Duke Heinrich of Braunschweig-Wolfenbüttel (as part of electoral Saxon political as well as ecclesiastical goals)[47] and theologians, including the faculty at Louvain and several individuals, provided him foils for critique of medieval religion.[48]

As rumors of the impending papal council spread again in 1545, this time justifiably, Elector John Frederick encouraged Luther to undermine the position of the papacy in print. His *Against the Roman Papacy, an*

---

[44] e.g. *On the Keys*, 1530, WA 30.2: 483.36–484.14, LW 40: 348–9; *The Le-gends of Saint John Chrysostom*, 1537, WA 50: 52–64; see pp. 90–1 above.

[45] *BSLK*, 427–33, *BC*, 307–9. Cf. S. Hendrix, *Luther and the Papacy, Stages in a Reformation Conflict*, Philadelphia, Fortress, 1981, 146–59; M. Edwards, *Luther's Last Battles: Politics and Polemics, 1531–1546*, Ithaca, Carvell University Press, 1983, 68–96; Headley, *Church History*, 181–223.

[46] H. Preuss, *Die Vorstellungen vom Antichrist im späteren Mittelalter, bei Luther, und in der konfessionellen Polemik*, Leipzig, Hinrichs, 1906, 4–82.

[47] Edwards, *Last Battles*, 38–67, 143–62.

[48] e.g. *Contra Latomus*, WA 8: 43–128, LW 32: 137–260; three treatises against Jerome Emser, WA 7: 262–5, 271–83, 621–88, LW 39: 111–15, 121–35, 143–238; one against Augustine Alveld, WA 6: 285–324, LW 39: 55–104.

Institution of the Devil[49] examined the papal claims to be supreme lord over Christendom, to stand above the judgment of all others in the church, and to have bestowed the imperial title on the German emperors. Carefully aimed at the popular audience, this treatise shed no new light on the issues but repeated Luther's earlier critique with a level of venomous vituperation that could serve only to rally those already supporting him, particularly princes who sought reinforcement for their position within the Empire. This, and other shorter treatises against the papacy from the final years of his life, demand reading in the context of Mark Edwards's observation that Luther wrote firmly convinced that God is the author of history, and with a 'robust sense of humor'. These treatises reflect his continuing learning and research into the history of the church. 'He was vulgar and abusive when he wished to be, moderate and calmly persuasive when it suited his purposes. . . . And all the treatises of his old age, even the most crude and abusive, contained some exposition of the Protestant faith. Luther could never just attack. He always had to profess and confess as well.'[50]

THE CHURCH IN ESCHATOLOGICAL CONFLICT

Integral to Luther's understanding of the church was his conviction that the church, as the people among whom God is forgiving sins, is also on its way to the resurrection of the body and the life everlasting, in the words of the Apostles' Creed.[51] This path through earthly life involves the struggle against all enemies of the faith, internal and external to believers. With the same intensity that he rejected papal claims to authority and power over the church, Luther denounced the Turks, who since before his birth had been making steady and rapid military gains in the Balkans, defeating Christian forces of the Hungarian king Louis in 1526 and besieging Vienna unsuccessfully in 1529. Such external foes of the gospel served Luther as an occasion for confessing his faith. He disavowed reacting to this serious threat to Christian Europe with a holy war, a crusade, counseling instead Christian prayer, and secular government's exercise of its God-given obligation to protect its subjects against this threat to life and to the faith of the people.[52]

---

[49] WA 54: 206–99, LW 41: 263–376; Edwards, *Last Battles*, 182–200.

[50] Edwards, *Last Battles*, 208.

[51] Aurelius, *Kirchenverständnis*, 122–3; Lohse, *Theology*, 325–35.

[52] Especially *On War Against the Turk*, 1526, WA 30.2: 107–48, LW 46: 161–205; *Military Sermon against the Turks*, 1529, WA 30.2: 160–97; and *Admonition to Prayer Against the Turks*, 1539, WA 51: 478–87. Cf. Edwards, *Last Battles*, 97–114, and G. Miller, 'Luther on the Turks and Islam', *LQ* 14 (2000), 79–97.

At the same time Luther viewed the Turks as not only Satan's servant and instrument but also God's scourge and rod to call people to repentance and to faith in Christ.[53] He took the Turkish threat to Christendom seriously, voluntarily paying the imperial tax appropriate for his property levied by the Saxon government, even though he felt that Christian Europe had brought down God's wrath upon itself for resisting the gospel and would pay the price through defeat.[54] He promoted Christian knowledge of Islam by writing on the subject and making available the text of the Qur'an and the critique of it by a fifteenth-century Dominican, Ricoldus.[55] Luther's warnings sometimes misrepresent facts about Islam, but the thrust of his warnings reminded people that they were living in the last times, when Satan's minions, including the pope, were storming against the church to do it maximum harm before Christ's return.

This same eschatological framework must be considered when reviewing Luther's attitudes toward the Jews. His first treatise on them defended his own belief in the virgin birth of Jesus, against accusations from Roman Catholic foes. It departed from the predominant polemic against Jewish people, arguing that Jews had understandably resisted papal superstition in earlier times. Luther expressed hope that with the revelation of the gospel in the Reformation, Jews would come to faith in the Messiah. Luther anticipated that conversions would happen if Jewish people properly understood Old Testament prophecies, which he read as predictions of Christ.[56] They did not, in significant numbers, but Luther never ceased giving counsel for pastors witnessing to Jews interested in coming to faith in Christ.[57] He welcomed Jewish converts and continued to remind readers that Jesus came from the Jewish people, God's chosen people.

However, disputes over messianic prophecies and other Old Testament interpretation aggravated Luther,[58] as did reports of what he regarded as blasphemous Jewish maligning of Jesus. Rumors of ritual murder and other crimes led him to fierce, vitriolic denunciations of Jewish theology as another Satanic threat, like that of the papacy and the Turks, to the remnant of Christ's people on earth. When in 1538 Count Wolfgang Schlick reported from Bohemia of Jewish attempts to convert Christians

---

[53] WA 30.2: 116.16–17, LW 46: 170.

[54] Letter to Elector Johann Friedrich, 25 March 1542, WABr 10: 17–23, #3727.

[55] Preface to *On the Rites and Customs of the Turks*, 1530, WA 30.2: 205–8; *Refutation of the Koran*, 1542, WA 53: 272–396; Edwards, *Last Battles*, 106–14.

[56] *That Jesus Christ was Born a Jew*, 1523, WA 11: 314–36, LW 45: 199–229; Lohse, *Theology*, 336–45.

[57] Letter to Heinrich Gnesius, 9 July 1530, WABr 5: 452, #1632.

[58] In his Genesis lectures he often disagreed with Jewish exegetes, e.g. WA 42: 271.30–4; 44: 198.6–20, LW 2: 14; 6: 267–8.

there, Luther wrote *Against the Sabbatarians*, calling Jews to repent under God's wrath and trust in Christ, with appeals to his interpretations of Old Testament prophecies.[59] Schlick's transmittal of a dialog in which a Jew and a Christian trade attacks elicited *On the Jews and their Lies*, in 1542, upon which followed *Schem Hamphoras (The Ineffabile Name) and Christ's Lineage* and *The Last Words of David* (2 Sam. 23: 1–7) in 1543.[60] Particularly the last of these focused on the doctrines of the Trinity and the person of Christ, with sharp critique of some Jewish exegesis but little reference to contemporary Judaism. However, the former two contained scurrilous, vicious attacks, as strong as those against the papacy and Turks, voicing Luther's sense of apocalyptic conflict in which the Jews fought for Satan's deceptions that were seeking to destroy the Christian faith as the Judgment approached. These treatises sold relatively poorly in his own time, Edwards demonstrates,[61] but they have served nefarious purposes in later times, with the rise of racial anti-Semitism, even though they ought to be read in the context of late medieval European anti-Jewish attitudes and his own fears of and hopes for the Jews. That context of hatred against the Jews does not excuse or justify Luther's harsh language, which contributed to Jewish suffering, but to evaluate him historically demands attention to the fact that the arguments in these treatises were to a significant extent exegetical.[62] From any twenty-first-century perspective, however, his tirades against the Jews remain inexcusable.

They do reflect the depth of the eschatological structure of his thinking, which expressed itself in several forms. Wittenberg fostered historical study in a number of ways, reflecting the escalating humanist interest of Melanchthon and others in historical texts and study of human action, particularly for its use as salutary examples for daily living.[63] Luther concerned himself foremost with the history of the church. In 1541 he published his *Computation of the World's Chronology*. It, like much of his preaching, reflected his belief that the end times had begun, that the final struggle to pervert God's truth through Satan's deception in its many forms was intensifying.[64]

Luther claimed to follow Augustine's view of history, especially in defining it as the record of enduring conflict between God's people and the

---

[59] *WA* 50: 312–37, *LW* 47: 65–99.

[60] *WA* 53: 417–552, *LW* 47: 137–306; *WA* 53: 579–648; *WA* 54: 28–100, *LW* 15: 267–352.

[61] Edwards, *Last Battles*, 136.

[62] Ibid., 28–142; cf. M. Brecht, *Martin Luther*, 3. vols., tr. James L. Schaaf, Philadelphia, Fortress, 1985–93, 3: 334–51.

[63] P. Fraenkel, *Testimonia Patrum. The Function of the Patristic Argument in the Theology of Philip Melanchthon*, Geneva, Droz, 1961, esp. 52–109.

[64] *WA* 53: 22–182. H.-M., Barth, *Der Teufel und Jesus Christus in der Theologie Martin Luther*, Göttingen, Vandenhoeck & Ruprecht, 1967, 82–123.

world, under Satan's control.[65] But, as Headley shows, Augustine's sharp distinction of the godly and the earthly cities differs from Luther's view of the church itself as the battlefield between God and Satan. Augustine distinguished the 'cities' on the basis of the object of their love; Luther on their adherence to God's Word, the object of their trust. 'Despite the grandeur of Augustine's view, it lacks the coherence, focus, and intensity which Luther achieved through his doctrine of the Word and his definition of the Church as a people of faith.'[66]

Luther understood human history as God's history, reflecting the Augustinian tradition he had learned.[67] His view of the long stretch of human events illustrates his belief that God is totally responsible for everything in his universe and that human creatures are also totally responsible for functioning as God designed them in caring for his universe. God is at work in mysterious fashion through human activity, even through sinful deeds.[68] Yet human beings dare not 'leave it to God'. They serve as his agents in history. Speaking of Noah's exercising his own responsibility for saving his family, Luther told the Wittenberg congregation, 'If you say, "God will sustain me," but get lazy and not work, it will not happen. It is true that he gives all things; he sustains and preserves everyone. But if you do not want to use what you are able to put to use, that is tempting God. . . . He will not perform a miracle for you when it is not necessary.'[69] In his Genesis lectures he repeated Augustine's observation that 'God governs the things he has created so that he nevertheless allows them to function with their distinctive impulses . . . God makes use of definite means and tempers his exercise of his miraculous powers so that he makes use of the service of nature and of natural means.'[70] Apart from very rare exercise of his 'absolute' power, God counts on people and angels to carry out his providential will in caring for creation and bringing the message of the gospel to others.[71] His presence in history often remains hidden; he works there under the appearance of opposites, permitting Satan to wreak havoc at times with no explanation.[72] Nonetheless, he is at work, choosing different individuals for different tasks.[73] Therefore, history often provided

---

[65] *WA* 42: 187.13–30; *LW* 1: 252.

[66] Headley, *Church History*, 67–8; M. Edwards, *Luther and the False Brethren*, Stanford, Stanford University Press, 1975, 112–26.

[67] *Preface to Galeatius Capella's History*, 1538, *WA* 50: 385.15–18, *LW* 34: 277–8; Headley, *Church History*, 1–55.

[68] *Bound Choice*, 1525, *WA* 18: 709.10–36, 712.1–38, *LW* 33: 175–6, 179–80.

[69] *Sermons on Genesis*, 1527, *WA* 24: 181.6/19–9/26.

[70] *WA* 42: 316.21–5, *LW* 2: 76; *WA* 42: 512.19–20, *LW* 2: 350. Cf. Augustine, *De Trinitate*, Book III, chapter 4. See a similar warning to students in *WA* 44: 461.37–462.5, and 463.22–32, *LW* 7: 219, 221–2.

[71] *WA* 43: 71.7–37, *LW* 3: 274–5.   [72] Barth, *Teufel*, 185–208.

[73] *WA* 10.1.1: 606.11–607.5.

Luther's teaching and preaching with examples of God's mercy and wrath, of human wisdom and folly, embodiments of God's law and plan for proper human conduct in this world. Luther's view of church history focused on the devil's unceasing attempts to undermine God's Word and its saving truth. In this struggle Scripture alone retained ultimate authority and absolute authenticity as the unfailingly reliable Word of God. Despite Luther's conviction that the oral Word taken from it is the living, active delivery of its message in native form, he turned alone to Scripture to adjudicate disagreement and to ground all proclamation. Nonetheless, voices of believers had secondary authority for him, particularly the voices of respected teachers. He appears to have kept on reading the ancient fathers as new editions appeared from humanist presses throughout his career.[74] Luther's criterion was not dependent on whether a teacher lived earlier or later; he believed that error had crept into the church's public teaching early as Satan assaulted it in apostolic times. He evaluated each teacher against Scripture's measuring-stick.[75] The same is true for councils. He devoted rather intense study to the council of Nicea and to other ancient creedal statements.[76] He also cited canon law and other elements of medieval tradition when it served to give historical support for his critique of papal practice.[77] But by the time of his interview with Cajetan in 1518, his experimentation with formulating public teaching had persuaded him that the scholastic assignment of authority to oral tradition in the custody of the church, that is the papacy, was wrong. The Holy Spirit works to preserve and propagate God's truth through Scripture, not such traditions.[78]

Luther summarized his position on tradition in two works prepared in reaction to the papal call for council. Extensive reading prepared him for placing his teaching in the catholic stream of doctrine; his works cite Eusebius, Rufinus, and Cassiodorus, among others, as well as recent works by the Franciscan Peter Crabbe on the councils (1538) and the humanist Bartolomeo Platina on the popes (1471–81). *The Three Symbols or Creeds of the Christian Church* (1538) affirmed his commitment to the creedal tradition in comments largely dedicated to the person of Christ, as presented in the Apostles and Athanasian Creeds and the medieval liturgical canticle, 'Te

---

[74] Headley, *Church History*, 162–94.

[75] Letters of 4 August 1530 and 28 December 1538 to Melanchthon; *WABr* 5: 525–7, #1674, and *WABr* 8: 334–45, #3285; *WA* 43: 226.8–227.6, 671.32–673.20, *LW* 4: 126–7; 5: 352–3; W. Bienert, ' "Im Zweifel näher bei Augustin?" Zum patristischen Hintergrund der Theologie Luthers', In D. Papandreou et al. (eds.), *Oecumenica et Patristica*, Stuttgart, Kohlhammer, 1989, 281–94; Headley, *Church History*, 170–6.

[76] Headley, *Church History*, 163–70; cf. *On Councils*, *WA* 50: 531.19–624.3, *LW* 41: 33–143; and *Creeds*, *WA* 50: 262–83, *LW* 34: 201–29.

[77] e.g. *WA* 50: 520.22–526.21, *LW* 41: 20–5.

[78] *WA* 2: 6–26, *LW* 31: 259–92; cf. Headley, *Church History*, 69–94.

Deum Laudamus' (presuming the Nicene Creed stands behind them). He counted the Apostles' Creed as 'truly the finest of all' confessions of faith, for it rightly presents Christ. Citing Augustine's dictum that 'Scriptures alone do not err. . . . I regard [others'] teaching true only if they can prove their statements through Scripture or reason', Luther regarded these creeds as secondary authorities, proper, clear expositions of the primary authority, Scripture.[79] This work was designed to demonstrate Luther's catholicity not only in its confession of the biblical truth but also in its condemnation of Christological errors, above all Arianism, a fourth-century denial of Christ's divinity. For the handing down of biblical teaching always stands under Satan's attack.[80]

On the Councils and the Church (1539) also devoted many pages to detailed review of the first four ecumenical councils and their faithful reproduction of biblical teaching in formulating Christological dogma against Arius, Macedonius, Nestorius, and Eutyches.[81] This work included a more critical assessment of conciliar authority in which—in the midst of the struggle against the gates of hell (Matt. 16: 18, referring to popes and kings who sometimes manipulate or tyrannize councils)—Christ defends his church.[82] Luther criticized the hypocrisy of papal supporters, who insisted on absolute conciliar authority but did not follow Nicea's prohibition of Christian participation in the military (among other examples) or even the first three mandates of the Council of Jerusalem (Acts 15: 19–20).[83] Luther defined the tasks of councils: they have no power to establish new articles of faith, good works, ceremonies, or ecclesiastical statutes. Councils such as Nicea defended biblical teaching; they did not formulate the church's doctrine.[84] They must restrain and condemn false teaching, evil works, idolatrous ceremonies, and tyrannous laws. They dare not interfere in secular government but may introduce ceremonies that are profitable for Christ's people. They should deal with matters of the faith, when it stands under threat.[85]

Luther recognized no unbroken line of prominent teachers in the church but affirmed that the presence of God's Word had preserved the church and the faithful throughout history. Just as in individual believers' lives the rhythm of law and gospel—of sin, repentance, and forgiveness—continues, so the church's history is marked by apostasy, recall to faith, and restoration of purer preaching.[86]

[79] *WA* 50: 524.12–24, *LW* 41: 25; cf. *WA* 50: 543.29–544.12, *LW* 41: 49.
[80] *WA* 50: 262–83, *LW* 34: 201–29.   [81] *WA* 50: 569.6–606.20, *LW* 41: 79–122.
[82] *WA* 50: 511.4–10, *LW* 41: 10.
[83] *WA* 50: 532.10–535.4, 560.11–569.5, *LW* 41: 34–8, 68–79.
[84] *WA* 50: 551.15–20, *LW* 41: 58.   [85] *WA* 50: 606.34–619.8, *LW* 41: 123–37.
[86] *WA* 42: 270.12–271.5, *LW* 2: 12–13; Headley, *Church History*, 101–5.

Several patterns for periodizing guided Luther's understanding of church history. Following Melanchthon's adaptation of the Augustinian schema of six ages of the church, Luther often divided the chronicle of God's people into the 'governances' of Adam, Noah, Abraham, David, Christ, and the pope. But at other times he spoke of three epochs: of the patriarchs, Abraham and the prophets, and Christ. Although he regarded the epoch of the patriarchs as a golden age at times, each period, Luther believed, had witnessed apostasy and God's gracious recall of his people to faith and obedience. Institutionally, the church had experienced a gradual decline with the increasing corruption of the papacy, but in its teaching it had experienced this pattern of apostasy and renewal in every age. Persecution accompanied apostasy the entire Christian era; Arius, Muhammad, and the papacy marked the focal points of this persecution.[87] Confidence that God would preserve the faithful remnant of his church in the end framed his conception of his own time.

Luther came to believe that he was following and completing the work of reformers such as Jan Hus and that God was renewing the clear proclamation of salvation in Christ through himself and his Wittenberg colleagues. Luther realized that he did not fully share all of Hus's positions; Hus had not identified the papacy itself as Antichrist. Luther did not catalog other differences of vital importance between the two (their understanding of justification and God's Word, for instance). But he did see himself as pursuing the reform of the church in Hus's train.[88]

Particularly in secular affairs God exercises his lordship in human history generally through the structures he has written into his creation, but occasionally he intervenes against those manipulating these structures for their own ends with great figures, Luther believed. He warned that those whom God sends to step outside normal procedures suffer severe temptation to become law unto themselves rather than to serve God's purposes, but his reading of history nonetheless led him to believe that battling evil at times involves 'heroic men' (*viri heroici*) who rise above the normal way of doing things to bring God's wisdom and counsel to worsening circumstances.[89]

All history takes place under God's governance but also reflects Satan's attempts to undermine God's rule. These battles continue in individual lives. Therefore, Luther's thought was eschatological in more than the sense of his expecting an imminent end to human history. His consciousness of living each day in God's presence, of God's judgment upon sin and his liberation of his chosen people, permeated his thinking. The whole life

---

[87] Headley, *Church History*, 106–61.

[88] *WA* 44: 744.21–5, 774.19–34, *LW* 8: 226, 266; Headley, *Church History*, 224–65.

[89] Wingren, *Vocation*, 154–60.

of Christians was to be a life of dying to sin and rising again through the forgiveness won by Christ's death and resurrection for living in new obedience. Satan mounts daily attacks against believers' trust in God's promise and his faithfulness.[90] The Holy Spirit daily counter-attacks, renewing that promise; believers daily counter-attack, mortifying sinful desires, repenting, clinging to the promise, and living holy lives out of its power. In this eschatological combat believers exercise full responsibility as God's instruments for affirming God's truth and rejecting Satan's lie as God's rule asserts itself, cutting through the mystery of continuing sin and evil in his world with the Word of truth and life.

This understanding of the End Times, already begun, did not prevent Luther from looking forward to the final consummation at the end of time, the world's time and the individual believer's time on earth.[91] He dealt with this personal eschaton in his own revision of the medieval genre of the *ars moriendi*, composed in 1519, and in sermons—funeral homilies and pericopes on Jairus's daughter, the son of the widow of Nain, and 1 Corinthians 15 above all—as well as personal conversations, letters of consolation, and treatments of martyred followers.[92] Sin causes death (Rom. 5: 12–21; 6: 23), he told students at table; it is 'cruel, hideous, monstrous', revealing God's wrath against sin, terrifying even believers although Christ has taken away their need to fear it.[93] But throughout his life, while very occasionally expressing his own fear of death, he generally expressed absolute confidence in the resurrection that Christ would bestow upon him and all believers, belying the inaccurate claim that he was 'caught between God and death'.[94] Nonetheless, his sorrowful reactions to the loss of loved ones, including his own parents and daughters and his gentle consolation of the dying and grieving,[95] confirm his observation: 'It is normal and right that a person should grieve, particularly when it concerns one's own flesh and blood, for God has not made us to be without feelings, to be like a stone or a piece of wood, but instead it is his will that we

---

[90] Ibid., 234–51; Barth, *Teufel*, 82–123.   [91] Bayer, *Theology*, 322–38.

[92] See W. Goez, 'Luthers "Ein Sermon von der Bereitung zum Sterben" und die spätmittelalterliche ars moriendi', *LuJ* 48(1981), 97–114; U. Mennicke-Haustein, *Luthers Trostbriefe*, Gütersloh: Gütersloher Verlagshaus, 1989; N. Leroux, *Martin Luther as Comforter: Writings on Death*, Leiden, Brill, 2007; R. Kolb, ' "Life is King and Lord over Death," Martin Luther's View of Death and Dying', in M. K. Groch and C. Niekus-Moore (eds.), *Tod und Jenseits in der Schriftkultur der Frühen Neuzeit*, Wiesbaden, Harrassowitz, 2008, 23–45.

[93] Kolb, ' "Life is King" ', 27–9.

[94] Kolb, ' "Life is King" ', *passim*, against R. Marius, *Martin Luther: The Christian between God and Death*, Cambridge, Mass., Harvard University Press, 1999. Marius reads a very few, selected sources, largely from Luther's earlier years, often without respect for context, to reach conclusions fitting for a dramatic, but false, argument.

[95] *WATR* 2.309, #2065; 4.441, #4709; 5.189–92, #5499; 5.185–7, #5490–1; *WABr* 5.240–1, #1529; 6.103–6, #1820; cf. Mennicke-Haustein, *Luthers Trostbriefe*.

weep and mourn. Otherwise it would be a sign that we did not love our own.'[96]

God remained for Luther, however, lord of death and life. He urged believers to trust completely in Christ's resurrection as the guarantee of their own resurrection (1 Thess. 4: 13; Rom 14: 8),[97] assuring them of God's presence, power over death, and love for them—even when it seemed that he was angry with them and punishing them through the death of loved ones or mortal illness.[98] Luther's sermons on death focused on this gospel comfort rather than using death as an occasion for speaking of the sinfulness that causes it. He also made it clear that death springs from unbelief, fostered by Satan, but often dramatically emphasized Christ's victory, with language filled with military descriptors of his triumph in the resurrection. Especially in treating 1 Corinthians 15, he spoke of the physical resurrection and glorification of the body.[99]

Sometimes Luther spoke of body and soul sleeping in the grave until the Last Judgment, sometimes of the soul's being in heaven until reunited with the body in the final resurrection. He repeated biblical phrasing that described death as sleep[100] but affirmed that believers immediately begin to enjoy heaven when they die.[101] His statements did not settle dogmatically on one description of the 'interim state' of God's people[102] but affirmed the certainty of eternal life with God and the bodily resurrection of the dead.[103]

Luther regarded both the eschatological course of history, which he thought was nearing its end, with all its cosmological dimensions, and the eschatological existence of all people, who live out their lives in the presence and sight of God, as vital for a proper understanding of daily life. The eschatological struggle of Satan against God's people explained something of the suffering believers incurred, and the triumph of Christ's resurrection gave them assurance that this life would issue into life forever with their Lord and with the company of those whom he had brought to faith.

Luther's views of the church and eschatology were inextricably bound together. He regarded human life as inherently communal, for God had

---

[96] *WABr* 8: 485.   [97] *WABr* 3: 498; 8: 280; 10: 227, 664, 699; 11: 113–14.

[98] *WABr* 4: 625; 5: 323; 6: 280, 383; 8: 353; 10: 227, 395; 11: 76.

[99] Kolb, ' "Life is King" ', 34–42.   [100] e.g. *WA* 49: 732.26–734.25.

[101] *WA* 53: 400.14–19. In the text of the fourth sermon on 1 Corinthians 15 from 1544, the editor Andreas Poach inserted, without basis in Georg Rörer's notes, 'Whether my body is dead or not makes no difference. My soul does not die, and the body will at the proper time again rise from the grave.' *WA* 49: 779.23–5.

[102] Lohse, *Theology*, 348.   [103] *WA* 49: 740.32–741.13.

not created human beings to be alone, and he recognized that God's people are joined in their Lord's battle against the evil that lies beyond human grasp but that daily attacks them and their God. Nonetheless, Christ binds his church together and has already won victory over sin and death, Satan's most formidable weapons. Though but a little flock, his people need have no fear living day by day in the shadow of their triumphant Lord.

10

Faith Active in Love: Christian Living on the Foundation of God's Calling and Command

As important as they were for him, Luther's faith focused neither on the afterlife nor on the individual's relationship with God alone. Trusting God—listening to him—enables faithful people to focus their lives on service to others, the righteousness of human performance that faith in Christ produces. His Ockhamist instruction prepared Luther to take the created order seriously and to perceive God's presence in it. His engagement with the Old Testament may have been the most significant factor that impelled him to a greater appreciation of life on earth in its ordinary dimensions and of God's providing, preserving care within and through the created order. Whatever its origins, his break with medieval views of the superiority of the 'sacred' over the 'profane' pioneered new ways of viewing life on this earth as well as the human relationship to God.

The story of Luther's saying that, if he knew the world would end tomorrow, he would plant a tree today, appeared more than two centuries after his death. Nonetheless, it reflects his attitude toward the relationship of this life and the next. And he would have planted the tree both to enjoy its beauty, as a reflection of God's goodness, and to produce fruit for the neighbor. He believed that God designed human beings to be in communion with him and serve one another. Therefore, he strove to cultivate the God-pleasing acts of love that both reflect God's love into his world and focus on the neighbor's need. He did so by instructing hearers and readers on God's commands for human life and the structures of daily living in which those commands should be performed. Although much of his program for society reflected social and political theories of his time, regarding which he demonstrated various degrees of expertise or lack thereof (and which address sixteenth-century problems long since disappeared), the theological roots and context of these developments must be noted, and Luther's impact on society not set aside because he is above all a theologian and not a political or social thinker. For, as John Witte observes, the Lutheran Reformation can be labeled 'both a theological and a legal reform movement';[1] it unleashed social and political waves of great significance.

Two events in 1525 provided critical moments that led Luther to reflect on Christian living in this world. His marriage in June to Katharina von Bora provided a showplace for his appreciation of God's gifts of sexuality and family. The peasant revolts that began in 1524, reached a climax in summer 1525, and ended in 1526 occasioned his application of his fear of disorder and violence to his assessment of secular authority as God's agent for limiting evil and promoting the good.

CALLED AND COMMANDED TO LOVE

Luther's view of family and economic life, secular authority, and ecclesiastical practice rested upon his radical revision of the Western Christian estimate of what is truly God-pleasing and of the relationship between religious activities and activities in other realms of daily life. This revision arose out of his experiences with the monastic way of life and the scholastic definition of what anthropologists label 'sacred' and 'profane'. Most religious systems define activities directed toward the divine, the 'sacred', as more effective for pleasing whatever deities they acknowledge than are 'profane' or everyday, mundane activities.

Medieval Christianity did not deny that believers could lead God-pleasing lives in any moral activities or areas of life, but most thinkers held that pilgrimages pleased God more than plowing, fasting more than feasting, and that monasticism or the priesthood had higher spiritual value than service to God and neighbor in other walks of life. Luther came to reject that view when the promise of monasticism to be a shorter, though steeper, path to peace of conscience and heavenly blessings failed him completely. Although he continued to count himself a monk by profession until his marriage, his criticism of monastic claims to be the most godly 'calling' or 'profession' became ever sharper in the late 1510s.[2] Instead, he ever more affirmed that God calls—formerly a technical term for God's bidding people to become celibate monks, priests, or nuns—every Christian

---

[1] J. Witte, *Law and Protestantism: The Legal Teachings of the Lutheran Reformation*, Cambridge, Cambridge University Press, 2002, 5.

[2] T. Wengert, ' "Per mutuum colloquium et consolationem fratrum": Monastische Züge in Luthers ökumenischer Theologie', in C. Bultmann, V. Leppin, and A. Lindner (eds.), *Luther und das monastische Erbe*, Tübingen, Mohr/Siebeck, 2007, 258–9.

to serve neighbors. They do so in the 'vocations' which God shaped for human beings in the home and economy, the civil community, and the church.

Three reasons emerge for his revaluation of what is truly God-pleasing in his departure from the traditional distinction of 'sacred' and 'profane'. First, he found many medieval activities in the 'sacred' realm to be without God's command but instead regulations imposed by human beings (Matt. 15: 9). Second, he believed that many 'sacred' activities distracted from proper service to neighbor in the callings God establishes for human life. Third, he experienced himself that these 'sacred' activities fundamentally served the self, striving to win God's favor, rather than serving God or neighbor. His understanding of salvation on the basis of God's grace alone, and his distinction of righteousness through that grace, appropriate for the relationship to God, from the righteousness of human performance, appropriate for service to other creatures, undercut the traditional understanding of 'sacred' and 'profane' realms. Instead, Luther taught that God is pleased with his chosen children for no other reason than his gracious will to love, unconditioned by any human performance. They are pleasing to him because of the trust he has instilled in their hearts (Rom. 14: 23), not because of the works that flow from that faith. Those works are indeed God's expectation for his people, but their object is not to please God nor to secure the performer's place in God's favor, but to serve the neighbor and other creatures.

Luther aided readers and hearers in determining how they should live according to God's will by providing a structure for that life and by explaining God's specific commands for it. The structure emerged out of medieval social theory, which posited that three distinct groups constitute human society: those who provide nourishment (*Nährstand, oeconomia*), insure order (*Wehrstand, politia*), and teach God's Word (*Lehrstand, ecclesia*). In each of these walks of life (*Stand, status*) (estates, stations, situations are other translations) human creatures exercise responsibilities (*Amt, officium*), which referred to both positions or 'offices' (such as mother, husband, ruler, subject), and the functions of those responsibilities (caring for children, levying or paying taxes, for example). Because Luther did not know that he was fashioning technical terminology, his usage of these terms, particularly of *Stand*, varies, sometimes meaning the entire Christian way of living, sometimes specific spheres of life. Initially, Luther placed each individual most often in only one *Stand*, but later in his life he usually assumed that all people have responsibilities in all three walks of life. Christians, he believed, realize that these responsibilities are gifts of God, 'callings' (*Beruf, vocatio*) into which God places believers in order to make his world run smoothly. Some scholars credit Luther with this new definition of the word

Beruf for the activities of daily life in all its aspects though some German mystics had foreshadowed this usage.[3]

God provides for his creation through human beings exercising their responsibilities; Luther dubbed people in their callings 'masks of God' because they support and sustain each other through daily activities of all kinds. In the mystery of being human creatures, people exercise total responsibility through the offices and assignments God has given them. At the same time he is totally responsible for providing and protecting his human creatures as he uses them as his instruments to care for one another, guiding them to practice his love in his world. Each office served unique purposes; God has woven them together into a rich tapestry that functions as a whole when all carry out their responsibilities properly. Different terms described the places of service into which God puts people. He gives them his grace and favor in their obligations (Latin *munus*) and obedience (*oboedientia*) as he preserves peace and public well-being through individuals who serve as his masks (*larvae*) in their roles (*personae*) or orders (*ordines*) and levels (*gradus*) in society.[4]

Some serve through lowly labor, others through governing and guiding, but none is more worthy in God's sight because of these activities. Christians are called to them, just as non-Christians are placed into their responsibilities, to serve others, not to gain advantage for themselves.[5] 'We are indeed all equal in God's sight,' the *Large Catechism* states, 'but among ourselves it is impossible for there not to be this sort of inequality and distinction according to [God's] order' between those placed in different situations and responsibilities.[6]

Therefore, Luther rejected a narrowly defined kind of 'imitation' of Christ, which some medieval theologians had used as a call to celibacy and religious occupations, as the model for the Christian life. Following Christ, Luther believed, meant embodying and exemplifying God's love, displayed indeed in Christ's self-sacrificial living, but *freed* to serve the neighbor according to God's plan and model for loving within the responsibilities of each human situation and apart from humanly devised expectations.[7]

---

[3] P. Althaus, *The Ethics of Martin Luther*, tr. R. Schultz, Philadelphia, Fortress, 1972, 39; F. Cranz, *An Essay on the Development of Luther's Thought on Justice, Law, and Society*, Cambridge, Mass., Harvard University Press, 1959, 153–78; G. Wingren, *Luther on Vocation*, tr. C. Rasmussen, Philadelphia, Muhlenberg, 1957, 1–3; O. Bayer, *Martin Luther's Theology: A Contemporary Interpretation*, tr. T. Trapp, Grand Rapids, Eerdmans, 2008, 116–49, 305–21; G. Ebeling, *Luther, an Introduction to his Thought*, tr. R. Wilson, Philadelphia, Fortress, 1970, 175–209.

[4] Genesis commentary, WA 44: 440.18–22, LW 7: 190; cf. WA 47: 452.5–453.11; WA 49: 604.30–614.9, LW 51: 348; WA 26: 505, LW 37: 365.

[5] Wingren, *Vocation*, 1–50, 123–43, 213–34; Althaus, *Ethics*, 36–42.

[6] BSLK, 587, BC, 401.   [7] Wingren, *Vocation*, 171–84.

God's creative activity and his plan for human creatures in all the variety in which he created them fashioned those structures. These structures hold society together and give individuals opportunity to fulfill their humanity in service to one another. Occasionally, God breaks through his established structures to combat human sinful devices with special 'heroes', but they always stand in danger of playing outside the rules contrary to God's will and thus bringing ruin upon themselves.[8]

Some accuse Luther of locking individuals into their situations in life, but his own upwardly mobile career from peasant's grandson to entrepreneur's son to law student and then university professor contradicts this. His thirst for contentment and peace did indeed impel him to urge readers and hearers to be satisfied with where God had placed them. Indeed, he censured moving into walks of life invented by human minds, such as monasticism. But he never protested assuming new assignments to different tasks when God calls.

Instructions for Christian living within life's situations constituted the conclusion and goal of Luther's *Small Catechism*. He entitled a series of Bible readings for the various callings of daily life 'The Household Chart of some Bible passages for all kinds of holy orders and walks of life . . . pertinent to their responsibility and service'.[9] Common medieval usage had denoted the monastic and priestly callings as 'holy orders and walks of life'; Luther overturned their precedence in the estimate of life he had previously held. He designated, above all, family life, but in essence all human activities exercised in godly fashion, as the ideal for Christian living and service.[10] This exaltation of the ordinary, which could not count as merit before God, replaced the exaltation of sacred activities designed precisely to do that. Luther's appreciation of the commonplace of God's created order flowed from his understanding of the two dimensions of human nature, the priority of trust in God in his definition of humanity, and his pastoral concern for cultivating repentance and providing peace of conscience through the proper distinction of law and gospel.

Luther's understanding of the three situations or 'hierarchies' of life in society is sometimes confused or equated with his so-called 'doctrine of the two kingdoms'. His use of 'two kingdoms' terminology did not constitute a 'doctrine' as such but rather a framework or presupposition through which various aspects of biblical teaching should be explained. Furthermore, Luther did not know that he was inventing technical vocabulary when he spoke of two 'kingdoms', so he rather casually used this language for at least three distinct concepts: the realms of God and Satan in conflict with each other; the two dimensions of human relationships, with God

---

[8] Althaus, *Ethics*, 160; Wingren, *Vocation*, 92–3, 156–61, 214–15.

[9] *BSLK*, 523, *BC*, 365.   [10] Wengert, ' "Per mutuum" ', 253–9.

and with his creatures; and occasionally, for the institutions of church and state, a usage reflecting medieval processing of Augustine's distinction of two cities.[11] It seems preferable to speak of the two 'kingdoms' of God and Satan, the two 'realms' or 'governments' of relationship to God and relationship to other creatures, and the two 'institutions' of church and secular government.

These three categories treat distinct elements in life but are interrelated. God and Satan battle for control of both sets of relationships. The church exists in the horizontal relationship of life in this world but brings God's power and presence for the vertical relationship into Christians' lives, while secular government exercises its God-given responsibilities only in the horizontal dimension of life (though this does not abolish its God-given responsibility for appropriate external support of the church). Life in the vertical 'government' centers on faith in God, in the 'horizontal' on love for others. Within the two realms exist distinct forms of governance, exercised through God's two words: the gospel governs the relationship between God and his children, the law governs relationships among his creatures, as his plan for life which prescribes proper human behavior. The gospel does, however, motivate Christian service in the horizontal, the law prescribes human trust with mind and heart in the vertical relationship. Behind his words of both gospel and law stands God, revealed in the vertical relationship in Jesus Christ, sometimes revealed, at others hidden, in the course of horizontal relationships.[12]

Luther's understanding of the purpose and modus operandi of these governments matured over the years. Initially, he regarded secular authority as only a measure against and necessitated by sin, but later he seems to have included it in the natural order of human life.[13] Not all scholars recognize that Luther placed the ongoing life of the church in the earthly realm; some texts from his writings justify this interpretation. But more consistently in accord with his understanding of the functions of law and gospel is his assertion that the church's life in delivering God's Word, especially the gospel, is conducted according to rules and regulations for human performance as Christians exercise their calling to serve within

---

[11] However, as he developed further, Luther 'developed a genuine political theory in a way that Augustine, whose ideas always remained in the realm of the nebulous and abstract, never did. Whereas Augustine's ideas were so vague as to be capable in subsequent centuries of being interpreted in a wide variety of different ways, Luther's were relatively clear, concrete, and unmistakable in their meaning', W. D. J. Cargill Thompson, *The Political Thought of Martin Luther*, Sussex, Harvester, 1984, 3. Selective use of elements of Luther's political utterances have led to gross misrepresentation of his political theory, too, e.g., in both the Second and Third Reichs, but see U. Siemon-Netto, *The Fabricated Luther: Refuting Nazi Connections and Other Modern Myths*, 2nd edn., Saint Louis, Concordia, 2007.

[12] Cargill Thompson, *Political Thought*, 36–61; Althaus, *Ethics*, 43–82.

[13] Althaus, *Ethics*, 112–18.

God's congregation of worshippers. Consistently throughout his career he insisted that both realms of life and ways of governing life stand under God; he rules in both and opposes Satan's efforts to pervert each into his own kingdom.[14]

Luther regarded love as the supreme command God gives his people for their conduct in all situations: love for others reflects God's image and his fundamental attitude toward his creation. His sermon on Genesis 1: 27 (1523/7) reminded hearers that human creatures are fashioned in God's image, that is, the heavenly image of humanity in Christ, 'who was a human being full of love, mercy, and grace, humility, patience, wisdom, light and everything good. His entire being was dedicated to serving everyone and harming no one. This image we must bear and conform ourselves to him.'[15] God's commands express specifics of his expectations for human performance of love and inform people on the general rules for living as a human being.

These commands are accessible, Luther believed, not only from Scripture but also from the knowledge of heart and conscience. God implanted this sense of right and wrong in his human creatures; all rational human beings seek to use reason to identify precisely what is proper and improper behavior. All cultures build systems of conduct for their members, which, despite all their differences, in general agree on the fundamental rules for behavior; Luther called this the 'law of nature', or 'natural law', or 'natural justice'.[16] Though Luther could refer to express biblical commands as 'God's law', he also used that designation for the sense of right and wrong in all people. He saw no essential difference in the behaviors expected by Moses in Scripture and the expectations of moral people for themselves and others everywhere at all times, expressed in the positive or statutory law they formulated from their God-implanted wisdom.[17] This law, summarized in the Golden Rule, demands mutual love, respect, regard, and concern. Christians must recognize that their practice of horizontal righteousness, though externally similar, is different in two respects from the 'civil righteousness' of others. First, non-Christians 'may also do all other works', but trusting God comes only from Holy Spirit.[18] Second, Christians add a willingness to suffer and sacrifice self to normal human love of others.[19]

[14] Althaus, *Ethics*, 54–62; F. Cranz, *An Essay on the Development of Luther's Thought on Justice, Law, and Society*, Cambridge, Mass., Harvard University Press, 1959, 116–53.

[15] WA 14: 111.5–6, 19–22; 24: 50.26–33.

[16] WA 18: 307.23–5, LW 46: 27. Scholars disagree as to whether Luther used these terms synonymously; Althaus's argument that he did seems convincing, *Ethics*, 25–35. Cf. Cargill Thompson, *Political Thought*, 79–90.

[17] Althaus, *Ethics*, 132–7.   [18] WA 6: 206, LW 44: 25.

[19] WA 18: 310.24–32, LW 46: 29.

God's creative design obligates Christians to obey his commands, but it also provides a good deal of room for personal and societal decision-making, choosing among several good possibilities to show love in specific instances. Therefore, Luther taught not only that God had freed his people from all that threatened them and for service to one another. He also maintained that that service or love for others sometimes involved decisions made in freedom from precise prescription. In life's horizontal dimension the human will can exercise some freedom in choosing the best possible way, often among several, to execute God's assignments to deliver love. Even in *Bound Choice* Luther affirmed that 'there are things free choice does by nature, such as eating, drinking, begetting, ruling'.[20] Freedom in Christ places the exercise of this choice within bounds of love, however. True freedom from the curse of the law, sin, and death enables believers 'to serve the other person through love, in accordance with Paul's commandment' by carrying out their responsibilities in their callings, helping the neighbor in every possible way, Luther commented on Galatians 5: 13 in 1535,[21] echoing his *Freedom of a Christian* fifteen years earlier.[22]

In all efforts to exercise callings responsibly and obey God's commands, human reason and wisdom must govern decision-making. Exercising wisdom depends on prayer, the call of faith for God's aid in practicing love properly and fruitfully.[23] Luther recognized that legalistic following of God's commands can occasionally create injustice despite good intentions. Therefore, he embraced Aristotle's concept of *epieikeia*, fairness. He believed it expressed Jesus's command to love others as people love themselves (Matt. 22: 39).[24] Luther strove for peace among people as they encountered one another, the kind of service he believed that God had designed human beings to render one another. He counseled contentment or satisfaction in fulfilling one's calling to help other people and care for their needs. In the practice of the virtues God commands, Joseph provided a model for Luther's contemporaries as a description of how God's people live.[25] This appeal to the exercise of the rationality and wisdom of individuals, particularly those exercising authority in society, reflects something of Germanic law executed on the basis of wisdom even though (or perhaps because) Roman law was replacing its use in Luther's day.[26] Christians exercise this wisdom as they practice God's commands within the callings

---

[20] WA 18: 752.7–8, LW 33: 240. Cf. Althaus, *Ethics*, 62–78.

[21] WA 40.2: 62.17–21, LW 27: 49–50.

[22] See pp. 80–1 above, and Wingren, *Vocation*, 93–106.

[23] Ibid., 184–99.   [24] e.g. WA 19: 632.8–24, LW 46: 102–3.

[25] WA 44: 704.13–706.17, LW 8: 171–4; Wingren, *Vocation*, 149–55, 162–71.

[26] G. Krodel, 'Luther and the Opposition to Roman Law in Germany', *LuJ* 58 (1991), 13–42; Witte, *Law*, 42–50.

that structure daily life in family and economic life, the church, and the political community.

'HIGHER THAN ANY OTHER WALK OF LIFE'—MARRIAGE AND FAMILY

Luther recognized that some people receive the gift of celibacy for the welfare of others, but God sustains society through his gift of marriage and family.[27] In explaining the Fourth Commandment in his *Large Catechism* he wrote, 'God has given this walk of life, fatherhood and motherhood, a special position of honor higher than that of any other walk of life under it.'[28] That laid the basis for his praise of obedient children, but he completed this explanation by reminding parents that this obedience is rendered not for their sake or to their praise but because God has called them to exercise responsibilities of this position earnestly and faithfully. Parents were not only to 'provide material support for their children' and servants 'but especially to raise them to the praise and honor of God'. 'Do not imagine that parental responsibility is a matter of your pleasure and whim. It is a strict commandment and injunction of God, who holds you accountable for it.' This is not only a matter of family honor or welfare. When families function well, people grow up to be 'good, capable citizens, virtuous women . . . good managers of the household . . . '.[29] The entire welfare of society depends on family life that corresponds to God's commands for parents and children. They begin, according to his *Small Catechism*'s 'Household Chart of Christian callings', with the admonition to parents not to provoke children to anger, 'lest they become fearful. Instead bring them up in the discipline and admonition of the Lord' (Eph. 6: 4), and to children to be obedient (Eph. 6: 1–3).[30] Because marriage and bearing children belong to created humanity and not exclusively to God's gifts of new life and salvation to his chosen children, Luther did not regard marriage as a sacrament, a tool for conveying God's mercy in Christ. Rather, it is the foundational situation of human life.[31] Luther's lectures often prepared students for preaching and teaching on God-pleasing family life; he often praised marriage and offered basic instruction on it from the pulpit. His writings dedicated to marriage-related topics, however, focused on specific societal problems of the day, above all, secret betrothals contracted

---

[27] Althaus, *Ethics*, 83–91.
[28] BC, 400, BSLK, 587. Cf. W. Lazareth, *Luther on the Christian Home*, Philadelphia, Muhlenberg, 1960, esp. 166–234.
[29] BSLK, 604–5, BC, 409–10.   [30] BSLK, 523–7, BC, 366.
[31] Althaus, *Ethics*, 89–90.

by children against their parents' will.[32] (These he condemned but also urged parents to refrain from forcing children into loveless marriages and to accept their childrens' chosen partners when love between the two existed.[33]) Through letters he offered support and consolation for those encountering problems with such betrothals or other marital difficulties.[34]

The love of parents for children and children for parents, Luther concluded, reflects the love of spouses for each other. In 1523 he emphasized the purpose of marriage in the reproduction of the human race. 'There is no greater unifying bond than that of men and women,' he told the Wittenberg congregation, for, he added to the printed version of his sermon, 'God has implanted it in human beings that there must be a man and a woman, and without this there can be no offspring. For women are created to support humanity, not for lust and abuse.'[35] By 1535 his monastic attitudes had faded; his own experience with his wife, Katharina von Bora, led him to expand his description of the blessings and purposes of marriage to include companionship and love, as well as the limitation of lust, with its negative consequences for society, in the complementarity of woman and man. 'Today after our nature has become corrupted by sin, woman is needed not only to secure increase but also for companionship and protection. The management of the household must take place under the administration of the women we cherish.'[36]

Luther's time as monk had deeply ingrained in him the feeling that the 'noble delight' of sexual intercourse had become something that physicians compare to epilepsy. Against those feelings he insisted that the sexual union of husband and wife is the most excellent and admirable activity in God's design for humanity even though sin has marred it with lust.[37] Preaching on Matthew 5: 7–29 (1528/9), he had described sexual desire in men and women as a gift of God, created by him as an integral part of humanity.[38] As part of his creation that changed with sin's advent in human life, sexuality still sometimes suffers the abuse of selfish lust even within marriage, as in every human activity, so Luther frequently assured hearers and readers

---

[32] *Sermon on the Estate of Marriage* (1519), WA 2: 166–71, LW 44: 7–14; *The Estate of Marriage* (1522), WA 10.3: 275–304, LW 45: 17–49; *Commentary on 1 Corinthians 7* (1523), WA 12: 92–142; *On Marriage Matters*, WA 30.3: 205–48, LW 46: 265–320; *Lecture on Psalm 128* (1532/3), WA 40.3: 269–309.

[33] *That Parents Should Not Compel their Children's Marriage* (1524), WA 15: 163–9, LW 45: 385–93.

[34] G. Ebeling, *Luthers Seelsorge an seinen Briefen dargestellt*, Tübingen, Mohr/Siebeck, 1997, 104–42.

[35] WA 14: 126.26–35; 24: 78.5–79.17.   [36] WA 42: 88.4–9, LW 1: 116.

[37] WA 42: 87.11–90.2, LW 1: 115–19.

[38] WA 32: 373.33–374.11, LW 21: 89; cf. *Large Catechism*, BSLK, 611–12, BC, 414.

of the forgiveness of this ever-present sin—an observation about human sinfulness more than about marriage.[39]

Two seemingly contrasting views of Eve mark his observations to students on Genesis 2. Luther himself was convinced that he was returning to a positive, biblical view of women that the exaltation of celibacy for nuns had obscured, although some modern scholars disagree. He did avoid the contempt for women found in some Renaissance authors. On the one hand, he told students in 1535, commenting on Genesis 2: 18, 'the woman was created by God's unique counsel, to show that this sex, too, is suited for the kind of life which Adam was expecting. . . . if the woman had not been deceived by the serpent and sinned, she would have been the equal of Adam in all respects. . . . She was in no respect inferior to Adam, whether you count the qualities of the body or those of the mind.'[40] Yet only a few weeks earlier, his monastic heritage asserted itself in his observation on Genesis 1: 27, 'Eve was a most excellent creature, like Adam in terms of God's image, that is, in righteousness, wisdom, and her general wholeness,' a 'most wonderful work of God but not equal to the man in glory or status'. Indeed, she shares the same divine image and likeness, the same dominion over everything, the same future life as Adam, but she was the moon to Adam's sun. 'This sex may not be excluded from any glory of human nature although she is below the male.'[41] Attempts at synthesizing these statements from a late-twentieth-century standpoint divide over whether the glass is half full or half empty: Luther earns praise for abandoning the diminution of women in medieval and Renaissance attitudes and blame for imprisoning women in the roles of wife and mother, depriving them of the monastic roles formerly present as alternatives.[42] However modern concerns lead us to judge such statements, Luther did appreciate women on a higher level than he had learned as a young man. His relationship with Katharina von Bora projected a model that made a profound impact on his students and society in general.[43] But in this case as in others he reflected that world in which he had been trained, however his attitudes had changed.

Luther's enthusiasm for God's gift of marriage suffered no diminution because of the hardships and suffering that inevitably befall couples. He knew of this first hand, for his relationship with Katharina and their children reflected and enhanced his embrace of family and sexuality as God's good gift. Their story concretizes this aspect of his theology with

---

[39] WA 10.2: 304.6–12, LW 45: 49; WA 34.1: 73.16–27.
[40] WA 42: 87.9–90.3, 50.6–11, 52.12–22; 87.20–9, 103.14–22, LW 1: 115, cf. 66, 69, 115–19, 137.
[41] WA 42: 51.36–52.22, LW 1: 69.
[42] S. Karant-Nunn and M. Wiesner-Hanks, *Luther on Women: A Sourcebook*, Cambridge, Cambridge University Press, 2003, 1–14.
[43] M. Treu, *Katharina von Bora*, Wittenberg, Drei Kastanien, 1995.

eloquent clarity. The stories in Genesis also gave him ample opportunity to demonstrate how marriage works. On the one hand, as they entertained the three messengers (Gen. 18), Abraham and Sarah showed that their home had 'nothing but grace and life'.[44] Nonetheless, Luther recognized the troubles that plagued their household and encouraged his students to be realistic but confident in God: 'inconveniences, vexations and various crosses are encountered in marriage. What does it matter? Is it not better that I please God in this manner? Does not God hear me when I call upon him? Does he not deliver me in misfortunes and bless me in various ways through my life's companion, the upright wife whom I have joined to myself?' For precisely in the trials of family life God hides himself and through them brings blessings.[45] The difficulties Abraham and Sarah experienced because God delayed giving them their son also disclosed godly aspects of life together. Sarah served as a model of Christian contentment and patience as she bore the burden of childlessness (Gen. 16).[46] Their squabble about Abraham's treatment of Ishmael (Gen. 21: 10–11) shows that both had honest and natural concerns, their dispute an example of their 'fear and obedience to God and true humility'. It provides comfort for spouses, 'that they may not think it strange if disputes arise among even the most affectionate and saintliest people. One should rather consider that in marriage there are such varied exercises in godliness and love.'[47] However, Luther also noted, referring to Isaac and Rebecca (Gen. 26: 8), that 'no disagreement and discord is bitterer and more horrible than between spouses or between brothers. On the other hand, if there is mutual love, mutual play and friendliness, that marriage is loved and praised everywhere by all, for that is rare because of the devil, who is its perpetual enemy, trying to disturb the divine union in whatever ways he can.' That can only happen when spouses live in love: 'a husband should conduct himself in a friendly and gentle manner toward his wife, not only in the bedroom but also in public. He should not be capricious, irascible, and surly, for examples of dissensions and harm done to others are noticed by people and cause them to fall into sin.' Instead, 'it is useful if there are such examples of friendliness and amiability among spouses, so that others also learn the habits of being pleasant, affable, and patient if any offense or trouble occurs'.[48] He condemned power plays in family life: 'Husbands generally are lions in their homes and are harsh toward wives and domestics. Similarly, wives generally domineer everywhere and regard their husbands as servants.' Both are foolish and wrong. Christians should follow the example of Abraham and Sarah in

---

[44] *WA* 43: 38.14–21, *LW* 3: 228. [45] *WA* 43: 140.16–20 and 140.28–141.3, *LW* 4: 6–7.
[46] *WA* 42: 578.22–581.18, *LW* 3: 42–6. [47] *WA* 43: 151.6–14, *LW* 4: 21–2.
[48] *WA* 43: 450.30–451.9, *LW* 5: 32; cf. the extension of these remarks, *WA* 43: 449.8–455.12, *LW* 30–8. In 1521 Luther had found in the examples of Jacob's family life in Genesis 30 a plan for marriage, *WA* 9: 412.7–11.

loving and respecting each other.[49] Husbands and wives shall 'treasure each other, become one, and serve each other', loving each other in harmony, 'cherishing each other totally, with perfect faithfulness'.[50] Although Luther recognized impotence, refusal of intercourse, incompatibility, and adultery as grounds for divorce, he opposed remarriage except in the first case.[51]

Spouses fulfill two vital roles, in loving each other and in raising children, above all in the true faith and Christian life. 'God does not make human beings from stones. He makes them from a man and a woman,' Luther reminded students in 1540.[52] He often instructed both parents and children in their mutual responsibilities to each other.[53] For family life, as an integral part of and key to humanity, carried and sustained all other aspects of society.

ECONOMIC LIFE

In Luther's late medieval European world the tasks of the household as a walk of life included all economic activities; 'family' embraced servants supporting the family and/or learning a trade in its midst. Luther had definite convictions about economic life, beginning with the relationships between employers and employees, extending to abuses perpetrated by the great trading companies and bankers of his day. Though sin made work burdensome and worrisome, honest effort in planting the garden and cultivating it with diligence belonged to the nature of humanity, Luther concluded in 1520.[54] Sinners wish to avoid the bitterness and burden of toil; indolence comes naturally to them. God's children recognize his calling in their work, the blessing of providing their own sustenance and that of others. Labor provides discipline for sinful desire and promotes patience and love for others. Therefore, in line with most medieval theologians, he condemned usury as a great evil, driven by sinful greed. He understood taking interest as contrary to Christian love, which freely loans money without expectation of gain through this sharing.[55] Greed perverts human enjoyment of life and relationships among people, enslaving sinners, turning

---

[49] *WA* 43: 128.25–37, *LW* 3: 354.

[50] *WA* 10.2: 299.5–14, *LW* 45: 43; *Large Catechism*, *BSLK*, 615–16, *BC*, 415–16.

[51] Althaus, *Ethics*, 97–9.   [52] *WA* 43: 344.15–17 and 24, *LW* 4: 291.

[53] Althaus, *Ethics*, 99–100.

[54] *WA* 7: 31.21–32, *LW* 31: 360; C. Lindberg, *Beyond Charity: Reformation Initiatives for the Poor*, Minneapolis, Fortress, 1993, 110–18.

[55] *On Trade and Usury* (1524), *WA* 15: 302.30–303.18, *LW* 45: 245–310; *On Psalm 128* (1532/3), *WA* 40.3: 179–283, *Church Postil* (1544), *WA* 22: 322.1–12; *Genesis Commentary*, *WA* 42: 152.1–160.27, *LW* 1: 203–15. Althaus, *Ethics*, 101–4.

them in upon themselves. Throughout his life Luther railed against it and the business practices it elicits, counseling instead the use of the believer's economic life to demonstrate and execute God's providing care,[56] highlighting specific temptations for peasants, nobles, artisans, and merchants.[57]

God calls both employers and employees to their respective responsibilities. Abraham's servant Eliezer modeled the ideal of his calling, Luther stated, lecturing on Genesis 24. He combined proper satisfaction with his service to Abraham with humility and modesty as well as faithfulness.[58] Always concerned with the contentment and confidence of his hearers, Luther observed that 'those who are placed more humbly in society should know that their calling carries with it the same honor and high regard as their masters and others placed more highly have, for whatever prestige or distinctions their superiors may command, the servants share with them; they participate in the same renown as the heroes whom they celebrate'.[59] He used Joseph's service in Potiphar's house and in Pharaoh's government[60] to depict for his students how to fulfill the calling of servant at various levels.

Closely connected to management and labor in Luther's mind was property. His sense of community and the primacy of love led him to ground his view of property in its usefulness for showing God's love to others. He often warned against the ease with which wealth and possessions become idols, the source of good and security for people,[61] and admonished hearers and readers to share their goods and support those in need.[62]

Some have suggested that his harsh criticism of early capitalistic practices in his day stemmed from his unfamiliarity with the workings of the system. True as that may be, his father's experiences in the smelting industry exposed young Martin to the underside of the capitalists' machinations. His censure of similar practices in local artisan production and shopkeeper sales suggest that his moral judgment knew well whereof he spoke. 'He recognized no mammonistic autonomy in business,' whether by grand capitalists or petty tradesmen, just as he recognized no 'Machiavellian autonomy in politics'.[63] All who served the public did so at God's call and behest and were obliged to do according to his rules.

---

[56] e.g. *WA* 15: 293–313, *LW* 45: 245–310; Althaus, *Ethics*, 108–11.

[57] R. Rieth, *'Habsucht' bei Martin Luther. Ökonomisches und theologisches Denken, Tradition und soziale Wirklichkeit im Zeitalter der Reformation*, Weimar, Böhlau, 1996.

[58] *WA* 43: 338.27–340.10, *LW* 4: 283–5.   [59] *WA* 43: 342.4–8, *LW* 4: 288.

[60] *WA* 44: 343.28–345.31, *LW* 7: 58–61; *WA* 44: 349.23–350.2, *LW* 7: 66–7; *WA* 44: 351.10–352.14, *LW* 7: 69–70.

[61] *Large Catechism*, BC, 387, BSLK, 561.   [62] Cf. Althaus, *Ethics*, 105–8.

[63] Ibid., 111.

POLITICS

The public service of governing society demanded the exercise of justice by those with the responsibilities of leadership and power and the discipline of order preserved through the obedience of those under these authorities. That obedience dare not, of course, involve disobeying God. Far from being the 'toady of princes', as is sometimes claimed, Luther's critical utterances regarding abuses of the responsibility of ruling probably outnumber his condemnation of the disorder wrought by subjects. The latter perhaps had more widespread impact on the public consciousness of his day. But his insistence that secular government is God's good gift to preserve peace and order for the entire community brought with it the insistence that rulers not abuse their responsibility. That makes the office of ruler difficult and dangerous, for power corrupts.[64] In first drafting his 'Household Chart' of Christian callings in 1529, Luther cited Romans 13: 1–2 and 4b to establish the obligation of obedience to temporal authority but undoubtedly presumed readers would think of the entire passage, which also defined temporal authority as existing for the benefit of good subjects and the punishment of evil. Not until 1542 did he add a section on 'what subjects owe the governing authorities', with Bible passages that placed praying for rulers, obeying them, and paying them taxes within the subjects' calling.[65]

Emperor Charles's summons of Luther to Worms hurled him—against his intention and will—into the midst of contemporary political maneuvering. The political milieu involved the impetus toward consolidation of personal power among German princes, who had been extending their control over the church in their lands in a manner parallel to Spanish and French kings during the fifteenth century. They had successfully assumed responsibility for enforcing Christian standards for behavior upon the populace and acquired the right to supervise and designate priests in their lands, largely at the expense of the German bishops.[66] This milieu also involved German national feelings, including resentment against perceived exploitation and domination by the papacy, rooted in more than five hundred years of tension between German emperors and princes and popes and papal legates to German lands. Whether the Ockhamist tradition that schooled Luther continued Ockham's own political views, fostered by his adherence to Ludwig of Bavaria in his bitter dispute with Pope John XXII in the 1330s, is unclear,[67] but German grievances against Rome loomed

[64] e.g., WA 11: 261, 271, 273, LW 45: 103, 120–1; WA 31.1: 198–200, 206, LW 13: 51–3, 59.

[65] BSLK, 524–5, BC, 365.

[66] J. Estes, *Peace, Order and the Glory of God: Secular Authority and the Church in the Thought of Luther and Melanchthon 1518–1559*, Leiden, Brill, 2005, 2–6.

[67] J. Kilcullen, 'The Political Writings', in P. Spade (ed.), *Cambridge Companion to Ockham*, Cambridge, Cambridge University Press, 1999, 302–25; W. Kölmel, *Wilhelm Ockham und seine kirchenpolitischen Schriften*, Essen, Wingen, 1962.

large in the consciousness of those with whom Luther associated as he was drawn closer to the Saxon court. He capitalized on the formal statement of those grievances in his *Open Letter to the German Nobility* in 1520.[68]

Charles's verdict of outlawry against Luther, and the opposition of rulers such as Henry VIII of England and the German dukes, George of Saxony and Heinrich of Braunschweig-Wolfenbüttel,[69] reinforced his critical stance toward governing authorities when they departed from proper exercise of their responsibility and perpetrated injustice toward those whom God had entrusted to their care. However, his overriding concern for public order drove him to fierce opposition to all breaches of the peace and stability of society. Peasant revolts had troubled parts of Germany in Luther's lifetime: thirty-four between 1509 and 1517, 112 between 1521 and 1523.[70] The disorder in Wittenberg in 1521 by Karlstadt's supporters exemplified the threat of law-breaking as a betrayal of his reform efforts in concrete form; Luther could view such disorder only as the devil's skulduggery to undermine reform in the world's last days.[71]

In early 1522 he issued *A Sincere Admonition to All Christians to Guard against Rebellion*, an admonition to princes to preserve public order as had Moses (Exod. 32: 38), even at the cost of violent suppression of rebellion (though he preferred combating evil with God's Word). For God's wrath descends on rebellious people that disrupt society and attempt to overthrow legitimate authority, which God establishes to punish evil and protect the upright (Rom. 13: 1–7; 1 Pet. 2: 13–14). God forbade rebellion, reserving 'revenge' for himself (Deut. 32: 35), but had commanded rulers to seek 'justice, and only justice shall you pursue' (Deut. 16: 20). His reading of history led Luther to state that rebellion 'never brings about the desired improvement'. It 'lacks discernment; it generally harms the innocent more than the guilty'. He viewed rebellion and disorder eschatologically, as tools of Satan to frustrate the gospel's spread in the world's last days.[72]

Proper conduct of life in the political realm continued to occupy Luther, as imperial and territorial officials struggled to deal with his cause. In mid-1522 he preached a sermon series on 1 Peter and addressed political obedience at 2: 13–17, as a natural part of the creature's creatureliness.[73]

---

[68] Estes, *Peace*, 18–20.

[69] M. Edwards, *Luther's Last Battles: Politics and Polemics, 1531–1546*, Ithaca, Carvell University Press, 1983, 38–67, 143–62. See also his response to the attack on his *Babylonian Captivity* published under the name of Henry VIII of England, WA 10.2: 180–222, 227–62.

[70] R. Scribner, 'The Reformation Movements in Germany', in G. Elton (ed.), *The New Cambridge Modern History*, vol. 2: *The Reformation 1520–1559*, Cambridge, Cambridge University Press, 1990, 86–7; T. Scott, *Town, Country, and Regions in Reformation Germany*, Leiden, Brill, 2005, 3–188.

[71] See p. 92 above; Estes, *Peace*, 42–4.

[72] WA 8: 679.35–681.30 (676–87), LW 45: 57–74.   [73] WA 12: 327.25–335.29.

In autumn Johann von Schwarzenberg, a counselor of the bishop of Bamberg, challenged Luther with several questions; Luther promised a treatise on political issues over which they disagreed.[74] In October he preached on God's establishment of governmental authority to the Saxon ruling family in Weimar and subsequently synthesized his thoughts in *On Temporal Authority* (1523). Romans 13 and 1 Peter 2 again laid the foundation for his assertion of the responsibility of governing authorities to keep peace and order in society, punishing evildoers, promoting the upright. Augustine's two cities shaped Luther's language and conceptualization of society divided between God's kingdom and the world's way of ruling, but the later contours of his own understanding of the responsibilities in this world to which God calls people were emerging. At this point he believed that Christians need no control by secular government but willingly submit to one another in love. Nevertheless, they should submit to rulers for the sake of the world, which needs protection against the disorder that the ungodly foment.

By 1530 Luther could write that 'temporal authority is a creation and ordinance of God and for us in this life it is a necessary office and estate which we can no more dispense with than with life itself since without it this life cannot continue'.[75] Therefore, while Christians for themselves turn the other cheek, those who are called to the responsibilities of preserving public peace and enforcing law must take in hand the sword against wickedness. Christ did not do so because his calling did not require it. Princes are to dedicate their lives to their subjects, aiding them, promoting their welfare, protecting them from courtiers who abuse them. They are to punish evildoers and act properly as God's servants. They should forbid public proclamation of heresy but cannot coerce people to believe properly.[76]

Luther expanded on these ideas in the 1530s, in comments on Psalms 82 and 101. Published in March 1530, in the midst of tension-filled discussions among Evangelical governments and theologians about the propriety of resistance against Emperor Charles should he move to suppress the Lutheran movement, the first commentary served as a 'mirror of princes'. The calling of princes is that of 'savior, father, rescuer', who aids his subjects, providing them protection and nourishment.[77] Church officials no longer could coerce governmental officials, Luther claimed, since the light of the gospel had also helped reveal the true distinctions between spiritual and temporal government. Godly order in society demands that subjects

---

[74] *WABr* 2: 600–1, #538.   [75] *WA* 30.2: 556.23–6, *LW* 46: 238.

[76] *WA* 11: 245–80, *LW* 45: 81–129; see B. Lohse, *Martin Luther's Theology*, tr. R. Harrisville, Minneapolis, Fortress, 1999, 151–9; Cargill Thompson, *Political Thought*, 62–78, 91–154; Althaus, *Ethics*, 112–54; and Estes, *Peace*, 37–41.

[77] *WA* 31.1: 205, 18–19 (189–218); Estes, *Peace*, 181–8.

obey authority and that authorities preserve peace and practice justice. Both are subject to God, who threatens and punishes disobedient subjects and tyrannous, arbitrary princes. This mirror of princes prescribed for them three godly activities: promoting God's Word and the salvation of the people whom God entrusts to him; aiding and promoting the welfare of the suffering, orphans, and widows; and protecting subjects from wickedness and violence, preserving peace. Luther condemned the princes' failure to uphold God's Word and provide the poor with justice and protection, and their wicked lives. He rebuked them for selfishly administering their office, driven by lust, malice, pride, and love of luxury.[78] To prevent princes from falling into such temptations Luther insisted upon the obligation of preachers to call rulers to repentance, arguing that it would be more subversive to good government if pastors let tyrants provoke the populace through misgovernment. For 'the office of preaching is not that of a courtier or hired hand. He is God's servant and minion.'[79]

Against the background of the Saxon government's execution of six Anabaptists, on 18 January 1530, on charges of sedition, Luther addressed the question of governmental suppression of heresy. Rulers should note three categories of heretics: those who simply hold false beliefs, those who encourage rebellion, and those who actively spread false teaching. The first should be tolerated since the sword cannot lead people to faith. Their rebellion earns the second punishment. The third also deserve punishment as public opponents of God's Word.[80] This position reflected earlier statements that asked princes to quash certain medieval catholic practices because they were blasphemous but insisted that force could not produce faith. Gradually Luther acceded to Melanchthon's position that Anabaptists could be executed because they rejected core teachings of the Christian faith. However, he continued to repeat that consciences dare not be coerced by secular rulers but must be won by proclamation of God's Word. Nonetheless, Anabaptist preachers that operated without a formal call to serve introduced disorder into the community, and rulers were to protect the church from such interference.[81] Luther counseled Lutheran preachers engaged in public disputes that unsettled the populace to yield and not disturb public order. He urged rulers to end public quarrels among preachers that concentrated not on God's Word but on practices and traditions and to end the activities of preachers who did not have a proper call to minister to a congregation.[82]

---

[78] WA 31.1: 189.21–196.3.   [79] WA 31.1: 196.19–198.18; cf. WA 51: 240.7–12.
[80] WA 31.1: 207.33–209.14.
[81] Estes, *Peace*, 185, 192; Cargill Thompson, *Political Thought*, 155–62.
[82] WA 31.1: 209.32–212.29.

The accession of John Frederick to the electoral throne (1532) gave Luther occasion in 1534 to use Psalm 101 to craft another mirror of princes, using David as the paradigm of princes, ignoring his vices, praising him as the model of virtues. Although John Frederick and Luther had a long, close friendship, the preacher held his prince to this ideal, implicitly critiquing the elector's vices and openly condemning the abuses of his counselors. David's example called princes to proper support for God's Word while leaving the tasks of the gospel to the pastors.[83] Luther's Genesis lectures, begun the next year, praise the virtues and proper activities of rulers. Luther praised Joseph and Pharaoh for their diligence, wisdom, bravery, humility, moderation, and similar virtues. Particularly important was Joseph's faith in God and his commitment to supporting the proclamation of his Word.[84] When rulers fail to exercise the responsibility to preserve the public order that all members of the community require, preachers should call them to their duty.[85] That is what he had done when central Germany threatened to be engulfed by rebellion in early 1525, earning in the process five centuries of criticism.

Luther commented on a number of spheres of community life in which rulers play special roles. Their call to defend peace and order necessitated, in a sinful world, the use of force against its enemies. This led Luther to encourage soldiers, so long as their military activity involved the defense of public order.[86] Every reform movement in the church raises moral sensitivities, often over the question of Christians in military service. Assa von Kram, a counselor and professional soldier serving Duke Ernst of Braunschweig-Lüneburg, laid his conscience qualms before Luther in mid-1525. Distractions delayed Luther's treatment of the question *Whether Soldiers Can Also Be Saved* until late 1526. Soldiers at the time were largely mercenaries; the time of feudal levies of nobles and their peasants had largely passed; national armies had not yet surfaced. Luther's answer reflected his anthropology of two dimensions of righteousness. He claimed that 'not since the apostles' time have the temporal sword and government been so clearly described or highly praised as by me'. He argued that believers in Christ recognize that as God's children they are called to serve others, and that may demand military service from some. Military professions are legitimate, godly callings so long as they follow rulers who are acting justly, that is, defending their people against unjust attacks from

---

[83] WA 51: 200–64; see the editors' comments on the relationship between Luther and John Frederick, p. 198; Estes, *Peace*, 193–205.

[84] WA 44: 415.15–21, 425.22–39, 427.18–22, 428.1–16, 432.26–8, 437.32–6, 444.10–39, 670.19–671.37, LW 7: 156–7, 170–3, 178–9, 186–7, 196–7; 8: 125–6.

[85] Althaus, *Ethics*, 147–51; Cargill Thompson, *Political Thought*, 112–18.

[86] Althaus, *Ethics*, 137–43.

their equals or suppressing disorderly subjects. Soldiers dare not participate in rebellion against a prince's overlord, for example, the emperor,
for that upsets godly order in society. In that case they must leave their
prince's service—something mercenaries could do—rather than disobey
God (Acts 5: 29).[87] Furthermore, war may never be waged on behalf of the
Christian faith; armed force should serve only to restore tranquility, not to
advance the cause of the gospel. Luther sharply criticized the concept of
crusade.[88]

Among the tasks God assigns to secular authorities who are Christian
was the care of the church. Scholars offer differing assessments of Luther's
understanding of the role Christian princes should play in the church's life.
Some emphasize the differences on church and secular authority between
him and Melanchthon; James Estes convincingly argues for their fundamental agreement even if sometimes on the basis of different rationales
and arguments.[89] Luther rejected the Erasmian ideal of a Christian state
for two reasons. He believed that non-Christian rulers, on the basis of wise
use of reason, can manage the mechanisms of governing society as well
as Christians can; he recognized how often Christian rulers fall victim to
sinful impulses to abuse power and ignore their God-given responsibilities.
Therefore, his thinking on this subject wove a delicate path through practical necessities, as he saw them, within his framework of callings in two
different walks of life: pastors and princes simply had different assignments
from God.

But pastors—pope and bishops—had failed. In 1520 Luther advanced
the argument that Christian secular rulers have an obligation to seek the
church's welfare and the pure preaching of the gospel. In emergency situations (terminology often assigned to Luther but not actually employed by
him) Christian rulers have the power as rulers and the calling as Christians
to exercise responsibility for the welfare of their churches. Indeed, the
dispensation of the gospel, in public preaching and absolution, for instance,
belongs alone to pastors, but in other matters secular authorities may
intervene and guide the church.

Over the years Luther came to accept the role of secular government
in the life of the church as an appropriate way of governing its life in this
world but always condemned governmental interference with the preachers' proclamation and exercise of his ministry of the gospel.[90] Luther's
definition of the church as the place where sheep hear the voice of the
shepherd led him to advocate local control of the congregation's life, but as

---

[87] *WA* 19: 623–62, *LW* 46: 93–137.   [88] *WA* 30.2: 111.13–117.5, *LW* 46: 165–70.
[89] Estes, *Peace, passim*, esp. 179–81, 205–12; Althaus, *Ethics*, 151–4.
[90] Estes, *Peace*, 9–30; cf. *WA* 6: 434.6–9, *LW* 44: 165.

his reforms took shape in villages and towns, it became obvious that not all congregations were able to manage their own affairs. By 1525 Luther was pressing Elector John to take a more active role in guiding church life.[91] His concern for the actual life of Christian people led him to find the best practical solution for the concrete problems of congregational life.

Luther's most controversial political utterances came in reaction to the most serious, widespread outbreak of violence in several regions as a new wave of peasant revolts broke out in 1524 and 1525, so many that scholars designate this the 'Peasants War'. Peasants near Memmingen composed the most widely used articles presenting their grievances in early 1525. At least two groups of peasants had named Luther as one potential judge of their cause, so in April he replied in his *Admonition to Peace: A Reply to the Twelve Articles of the Swabian Peasants*. Its first section blamed tyrannous princes and bishops for 'this disastrous rebellion'. God's wrath was coming upon them for not properly caring for their subjects and treating them unjustly. Both their suppression of the gospel and their economic injustices cried out to God for rectification. However, Luther also counseled the peasants that God had called them to obedience and that violence threatened the innocent more than the guilty. He criticized their claiming to be a 'Christian' organization when seeking temporal justice. What is right in this world is right whether practiced by Christians or 'heathen, Jews, or Turks'. Therefore, Christians should seek justice, not claim special rights as Christians. He also feared that association with violence would misrepresent and damage the Reformation. Injustice by princes does not justify the injustice that rebellion inevitably causes. Christians suffer wrong and combat evil with prayer, not with armed force (Rom. 12: 19; 1 Cor. 6: 1–2; 2 Cor. 10: 4; 12: 9; Matt. 5: 44). In the midst of suffering God is with them.

In evaluating the twelve articles, Luther granted that local congregations should have the right to choose their own pastors but counseled exile over revolt should rulers refuse. He did not recognize the community's right to the tithe their lords collected and contradicted the belief that serfdom is in and of itself wrong, referring readers to the position of his friend Urbanus Rhegius, published earlier in 1525.[92] On the other issues, rights to hunt, fish, use wood from forests, rents, taxes, and the like, he yielded to the lawyers, whom he regarded as the competent judges in such matters.[93]

---

[91] See pp. 153–4 above; Estes, *Peace*, 30–52.

[92] *Von leibaygenschaft oder knechthait* . . . , s.l., 1525. See R. Kolb, 'The Theologians and the Peasants: Conservative Evangelical Reactions to the German Peasants Revolt', *ARG* 69 (1978), 103–31.

[93] *WA* 18: 291–334, *LW* 46: 17–43; M. Edwards, *Luther and the False Brethren*, Stanford, Stanford University Press, 1975, 60–81.

Luther's treatise did nothing to stem the rising tide of peasant violence. By early May he had experienced firsthand in the countryside around his hometown in Mansfeld county the threatening mood of peasants. Relatives had reported their fears of the rebels. Erfurt and other towns had surrendered to rebel groups; castles and monasteries had been burned and plundered. Elector Frederick lay on his deathbed, his government paralyzed. In early May Luther wrote *Against the Robbing, Murdering Hordes of Peasants*, in which he urged governments to restore order against Satan's machinations. The peasants had broken their oaths of allegiance, perpetrated violence like a fire devastating the entire land, and cloaked their sin under the name 'Christian brethren', misrepresenting what Christian freedom means. They also coerced others into supporting them, making victims of their fellow peasants. To correct the situation, Luther insisted, those charged with maintaining peace and order had first to offer the rebels an opportunity to come to terms. If they refused, rulers should 'smite, slay, and stab' those who were visiting destruction upon the land so that they might 'release, rescue, help' all whom the rebels were victimizing, including fellow peasants who were being coerced into rebellion.[94] For, Luther noted, the end of the world was at hand.

Central German governments, including Saxony, did not need Luther's urging. They struck back; at Frankenhausen on 15 May thousands fell in battle, among them Thomas Müntzer. Protests from some supporters and from Roman Catholic opponents evoked Luther's *Open Letter on the Harsh Book against the Peasants* in summer 1525. There he insisted that the need for public order exceeded all other considerations in the face of murderous rebellion. He rejected the charge of simply wanting to earn the princes' good graces, emphasizing his commitment to order and justice. Without remorse for his call to arms, he stated that suppression of violence is necessary to preserve the populace from greater suffering. But he also closed this tract with a condemnation of 'furious, raving, senseless tyrants' who could not get their fill of blood after their victories. He remanded them to the devil and to hell.[95] Luther's opponents gloated that he had sacrificed the support of the peasantry through his stand. However, Franz Lau demonstrated that the attraction of his ideas did not diminish among the populace in most places in the years following 1525 even though the maturing reform movement took on other institutional forms, with more and more governments embracing the Wittenberg Reformation.[96]

Luther always had presumed that Christians had the obligation to disobey secular authorities when they transgressed God's commandments.

---

[94] *WA* 18: 357–61, *LW* 46: 49–55.   [95] *WA* 18: 384–401, *LW* 46: 63–85.

[96] F. Lau, 'Der Bauernkrieg und das angebliche Ende der Lutherischen Reformation als spontaner Volksbewegung', *LuJ* 26 (1959), 109–34.

He first formulated the right and responsibility to resist authority which God has given Christians in terms of resisting ecclesiastical authorities, as early as 1520; in 1521 his *Instruction to Penitents concerning the Forbidden Books of Dr. M. Luther* had advised pious readers to ignore father-confessors who forbade them to read his books.[97] But for a decade he limited this resistance to passive defiance of ungodly exercise of authority. In the 1530s he reluctantly and seemingly halfheartedly conceded to the lawyers of his princely supporters that German law might permit active resistance by inferior authorities, such as princes and cities, against the emperor. This question first confronted the Wittenberg team soon after the Edict of Worms. Elector Frederick approached Luther's colleague Nikolaus von Amsdorf, a member of the lower nobility from a family that had served the Wettin princes for several generations, with a request for his theologians' opinions on the propriety of his defending his people from the forceful reimposition of papal control over their churches. Luther's conditions for Frederick's use of force against the emperor rendered it virtually impossible. Melanchthon and Bugenhagen were somewhat more open to defense of the gospel with the sword against the emperor. Amsdorf agreed that individual believers must suffer persecution and not contribute to rebellion, but he argued that the office of prince requires seeking the people's welfare also with the sword, even against the emperor.[98]

Luther's argument rested on his conviction that God had placed rulers in their office (and only God could replace them), on his deep-seated dread of disorder, and on his fear that revolt would discredit his Reformation as the eschatological battle intensified before the ever-nearer Judgment Day. This remained Luther's position until October 1530. Then, in the wake of the imperial threat to execute the Edict of Worms and proceed with military force against Evangelical governments, the Protestant princes persuaded the Wittenberg theologians to accept the argument that the German constitution and the office of subordinate ruler permitted armed resistance to the emperor when he failed to uphold his oath of office and execute that office properly. Luther continued to insist that he had not changed his convictions but conceded competence in the question to the jurists, who could better appraise the legal and political situation.[99]

The dire situation of late 1530 moved Luther to compose a *Warning to His Dear German People*. It formally rejected rebellion but, in Mark Edwards's words, through the polemical force of the treatise 'favored

---

[97] WA 7: 290–7, LW 44: 223–9; Althaus, *Ethics*, 124–32; Estes, *Peace*, 10–13.

[98] WABr 12: 35–45.

[99] Edwards, *Last Battles*, 20–37; W. Cargill Thompson, 'Luther and the Right of Resistance to the Emperor', in D. Baker (ed.), *Studies in Church History*, Oxford, Blackwell, 1975, 159–202; cf. Ebeling, *Seelsorge*, 63–77.

resistance. In fact, it was an incitement to resistance.'[100] For Luther increasingly applied his understanding of calling to the question of subordinate political figures' relationship to the emperor. If the emperor was functioning no longer as emperor but as toady of the pope, he could and should be resisted, called back to proper exercise of his calling.[101] Edwards interprets Luther's evolving position as 'more comfortable with the positive law argument but never fully satisfied', even as he joined his Wittenberg colleagues in 1536 and 1538 in opinions advocating resistance partly on the basis of a natural law right to self-defense.[102] He preferred his argument from the calling and responsibility of the emperor, as seems clear in his letter to the Brandenburg pastor Johann Ludicke in February 1539.[103] In a disputation on the 'Three Hierarchies, Church, State, and Household' of April 1539 he dismissed the pope's authority since he, not God, had created his position or walk of life. Therefore, resisting the pope and his supporters was justified, particularly as the Last Day approached.[104] In these writings Luther continued to struggle with his own recognition that such legal questions were beyond his competence, the genuine threat of military action against his cause by Roman Catholic opponents, and his convictions regarding the sinfulness of resistance to higher governmental authority. His resolution of this dilemma shows how he reformulated a position when changing perceptions of his context conflicted with his previous beliefs. He struggled to maintain his underlying principle while recognizing that his earlier position had not addressed all related concerns as circumstances actually framed them.

Luther also reflected the structures of societal development at his time in his assigning governments' roles in education and social welfare. During the fifteenth century many municipalities in Germany had introduced reforms of the often rather disparate and disorganized options for aiding the poor and ill in a community that had grown up in the Middle Ages. Wittenberg attained a more centralized, uniform system while Luther was at the Wartburg. Upon his return he became consultant to the town of Leisnig, near Leipzig. He advised its citizens on their right to call their own pastor, their worship forms, and their program for social welfare. He found biblical basis for a common 'chest' or 'fund' to support poor relief and care of the sick in the apostles' actions (e.g. Acts 2: 44–5; 4: 32–5). Monastic properties, in so far as the heirs of the original donors did not require them for their own needs, should support a just administration of aid governed

---

[100] Edwards, *Last Battles*, 29.   [101] WA 30.3: 291.20–309.6, LW 47: 30–41.
[102] Edwards, *Last Battles*, 30–1.
[103] WABr 8: 366–8, #3297; Edwards, *Last Battles*, 31–3.
[104] WA 39.2: 39–89; Edwards, *Last Battles*, 33–5.

by Christian love. But he did not offer details on how to administer such funds. That he left to responsible municipal officials.[105]

Luther's instructions on education contained more detail and theological grounding. His concept of Christianity as a faith based on God's Word gave impulse to improving and broadening the educational foundations of the population. That became part of his preaching and program in the years of consolidation following Worms. In the wake of the Saxon visitations he renewed his original published call for better schooling of 1524 in a sermon readied for publication in 1530. Satan endeavors to harm both society and the faith by disrupting education or depriving as many of it as possible, he observed. The Germans dare not bypass the opportunities the Reformation was giving to establish and expand schools. For God commands that parents educate their children (Ps. 78: 5–6; Deut. 32: 7); God's wrath falls upon parents who neglect that part of their calling. The church depends on educated young men for pastors; secular government requires them for administration of public affairs. Luther stressed the importance of training in ancient languages, reflecting his sympathies for humanistic educational reform, to which Melanchthon was contributing so much. He argued that schooling was vital for girls as well as boys; both boys and girls could spare time for schooling alongside their learning a trade and the conduct of the household.[106]

This advice reflects the structure that guided his entire address of the Christian life in its horizontal dimension, the pursuit of virtue, obedience to God's commands, within the context the Creator had fashioned for human living in the callings issued in each walk of life. Luther believed that fallen human creatures could fully live out such a life only when moved by trust in Christ, but he was also convinced that all people should strive to live in the civil righteousness that conformed to God's plan for human action. Such works did not make believers or unbelievers righteous in God's sight. But those who trusted God's Word of assurance that the Holy Spirit had made them righteous by faith were to know that the fruits of faith inevitably proceeded from that gift of God's grace that recreated them as children of God.

---

[105] 'Preface to the Leisnig Ordinance of a Common Chest', WA 12: 11–20, LW 45: 169–76; Lindberg, *Beyond Charity*, 85–127.

[106] *To the Councilmen of all Towns in German Lands: That They Establish and Maintain Christian Schools* (1524), WA 15: 27–53, LW 45: 347–78; *A Sermon on Keeping Children in School* (1530), WA 30.2: 517–88, LW 46: 213–58; see I. Asheim, *Glaube und Erziehung bei Luther*, Heidelberg, Quelle/Meyer, 1961.

Conclusion: Martin Luther, Confessor of the Faith and Pastor of God's People

Martin Luther commands attention, respect, and criticism in modern societies around the world even though his social and cultural significance projects itself in muted and mutated tones at the beginning of the twenty-first century. His breakthrough out of the medieval distinction of sacred and profane realms contributed to the higher evaluation of family life, economic service, and political leadership that marks contemporary Western cultures, although these secularized societies largely ignore the foundations he presumed for these walks of life in God's institution and ordering of human life. These societies are replacing his view of the callings of daily life, as God's summons to serve others, with a focus on personal rights and individual freedoms. Yet Luther's bold reinterpretation of relationships among human beings cannot totally be read out of Western perceptions of what it means to be human. However, his cultural contributions to German language and literature and his love of music that brought Johann Sebastian Bach and a rich musical tradition in its train strike different chords of response in the twenty-first century because the stage of world history as seen from Western eyes has expanded to embrace many more cultures than appeared there even a half-century ago.

Nonetheless, Luther continues to command attention in this new century. That is true above all because he continues to challenge Christians and others to think through afresh what it means to be human as individuals and in community. Luther continues to challenge his readers to think through anew their understanding of the nature of God and his disposition toward human creatures, indeed of the fundamental structure of reality. In the course of daily life they experience in various ways what Luther regarded as the eschatological intersection of what God has already done in Jesus Christ and what he promises to do in the consummation of all things. The reformer's sober assessment of human fault and the larger specter of evil does not seem as unrealistic in the wake of the Holocaust as optimistic Western Europeans and North Americans once thought. His assessment of human worth and dignity takes account of sin and enables believers to recognize what is wrong in themselves. This assessment also enables them to acknowledge the value God has placed on their lives by choosing them as his own and coming to die and rise for them in Jesus Christ. In postmodern terms his view of God's speaking through his oral, written, and sacramental Word, to perform his will and create new identities for people sick and tired of their old identities, demands reassessment of how all Christians communicate their faith in their God, a God of conversation and community.

Like all thinkers, Luther spoke within his specific historical context. Luther's conception of God's reality never lost the marks of the Ockhamist engagement with the person of the Creator, who had come to rescue his human creatures from the mystery of evil and restore them to their full enjoyment of his gift of humanity. Those marks include not only his negative reaction against his instructors putting the critical burden of righting his life upon his own shoulders. Among these marks are also the Ockhamist focus on human language and especially its emphasis on God's power and his desire to be conversing with and in communion with his human creatures. Luther's own solution to the dilemma and mystery of evil in human life highlighted the biblical sense of God's power and presence in the seeming weakness and foolishness of God's triumph over evil through the cross of Christ. Not only his scholastic training but also the pious study and exercise of his monastic years shaped his way of thinking. Significant elements took form through his engagement with the tradition of the church in the likes of Augustine and Bernard, the aids for biblical study supplied by humanists from Reuchlin to Melanchthon, and the personal engagement with his colleagues from Staupitz to Melanchthon and the entire Wittenberg circle.

Luther's personality—his scrupulosity, his intense personal relationships, among other factors—coupled with his biblical studies, molded his practice of theology as he mined the biblical text and applied it to the lives of Christian people. He regarded them as caught in the mystery of the continuation of sin and evil after God had baptized them into a new identity wrought by Christ's death and resurrection.

His theology took shape within the context of both the practice of the disputation, which sought truth through confrontation, and his feelings of betrayal at the hands of both pope and false brethren. The popes had failed to be pastors to God's people; a variety of false brethren had found another path to reform or another interpretation of critical aspects of the message of Scripture. His theology took shape less within the theoretical strictures of university theology than in pastoral practice, caring for the tender consciences of sinners sharing his terror and despair under the judgment of a wrathful God. In the Word of God, as it expresses God's essence, presence, and power, in Christ's cross, and in words of forgiveness and life delivered in oral, written, and sacramental forms, Martin Luther found answers to life's most pressing, oppressing, problems. Those answers he confessed before parishioners, students, and even Emperor Charles himself. As confessor of the faith and pastor of God's people he spoke and wrote that God's people might know God, revealed in Christ Jesus, and live in the joy and peace that he gives.

Bibliography

Aland, K., *Die Thesen Martin Luthers*, Gütersloh, Mohn, 1983

Althaus, P., *The Ethics of Martin Luther*, tr. R. Schultz, Philadelphia, Fortress, 1972

—— *The Theology of Martin Luther*, tr. R. Schultz, Philadelphia, Fortress, 1966

Arand, C., 'Luther on the Creed', *LQ* 20 (2006), 1–25

—— *That I May Be His Own: An Overview of Luther's Catechisms*, Saint Louis, Concordia, 2000

Asendorf, U., *Luther and Hegel*, Wiesbaden, Steiner, 1982

Aulén, G., *Christus Victor: An Historical Study of the Three Main Types of the Idea of Atonement*, tr. A. Hebert, New York, Macmillan, 1961

Aurelius, C., 'Luther in Sweden', *Word & World* 18 (1998), 299–306

—— *Verborgene Kirche. Luthers Kirchenverständnis aufgrund seiner Streitschriften und Exegese 1519–1521*, Hanover, Lutherisches Verlagshaus, 1983

Bagchi, D., *Luther's Earliest Opponents, Catholic Controversialists, 1518–1525*, Minneapolis, Fortress, 1991

Barth, H.-M., *Der Teufel und Jesus Christus in der Theologie Martin Luthers*, Göttingen, Vandenhoeck & Ruprecht, 1967

Bayer, O., *Martin Luther's Theology: A Contemporary Interpretation*, tr. T. Trapp, Grand Rapids, Eerdmans, 2008

—— *Promissio. Geschichte der reformatorischen Wende in Luthers Theologie*, Göttingen, Vandenhoeck & Ruprecht, 1971

—— *Schöpfung als Anrede*, Tübingen, Mohr / Siebeck, 1990

Bielfeldt, D., M. Mattox, and P. Hinlicky, *The Substance of the Faith: Luther's Doctrinal Theology for Today*, Minneapolis, Fortress, 2008

Beißer, F., *Claritas scripturae bei Martin Luther*, Göttingen, Vandenhoeck & Ruprecht, 1966

Bell, T., *Divus Bernhardus. Bernhard von Clairvaux in Martin Luthers Schriften*, Mainz, Zabern, 1993

Bienert, W., ' "Im Zweifel näher bei Augustin?" Zum patristischen Hintergrund der Theologie Luthers', in D. Papandreou, W. A. Bienert, and K. Schäferdiek (eds.), *Oecumenica et Patristica*, Stuttgart, Kohlhammer, 1989, 281–94

Bluhm, H., *Luther, Translator of Paul: Studies in Romans and Galatians*, New York, Lang, 1984

—— *Martin Luther, Creative Translator*, Saint Louis, Concordia, 1965

Bolliger, D., *Infiniti contemplatio: Grundzüge der Scotus- und Scotismusrezeption im Werk Huldrych Zwinglis*, Leiden, Brill, 2003

Bornkamm, H., *Luther im Spiegel der deutschen Geistesgeschichte*, Heidelberg, Quelle / Meyer, 1955

Brecht, M., *Die frühe Theologie des Johannes Brenz*, Tübingen, Mohr / Siebeck, 1966

—— 'Luthers neues Verständnis der Buße und die reformatorische Entdeckung', *Zeitschrift für Theologie und Kirche* 101 (2004), 281–91

—— *Martin Luther*, 3 vols., tr. James L. Schaaf, Philadelphia, Fortress, 1985–93

—— and C. Peters, *Martin Luther. Annotierungen zu den Werken des Hieronymus*, *Archiv zur Weimarer Ausgabe*, Cologne, Böhlau, 2000

Buchholz, A., *Schrift Gottes im Lehrstreit. Luthers Schriftverständnis und Schriftauslegung in seinen drei großen Lehrstreitigkeiten der Jahre 1521–28*, Frankfurt am Main, Lang, 1993

Cargill Thompson, W. D. J., 'Luther and the Right of Resistance to the Emperor', in D. Baker (ed.), *Studies in Church History*, Oxford, Clarendon, 1975, 159–202

—— *The Political Thought of Martin Luther*, Sussex, Harvester, 1984

Cochlaeus, J., *Commentaria De Actis et Scriptis Martini Luther*, Mainz, 1549; ET *Luther's Lives*, tr. E. Vandiver, R. Keen, and T. D. Frazel, Manchester, Manchester University Press, 2002

Cohn, N., *The Pursuit of the Millennium*, 3rd edn., Oxford, Oxford University Press, 1970

Cranz, F., *An Essay on the Development of Luther's Thought on Justice, Law, and Society*, Cambridge, Mass., Harvard University Press, 1959

Dettloff, W., *Die Entwicklung der Akzeptations- und Verdienstlehre von Duns Scotus bis Luther*, Münster, Aschendorff, 1963

Dieter, T., *Der junge Luther und Aristoteles. Eine historisch-systematische Untersuchung zum Verhältnis von Theologie und Philosophie*, Berlin, de Gruyter, 2001

Dingel, I., *Concordia controversa, Die öffentlichen Diskussionen um das lutherische Konkordienwerk am Ende des 16. Jahrhunderts*, Gütersloh, Gütersloher Verlagshaus, 1996

—— 'Die Rolle Georg Majors auf dem Regensburger Religionsgespräch von 1546', in *idem* and G. Wartenberg (eds.), *Georg Major (1502–1574), Ein Theologe der Wittenberg Reformation*, Leipzig, Evangelische Verlagsanstalt, 2005, 189–206

—— 'Strukturen der Lutherrezeption am Beispiel einer Lutherzitatensammlung von Joachim Westphal', in W. Sommer (ed.), *Kommunikationsstrukturen im europäischen Luthertum der Frühen Neuzeit*, Gütersloh, Gütersloher Verlagshaus, 2005, 32–50

Doerne, M., 'Gottes Ehre am gebundenen Willen. Evangelische Grundlagen und theologische Spitzensätze in *De servo arbitrio*', *LuJ* 20 (1938), 45–92

Dost, T., *Renaissance Humanism in Support of the Gospel in Luther's Early Correspondence*, Aldershot, Ashgate, 2001

Dykema, P., and H. Oberman (eds.), *Anticlericalism in Late Medieval and Early Modern Europe*, Leiden, Brill, 1994

Ebeling, G., 'The Beginnings of Luther's Hermeneutics', *LQ* 17 (1993), 129–58, 315–38, 451–68

—— *Evangelische Evangelienauslegung, eine Untersuchung zu Luthers Hermeneutik*, 3rd edn., Tübingen, Mohr/Siebeck, 1991

—— *Luther, an Introduction to his Thought*, tr. R. Wilson, Philadelphia, Fortress, 1970

—— *Luthers Seelsorge an seinen Briefen dargestellt*, Tübingen, Mohr/Siebeck, 1997

—— *Lutherstudien*, 3 vols., Tübingen, Mohr/Siebeck, 1971–89

Edwards, M., *Luther and the False Brethren*, Stanford, Stanford University Press, 1975

—— *Luther's Last Battles: Politics and Polemics, 1531–1546*, Ithaca, Cornell University Press, 1983

Edwards, M., *Printing, Propaganda, and Martin Luther*, Berkeley, University of California Press, 1994

Elert, W., 'Deutschrechtliche Züge in Luthers Rechtfertigungslehre', in M. Keller-Hüschemenger (ed.), *Ein Lehrer der Kirche, Kirchlich-theologische Aufsätze und Vorträge von Werner Elert*, Berlin, Lutherisches Verlagshaus, 1967, 23–31

Erasmus, D., *Collected Works*, Toronto, University of Toronto Press, 1974–

—— *De libero arbitrio ΔIATPIBH; siue Collectae . . .* , Augsburg, Ruff/Grimm, 1524

—— *Hyperaspistae liber secundus . . .* , Nuremberg, Petreius, 1527

—— *Hyperaspistes Diatribae Aduersus Seruum Arbitrium Martini Lutheri . . .* , Cologne, Quentel, 1526

—— *Opera omnia*, Louvain, 1703–6

Erikson, E., *Child and Society*, New York, Norton, 1950

—— *Young Man Luther: A Study in Psychoanalysis and History*, New York, Norton, 1958

Estes, J., *Peace, Order and the Glory of God: Secular Authority and the Church in the Thought of Luther and Melanchthon 1518–1559*, Leiden, Brill, 2005

Flogaus, R., *Theosis bei Palamas und Luther*, Göttingen, Vandenhoeck & Ruprecht, 1997

Forde, G., *The Captivation of the Will*, Grand Rapids, Eerdmans, 2005

—— *On Being a Theologian of the Cross, Reflections on Luther's Heidelberg Disputation, 1518*, Grand Rapids, Eerdmans, 1997

—— 'When Old Gods Fail: Martin Luther's Critique of Mysticism', in *idem, The Preached God*, M. C. Mattes and S. D. Paulson (eds.), Grand Rapids, Eerdmans, 2007, 56–68

Fraenkel, P., *Testimonia Patrum: The Function of the Patristic Argument in the Theology of Philip Melanchthon*, Geneva, Droz, 1961

Gerrish, B., *Grace and Reason: A Study in the Theology of Luther*, Oxford, Clarendon, 1962

Goez, W., 'Luthers "Ein Sermon von der Bereitung zum Sterben" und die spätmittelalterliche ars moriendi', *LuJ* 48 (1981), 97–114

Grane, L., *Contra Gabrielem. Luthers Auseinandersetzung mit Gabriel Biel in der Disputatio Contra Scholasticam Theologiam 1517*, s.l., Gyldendal, 1962

—— *Martinus Noster: Luther in the German Reform Movement 1518–1521*, Mainz, Zabern, 1994

—— *Modus loquendi theologicus. Luthers Kampf um die Erneuerung der Theologie (1515–1518)*, Leiden, Brill, 1975

—— A. Schindler, and M. Wriedt (eds.), *Auctoritas Patrum: Contributions on the Reception of the Church Fathers in the 15th and 16th Century*, 2 vols., Mainz, Zabern, 1993, 1998

Grimm, J. and W. (eds.), *Deutsches Wörterbuch*, Leipzig, Herzel et al., 1854–1960

Grönvik, L., *Die Taufe in der Theologie Martin Luthers*, Åbo, Åbo Akademi, 1968

Hägglund, B., 'Die Frage der Willensfreiheit in der Auseinandersetzung zwischen Erasmus und Luther', in A. Buck (ed.), *Renaissance—Reformation. Gegensätze und Gemeinsamkeiten*, Wiesbaden, Harassowitz, 1984

Haemig, M., 'Elizabeth Cruciger (1500?–1535): The Case of the Disappearing Hymn Writer', *SCJ* 22 (2001), 21–44

Härle, W., 'Die Entfaltung der Rechtfertigungslehre Luthers in den Disputationen von 1535 bis 1537', *LuJ* 71 (2004), 211–28

Haikola, L., *Gesetz und Evangelium bei Matthias Flacius Illyricus. Eine Untersuchung zur lutherischen Theologie vor der Konkordienformel*, Lund, Gleerup, 1952

Hamm, B., *Frömmigkeitstheologie am Anfang des 16. Jahrhunderts. Studien zu Johannes von Paltz und seinem Umkreis*, Tübingen, Mohr/Siebeck, 1982

—— and V. Leppin (eds.), *Gottes Nähe unmittelbar erfahren. Mystik im Mittelalter und bei Martin Luther*, Tübingen, Mohr/Siebeck, 2007

—— B. Moeller, and D. Wendebourg, *Reformations-Theorien. Ein kirchenhistorischer Disput über Einheit und Vielfalt der Reformation*, Göttingen, Vandenhoeck & Ruprecht, 1995

Headley, J., *Luther's View of Church History*, New Haven, Yale University Press, 1963

Hendrix, S., 'Deparentifying the Fathers: The Reformers and Patristic Authority', in Grane et al., *Auctoritas Patrum*, 1: 55–68

—— *Ecclesia in Via: Ecclesiological Developments in the Medieval Psalms Exegesis and the Dictata super Psalterium (1513–1515) of Martin Luther*, Leiden, Brill, 1974

—— *Luther and the Papacy, Stages in a Reformation Conflict*, Philadelphia, Fortress, 1981

—— 'Luther's Impact on the Sixteenth Century', *SCJ* 16 (1985), 3–14

—— *Recultivating the Vineyard: The Reformation Agendas of Christianization*, Louisville, Westminster John Knox, 2004

Herrmann, E., ' "Why then the Law?" Salvation History and the Law in Martin Luther's Interpretation of Galatians 1513–1522', Ph.D. dissertation, Concordia Seminary, Saint Louis, 2005

Holl, K., *Gesammelte Aufsätze zur Kirchengeschichte*, Tübingen, Mohr/Siebeck, 1928–32

Janz, D., *Luther and Late Medieval Thomism*, Waterloo, Wilfrid Laurier University Press, 1983

—— *Luther on Thomas Aquinas: The Angelic Doctor in the Thought of the Reformer*, Stuttgart, Steiner, 1989

Jenny, M., *Luthers geistliche Lieder und Kirchengesänge*, Cologne, Böhlau, 1985

Junghans, H., *Der junge Luther und die Humanisten*, Göttingen, Vandenhoeck & Ruprecht, 1985

Kalme, G., ' "Words Written in Golden Letters"—a Lutheran Reading of the Ecumenical Creeds', Ph.D. dissertation, Concordia Seminary, Saint Louis, 2005

Karant-Nunn, S., *The Reformation of Ritual: An Interpretation of Early Modern Germany*, London, Routledge, 1997

—— and M. Wiesner-Hanks (eds.), *Luther on Women: A Sourcebook*, Cambridge, Cambridge University Press, 2003

Kilcullen, J., 'The Political Writings', in P. Spade (ed.), *The Cambridge Companion to Ockham*, Cambridge, Cambridge University Press, 1999, 302–25

Kittelson, J., 'Successes and Failures in the German Reformation: The Report from Strasbourg', *ARG* 73 (1982), 153–75

Köhler, W., *Zwingli und Luther*, 2 vols., Leipzig, Heinsius, 1924, Gütersloh, Bertelsmann, 1953

Kohls, E., *Die Theologie des Erasmus*, 2 vols., Basel, Reinhardt, 1966

Kolb, R., *Bound Choice, Election, and Wittenberg Theological Method From Martin Luther to the Formula of Concord*, Grand Rapids, Eerdmans, 2005

—— 'Die Zweidimensionalität des Mensch-Seins Die zweierlei Gerechtigkeit in Luthers *De votis monasticis Judicium*', in C. Bultmann, V. Leppin, and A. Lindner (eds.), *Luther und das monastische Erbe*, Tübingen, Mohr/Siebeck, 2007, 207–20

—— 'From Hymn to History of Dogma: Lutheran Martyrology in the Reformation Era', in J. Leemans (ed.), *More than a Memory: The Discourse of Martyrdom and the Construction of Christian Identity in the History of Christianity*, Louvain, Peeters, 2005, 301–13

—— 'God Kills to Make Alive: Romans 6 and Luther's Understanding of Justification (1535)', *LQ* 12 (1998), 33–56

—— 'God's Gift of Martyrdom: The Early Reformation Understanding of Dying for the Faith', *Church History* 64 (1995), 399–411

—— ' "Life is King and Lord over Death," Martin Luther's View of Death and Dying', in M. K. Groch and C. Niekus-Moore (eds.), *Tod und Jenseits in der Schriftkultur der Frühen Neuzeit*, Wiesbaden, Harrassowitz, 2008, 23–45

—— 'Luther's Theology of the Cross Fifteen Years after Heidelberg: Lectures on the Psalms of Ascent', *Journal of Ecclesiastical History* (forthcoming)

—— *Martin Luther as Prophet, Teacher, and Hero*, Grand Rapids, Baker, 1999

—— 'Ministry in Martin Luther and the Lutheran Confessions', in T. Nichol and M. Kolden (eds.), *Called and Ordained*, Minneapolis, Fortress, 1990, 49–66

—— 'The Theologians and the Peasants: Conservative Evangelical Reactions to the German Peasants Revolt', *ARG* 69 (1978), 103–31

—— and C. Arand, *The Genius of Luther's Theology: A Wittenberg Way of Thinking for the Contemporary Church*, Grand Rapids, Baker, 2008

Kölmel, W., *Wilhelm Ockham und seine kirchenpolitschen Schriften*, Essen, Wingen, 1962

Krodel, G., 'Erasmus–Luther: One Theology, One Method, Two Results', *Concordia Theological Monthly* 41 (1970), 648–67

—— 'Luther and the Opposition to Roman Law in Germany', *LuJ* 58 (1991), 13–42

Lau, F., 'Der Bauernkrieg und das angebliche Ende der Lutherischen Reformation als spontaner Volksbewegung', *LuJ* 26, (1959), 109–34

Lazareth, W., *Luther on the Christian Home*, Philadelphia, Muhlenberg, 1960

Leder, H.-G., 'Luthers Beziehungen zu seinen Wittenberger Freunden', in H. Junghans (ed.), *Leben und Werk Martin Luthers von 1526 bis 1546*, Göttingen, Vandenhoeck & Ruprecht, 1983, 1: 419–40

Leppin, V., 'Geburtswehen und Geburt einer Legende. Zu Rörers Notiz vom Thesenanschlag', *Luther* 78 (2007), 145–50

—— *Martin Luther*, Darmstadt, Wissenschaftliche Buchgesellschaft, 2006

—— ' "Omnem vitam fidelium penitentiam esse voluit", Zur Aufnahme mystischer Tradition in Luthers erster Ablaßthese,' *ARG* 93 (2003), 7–25

—— 'Transformationen spätmittelalterlicher Mystik bei Luther', in Hamm and Leppin, *Gottes Nähe*, 165–85

Leroux, N., *Martin Luther as Comforter: Writings on Death*, Leiden, Brill, 2007

Lieberg, H., *Amt und Ordination bei Luther und Melanchthon*, Göttingen, Vandenhoeck & Ruprecht, 1962

Lienhard, M., *Luther: Witness to Jesus Christ, Stages and Themes of the Reformer's Christology*, tr. E. Robertson, Minneapolis, Augsburg, 1982

Lindberg, C., *Beyond Charity: Reformation Initiatives for the Poor*, Minneapolis, Fortress, 1993

Lohse, B., *Martin Luther's Theology*, tr. R. Harrisville, Minneapolis, Fortress, 1999

—— 'Philipp Melanchthon in seinen Beziehungen zu Luther', in H. Junghans (ed.), *Leben und Werk Martin Luthers von 1526 bis 1546*, Göttingen, Vandenhoeck & Ruprecht, 1983, 1: 403–18

Lotz, D., *Ritschl and Luther: A Fresh Perspective on Albrecht Ritschl's Theology in the Light of His Luther Study*, Nashville, Abingdon, 1974

Mannermaa, T., *Christ Present in Faith: Luther's View of Justification*, Minneapolis, Fortress, 2005

—— *Der im Glauben gegenwärtige Christus. Rechtfertigung und Vergottung*, Hanover, Lutherisches Verlagshaus, 1989

Marius, R., *Martin Luther: The Christian between God and Death*, Cambridge, Mass., Harvard University Press, 1999

Maschke, T., 'The Understanding and Use of Allegory in the Lectures on the Epistle of Saint Paul to the Galatians by Doctor Martin Luther', Ph.D. dissertation, Marquette University, 1993

Mau, R., 'Die Kirchenväter in Luthers früher Exegese des Galaterbriefes', in Grane et al., *Auctoritas Patrum*, 41: 117–27

Mennicke-Haustein, U., *Luthers Trostbriefe*, Gütersloh, Gütersloher Verlagshaus, 1989

Miller, G., 'Luther on the Turks and Islam', *LQ* 14 (2000), 79–97

Moeller, B., 'Das Berühmtwerden Luthers', *Zeitschrift für historische Forschung* 15 (1988), 65–92

—— 'Die Rezeption Luthers in der frühen Reformation', *LuJ* 57 (1990), 57–71

—— *Imperial Cities and the Reformation*, tr. H. Midelfort and M. Edwards, Jr., Philadelphia, Fortress, 1972

—— 'Luther in Europe: His Works in Translation 1517–1546', in E. I. Kouri and T. Scott (eds.), *Politics and Society in Reformation Europe: Essays for Sir Geoffrey Elton on his Sixty-Fifth Birthday*, New York, St. Martin's Press, 1987, 235–51

Mostert, W., 'Luther, Martin. III. Wirkungsgeschichte', *TRE* 21, Berlin, de Gruyter, 1991, 567–94

Nagel, N., '*Sacramentum et Exemplum* in Luther's Understanding of Christ', in C. Meyer (ed.), *Luther for an Ecumenical Age*, Saint Louis, Concordia, 1967, 172–99

Nielsen, K., *Simul, Das Miteinander von Göttlichem und Menschlichem in Luthers Theologie*, Göttingen, Vandenhoeck & Ruprecht, 1966

Oberman, H., *The Harvest of Medieval Theology: Gabriel Biel and Late Medieval Nominalism*, Durham, Labyrinth, 1983

—— *Luther: Man between God and the Devil*, tr. E. Waliser-Schwarzbart, New Haven and London, Yale University Press, 1989

Oberman, H., 'Simul gemitus et raptus: Luther und die Mystik', in I. Asheim (ed.), *Kirche, Mystik, Heiligung und das Natürliche bei Luther*, Göttingen, Vandenhoeck & Ruprecht, 1966, 20–59

Ocker, C., *Biblical Poetics before Humanism and Reformation*, Cambridge, Cambridge University Press, 2002

Ozment, S., *Homo Spiritualis: A Comparative Study of the Anthropology of Johannes Tauler, Jean Gerson and Martin Luther (1509–16) in the Context of their Theological Thought*, Leiden, Brill, 1969

—— *The Reformation in the Cities: The Appeal of Protestantism to Sixteenth-Century Germany and Switzerland*, New Haven, Yale University Press, 1975

Pelikan, J. (ed.), *Interpreters of Luther*, Philadelphia, Fortress, 1968

Peters, A., *Kommentar zu Luthers Katechismen*, 5 vols., ed. G. Seebaß, Göttingen, Vandenhoeck & Ruprecht, 1991

Peters, C., *Apologia Confessionis Augustanae*, Stuttgart, Calwer, 1997

Peura, S., *Mehr als Mensch? Die Vergöttlichung als Thema der Theologie Martin Luthers von 1513 bis 1519*, Mainz, Zabern, 1994

Prenter, R., *Creation and Redemption*, tr. T. Jensen, Philadelphia, Fortress, 1967

Preus, J., *From Shadow to Promise: Old Testament Interpretation from Augustine to the Young Luther*, Cambridge, Belknap, 1969

Preuss, H., *Die Vorstellungen vom Antichrist im späteren Mittelalter, bei Luther, und in der konfessionellen Polemik*, Leipzig, Hinrichs, 1906

Rieske-Braun, U., *Duellum mirabile. Studien zum Kampfmotiv in Martin Luthers Theologie*, Göttingen, Vandenhoeck & Ruprecht, 1999

Rieth, R., *Habsucht bei Martin Luther. Ökonomisches und theologisches Denken, Tradition und soziale Wirklichkeit im Zeitalter der Reformation*, Weimar, Böhlau, 1996

Rosin, R., *Reformers, the Preacher, and Skepticism: Luther, Brenz, Melanchthon, and Ecclesiastes*, Mainz, Zabern, 1997

Rupp, E., *The Righteousness of God: Luther Studies*, London, Hodder & Stoughton, 1953

Saarinen, R., *Gottes Wirken auf Uns. Die tranzendentale Deutung des Gegenwarts Christi, Motivs in der Lutherforschung*, Wiesbaden, Steiner, 1989

Sasse, H., *This is My Body*, Minneapolis, Augsburg, 1959

Schwarz, R., *Fides, spes, et caritas beim jungen Luther, unter besonderer Berücksichtigung der mittelalterlichen Tradition*, Berlin, de Gruyter, 1962

Schwarzwäller, K., *Theologia crucis, Luthers Lehre von Prädestination nach De servo arbitrio*, 1525, Munich, Kaiser, 1970

—— 'Verantwortung des Glaubens. Freiheit und Liebe nach der Dekalogauslegung Martin Luthers', in D. Bielfeldt and K. Schwarzwäller (eds.), *Freiheit als Liebe bei/Freedom as love in Martin Luther*, Frankfurt am Main, Lang, 1995, 133–58

Scott, T., *Town, Country, and Regions in Reformation Germany*, Leiden, Brill, 2005

Scribner, R., 'The Reformation Movements in Germany', in G. Elton (ed.), *The New Cambridge Modern History*, vol. 2: *The Reformation 1520–1559*, Cambridge, Cambridge University Press, 1990

Seckendorf, V., *Commentarius historicus et apologeticus de Lutheranismo, sive De reformatione religionis doctori D. Martini Lutheri*, Frankfurt am Main and Leipzig, Gleditsch, 1688–92

Sider, R., *Andreas Bodenstein von Karlstadt: The Development of His Thought*, Leiden, Brill, 1974

Siemon-Netto, U., *The Fabricated Luther: Refuting Nazi Connections and Other Modern Myths*, 2nd edn., Saint Louis, Concordia, 2007

Siggins, I., *Luther and his Mother*, Philadelphia, Fortress, 1981

—— *Martin Luther's Doctrine of Christ*, New Haven, Yale University Press, 1970

Smirin, M., *Die Volksreformation des Thomas Münzer und der grosse Bauernkrieg*, Berlin, Dietz, 1952

Spangenberg, C., *Theander Lutherus. Von des werthen Gottes Manne Doctor Martin Luthers Geistlicher Haushaltung vnd Ritterschafft*, Ursel, Heinrich, 1589

Spitz, L., 'The Third Generation of German Humanists', in A. R. Lewis (ed.), *Aspects of the Renaissance: A Symposium*, Austin, University of Texas Press, 1967, 105–21

Stayer, J., *Martin Luther, German Saviour: German Evangelical Theological Factions and the Interpretation of Luther, 1917–1933*, Montreal and Kingston, McGill-Queens University Press, 2000

Steinmetz, D., *Luther and Staupitz*, Durham, NC, Duke University Press, 1980

Steinmetz, M., *Deutschland von 1476 bis 1648*, Berlin, Deutscher Verlag der Wissenschaften, 1965

Stephan, H., *Luther in den Wandlungen seiner Kirche*, Giessen, Töpelmann, 1907

Stolt, B., 'Martin Luther on God as Father', *LQ* 8 (1994), 385–95

Strauss, G., *Luther's House of Learning: Indoctrination of the Young in the German Reformation*, Baltimore, Johns Hopkins University Press, 1978

Thompson, M., *A Sure Ground on Which to Stand: The Relation of Authority and Interpretive Method in Luther's Approach to Scripture*, Carlisle, Paternoster, 2004

Tolpingrud, M., 'Luther's Disputation Concerning the Divinity and the Humanity of Christ', *LQ* 10 (1996), 151–78

Tracy, J., 'Two Erasmuses, Two Luthers: Erasmus' Strategy in Defense of *De libero arbitrio*', *ARG* 78 (1987), 37–60

Treu, M., 'Der Thesenanschlag fand wirklich statt', *Luther* 78 (2007), 140–4

—— *Katharina von Bora*, Wittenberg, Drei Kastanien, 1995

—— 'Waschhaus—Küche—Prioret. Die neuen archäologischen Funde am Wittenberger Lutherhaus', *Luther* 76 (2005), 132–40

Trigg, J., *Baptism in the Theology of Martin Luther*, Leiden, Brill, 1994

Vajta, V., *Luther on Worship*, Philadelphia, Muhlenberg, 1958

Vercruysse, J., *Fidelis Populus*, Wiesbaden, Steiner, 1968

—— 'Luther in der römisch-katholischen Theologie und Kirche', *LuJ* 63 (1996), 103–28

Watson, P., *Let God be God! An Interpretation of the Theology of Martin Luther*, Philadelphia, Muhlenberg, 1947

Wengert, T., *Human Freedom, Christian Righteousness: Philip Melanchthon's Exegetical Dispute with Erasmus of Rotterdam*, Oxford, Oxford University Press, 1998

Wengert, T., *Law and Gospel: Philip Melanchthon's Debate with John Agricola of Eisleben over Poenitentia*, Grand Rapids, Baker, 1997

—— 'Luther neben Melanchthon, Melanchthon neben Luther', *LuJ* 66 (1999), 55–88

—— 'The Marks of the Church in the Later Luther', in G. Lathrop and T. Wengert (eds.), *Christian Assembly: Marks of the Church in a Pluralistic Age*, Minneapolis, Fortress, 2004, 81–112

—— ' "Per mutuum colloquium et consolationem fratrum": Monastische Züge in Luthers ökumenischer Theologie,' in C. Bultmann, V. Leppin, and A. Lindner (eds.), *Luther und das monastische Erbe*, Tübingen, Mohr/Siebeck, 2007, 243–68

—— *Philip Melanchthon's Annotationes in Johannem in Relation to its Predecessors and Contemporaries*, Geneva, Droz, 1987

White, G., *Luther as Nominalist: A Study of the Logical Methods Used in Martin Luther's Disputations in the Light of their Medieval Background*, Helsinki, Luther-Agricola-Society, 1994

Wingren, G., *Luther on Vocation*, tr. C. Rasmussen, Philadelphia, Muhlenberg, 1957

Witte, J., *Law and Protestantism: The Legal Teachings of the Lutheran Reformation*, Cambridge, Cambridge University Press, 2002

Wriedt, M., *Gnade und Erwählung, eine Untersuchung zu Johann von Staupitz und Martin Luther*, Mainz, Zabern, 1991

Zeeden, E., *Martin Luther und die Reformation im Urteil des deutschen Luthertums*, 2 vols., Freiburg im Breisgau, Herder, 1952

Zickendraht, K., *Der Streit zwischen Erasmus und Luther über die Willensfreiheit*, Leipzig, Hinrichs, 1901

Zur Mühlen, K.-H., 'Die Auctoritas patrum in Martin Luthers Schrift "Von den Konziliis und Kirchen" (1539)', in Grane et al., *Auctoritas patrum*, 2: 141–52

—— 'Die Rezeption von Augustins "Tractatus in Joannem 80,3" im Werk Martin Luthers', in Grane et al., *Auctoritas Patrum*, 1: 271–81

—— *Nos Extra Nos. Luthers Theologie zwischen Mystik und Scholastik*, Tübingen, Mohr/Siebeck, 1972

Index

Index of Scripture passages